# PATRIARCHALISM IN POLITICAL THOUGHT

# GORDON J. SCHOCHET

# PATRIARCHALISM IN POLITICAL THOUGHT

*The Authoritarian Family and*
*Political Speculation and Attitudes*
*Especially in Seventeenth-Century England*

Basic Books, Inc., Publishers  ·  New York

Library of Congress Catalog Card Number: 74–14110

SBN: 465–05455–2

Manufactured in Great Britain

# LOIS

# Contents

# Preface

Almost twenty years ago, a copy of Sir Robert Filmer's *Patriarcha* came into my hands quite fortuitously: the bookstore of the Johns Hopkins University had ordered the wrong edition of Locke's 'Second Treatise' for my freshman history course. And so, instead of the 'Second Treatise' alone, which was all we were to read, I purchased the *Two Treatises* along with *Patriarcha* in a volume edited by Thomas I. Cook. One of the most significant events of that winter, for me, was a severe snow storm that kept me house-bound for three or four days. I soon ran out of science fiction and decided to read ahead in my courses, eventually exhausting my assignments. As a compulsive reader, I had no choice but to read Filmer and the 'First Treatise'. After the snows melted, I promptly forgot about patriarchalism—or so I thought. A few weeks later, when we discussed Locke in my history course, the instructor misrepresented Filmer's arguments in ways that an impatient college freshman simply could not abide. And so I corrected him. 'Have you read Filmer?' he asked. 'Yes,' I replied, brashly waving my copy, 'Have you?'

The need to get patriarchalism straight—to rescue it from Locke's distortions and from its exclusive association with Filmer —has been a growing preoccupation of mine, and the obsession starts in that history class. The process of transforming an obsession into a book has been long and arduous, but it has been rewarding and often quite pleasant as well. The result is not to be measured merely by the pages that follow; it is also the many friends I have made, the thrills of discovery, and countless other experiences.

This book and I together owe more than can ever be fully acknowledged to the three men who have guided my research and academic development—Thomas I. Cook, Benjamin E. Lippincott, and Peter Laslett, my teachers and friends. Their lasting friendship is one of my most valued possessions. Tommy Cook, then at Johns Hopkins and now at the University of Texas at El Paso and the editor of that edition of Locke and Filmer, introduced me to political philosophy as well as to serious research and created my love of the seventeenth century. Ben Lippincott carefully taught me how to read political philosophy and attempted to put me on writing terms with the English language. His magnificent and demanding seminar, 'Readings in the Classics of Politics', was one of the truly great courses at the University of Minnesota and remains the standard for all my teaching and writing. Peter Laslett, who supervised my research and eased my life in Cambridge and intrigued me with his important and fascinating work on the history of social structure, has been a patron of this book from the very start. He read and commented on several versions of the manuscript and even suggested still more changes in the proofs; I doubt that this book would have been published without his support. The encouragement of these men and their continuing confidence have been most important to me through some very difficult times.

Others have been more than generous with their time and interest, and I can only mention a few. Richard Schlatter of Rutgers University commented extensively and helpfully on an early version of the manuscript and did much to improve my writing. My good friends Judson James, now of Virginia Polytechnic Institute, and Gerald Pomper, the absolute model of an ideal colleague, each read several chapters and offered valuable advice. Kenneth Einstein valiantly assisted—no, I assisted him!—with the proof-reading and the index. Bill and Dorothy Hathaway, special and extraordinary friends too seldom seen, have never read one word of this book, but none of it would have been written without them.

It is a pleasure to record my indebtedness to the cooperative and cheerful staff of the Anderson Room of the Cambridge University Library, where most of my research was done. John Harrison and John Morris provided much assistance at the University Library as well. It was a sheer delight for the awe-struck, Anglophilic American to work in the restored Duke Humphry Reading Room of the Bodleian Library at Oxford from which, as my fancy would have it, I was sent scurrying at closing time by the same bell that three hundred years earlier had evicted the very men whose pamphlets I was then reading. The Bodleian staff, especially Dr. D. M. Barrett, was very helpful, as were the staffs of the North Reading Room of the British Museum, the Library of Trinity College, Cambridge, and the William Andrews Clark Memorial Library. My own University Library at Rutgers has provided a secluded study space for the past few years and has been more than tolerant of my needs.

A Fulbright Fellowship to Trinity College, Cambridge (Sir Robert Filmer's College), in 1962–63 supported my initial research, and a Fellowship from the Graduate School of the University of Minnesota allowed me to write much of the first draft. The second stage of the research was begun in 1966 while I held a Summer Fellowship from the William Andrews Clark Memorial Library in Los Angeles. (The Clark Library is to be commended for sponsoring summer seminars for junior scholars. With book prices soaring and the excellent facilities of the Huntington Library nearby, the Clark Library staff wisely decided that some of its resources should be spent on these seminars rather than on more books.) The generous and continuing support of the Research Council of Rutgers University and the advice and encouragement of its Associate Director, C. F. Main, have been extremely important: a Summer Faculty Fellowship in 1967 made possible a second trip to England, and a Research Council grant has paid part of the costs of publication. My gratitude to all these sources is immense.

Previously published portions of this book are reprinted here in different form with permission from the *Political Science Quarterly*, 82 (September 1967), 427–45; *John Locke: Problems and Perspectives*, ed. J. W. Yolton (Cambridge: Cambridge University Press, 1969); and the *Historical Journal*, 13: 3 (Autumn 1969). Members of the Columbia University Faculty Seminar in Social and Political Theory responded with gratifying encouragement to a summary of some of the ideas that now make up chapters 1 and 3.

For subsidies and much else, I am indebted to my parents, Dave and Goldie Schochet, and to my in-laws, Stanley and Vivian Klein. Michael and Deborah Schochet, now nearly six and two and a half, could hardly have made any direct contributions to this book, but they helped sustain me through the agonies of revision. My greatest debt is to my wife, Lois, who has had to tolerate and read about patriarchalism too long. Editor, critic, and sometimes collaborator, she has been through

# I

# Patriarchalism and Political Theory

I

The patriarchal political theory brings to mind the name of Sir Robert Filmer, the seventeenth-century English royalist, whose posthumously published *Patriarcha* is regarded as the highest expression of that doctrine. But Filmer is one of those historical figures who is more known about than known and whose writings are more talked about than read. In essence, Filmer's theory was a defense of divine right absolutism on the ground that the political order of Stuart England had evolved from the family; magistrates were therefore entitled to the same filial obedience that children owed to their fathers. These political arrangements were sanctioned by God, and Sir Robert fortified his argument by tracing all legal authority back to the divinely ordained fatherly power of Adam.

What there is of Filmer's reputation is due chiefly to the commentary of John Locke, for it was against Sir Robert's patriarchalism that Locke's famous *Two Treatises of Government* were directed. Indeed, according to the view of G. C. Robertson, which has been a dogma until very recently, Filmer was 'saved . . . from oblivion' by Locke's criticisms.[1] This assessment was endorsed by Sir Frederick Pollock[2] and echoed by Harold Laski's claim that 'Filmer might never have been known had not Locke thus honoured him by retort'.[3] Locke himself said of

[1] George Croom Robertson, *Hobbes* (London, 1886), p. 209.
[2] Sir Frederick Pollock, 'Locke's Theory of the State', *Proceedings of the British Academy, 1903–1904*, reprinted in *Political Thought in Perspective*, ed. William Ebenstein (New York, 1957), p. 291.
[3] Harold Laski, *Political Thought in England: Locke to Bentham*, Home University Library, reprinted (London, 1949), pp. 29–30.

Filmer's books, 'There was never so much glib nonsense put together in well sounding English,' and the reader of the *Two Treatises* was challenged to 'try whether he can, with all his Skill, make Sir Robert intelligible, and consistent with himself, or common sense'.[4] Of the justification of absolutism in Sir Robert's *Patriarcha*, Locke was 'mightily surprised, that in a Book, which was to provide Chains for all Mankind, I should find nothing but a Rope of Sand, useful perhaps, to such, whose Skill and Business it is to raise a Dust. . .'.[5] Locke's polemic caricature of his opponent is very nearly received opinion. The word that has most frequently been used to describe both Filmer and patriarchalism is 'absurd'. So speak such noted commentators as A. J. Carlyle,[6] Leslie Stephen,[7] and Vernon L. Parrington,[8] almost with one voice. Laski wonders 'why Locke should have wasted the resources of his intelligence upon so feeble an opponent'.[9] His puzzlement is shared by C. E. Vaughan, who, in addition, describes Filmer as 'pedantic and rather fatuous'.[10]

Against this background, it is no wonder that Filmer and the patriarchal political theory have received little serious scholarly attention. Any notice at all has been devoted to Filmer rather than to political patriarchalism. As J. W. Allen, one of Sir Robert's few apologists—and the most enthusiastic of that select group—remarks, 'What is called [Filmer's] patriarchal theory was, in fact, no more than an argument from history. It was, I admit, a shockingly bad one; but it was *not in the least essential to his system of ideas.*'[11] This deprecated, unessential patriarchal

---

[4] John Locke, *Two Treatises on Government* (1690), ed. Peter Laslett (Cambridge, 1960), Preface, p. 156. Original text in Italics. All subsequent references will be to this edition, cited throughout by book and section number as Locke, *Two Treatises.*

[5] Ibid., I, 1.

[6] A. J. Carlyle, *Political Liberty: A History of the Conception in the Middle Ages and Modern Times* (Oxford, 1941), pp. 36, 38, and 122. See also pp. 36–44 in general.

[7] Leslie Stephen, *History of the English Thought in the Eighteenth Century*, 3rd ed., paperbound reprint, 2 vols. (New York, 1962), II, 114.

[8] Vernon L. Parrington, *Main Currents in American Thought*, paperbound, 2 vols. (New York, 1954), I, 193.

[9] Laski, *Locke to Bentham*, p. 29.

[10] C. E. Vaughan, *Studies in the History of Political Philosophy Before and After Rousseau*, ed. A. G. Little, 2 vols. (Manchester, 1925), I, 130.

[11] J. W. Allen, 'Sir Robert Filmer', *The Social and Political Ideas of Some*

doctrine is thus relegated to the status of a mere footnote in the history of political thought. George H. Sabine remarks in his influential text, 'Had Filmer not discredited himself with his absurd argument about the royal power of Adam, he might have been a rather formidable critic.'[12] Similarly, after calling *Patriarcha* the 'best English version' of the theory of the divine right of kings, John Plamenatz says, 'Of Filmer, more truly than of any other exponent of the doctrine, we can say that he is more impressive when he attacks others than when he defends himself.'[13] Another scholar, Perez Zagorin, tells us, 'When we turn to Filmer's criticism of the doctrine of popular sovereignty, we see him at his keenest.'[14] And Peter Laslett, Filmer's twentieth-century editor and biographer, comments on 'the destructive cast' of Sir Robert's thought and notes that he had the 'capacity for seeing straight through the arguments of others without being aware of his own extraordinary irrationality'.[15] To these evaluations should be added the recent appraisal by Wilfred Harrison, who says that Filmer 'was not a very influential writer' and, quite incorrectly, that his patriarchal theory was 'highly individual'.[16]

Except for Harrison's unwitting historical error and Allen's exaggerated efforts to distinguish between Filmer and a theory that is, by common consensus, 'absurd'—to say nothing of unusual and irrelevant—all these observations about Filmer are essentially correct. But the very fact that they are correct has

---

*English Thinkers of the Augustan Age, A.D. 1650–1750*, ed. F. J. C. Hearnshaw (London, 1928), p. 46. Emphasis added.

[12] George H. Sabine, *A History of Political Theory*, 3rd ed. (New York, 1961), p. 513. Sabine devotes little more than one page to Filmer, and it is impossible from his account to reconstruct the positive part of the patriarchal theory.

[13] John Plamenatz, *Man and Society: A Critical Examination of Some Important Social and Political Theories from Machiavelli to Marx*, 2 vols. (London, 1963), I, 173.

[14] Perez Zagorin, *A History of Political Thought in the English Revolution* (London, 1954), p. 198.

[15] Peter Laslett, 'Sir Robert Filmer: The Man versus the Whig Myth', *William and Mary Quarterly*, 3rd ser., V (1948), 546.

[16] Wilfred Harrison, *Conflict and Compromise: History of British Political Thought, 1593–1900* (New York, 1965), p. 34. See also Zagorin, *History of Political Thought*, p. 196, and R. W. K. Hinton, 'Husbands, Fathers and Conquerors', *Political Studies*, XV (1967), 297 and 299.

led commentators to disregard Sir Robert's positive doctrine, the patriarchal justification of political authority. Thus, there has been no attempt to relate this theory to the arguments advanced by other thinkers or to determine the proper place of patriarchalism in the political thought of seventeenth-century England. In fact, an entire tradition of political expression has been neglected to the point of suppression, and we cannot appreciate how pervasive this particular 'absurdity' was.

However, the situation is beginning to change. Since Filmer's political works were republished in 1949[17]—for the first time since 1696—there have been a slowly growing and almost grudging recognition that Sir Robert was not the only spokesman for the patriarchal point of view as well as an expanding realization that the doctrine must be accorded some status in the development of Stuart political theory.[18] As J. G. A. Pocock points out, the patriarchal doctrine 'did not sound absurd to its opponents'.[19] Despite his mocking derisions, Locke took Filmer seriously enough to write a detailed criticism. He was joined by his friend James Tyrrell, a competent Whig historian, and by the fiery republican, Algernon Sidney, both of whom wrote lengthy attacks on Sir Robert. To understand why this should have been the case and to appreciate just what Locke and the others had to refute, it is necessary to examine patriarchalism on its merits as a meaningful justification of political obligation. The importance of this theory can only be determined by placing it in its own times and by analyzing it in relation to competing systems of political thought as well as to its own tradition.

---

[17] Sir Robert Filmer, *Patriarcha and Other Political Works*, ed. Peter Laslett, Blackwell's Political Texts (Oxford, 1949). Unless otherwise indicated, all references to Filmer will be to this edition, which contains seven of Sir Robert's tracts. Citations will be by the name of the specific work, and the collection itself will be referred to as Filmer, *Political Works*.

[18] See, for instance, J. G. A. Pocock, *The Ancient Constitution and the Feudal Law* (Cambridge, 1957), pp. 145–59 and 187–90; J. H. M. Salmon, *The French Religious Wars in English Political Thought* (Oxford, 1959), pp. 110–13 *et passim*; W. H. Greenleaf, *Order, Empiricism, and Politics: Two Traditions of English Political Thought, 1500–1700* (Oxford, 1964), pp. 80–94; and R. W. K. Hinton, 'Husbands, Fathers and Conquerors', *Political Studies*, XV (1967), 291–300, and XVI (1968), 55–67.

[19] Pocock, *Ancient Constitution*, p. 189.

2

The purpose of this book, then, is to set the political ideas associated with Sir Robert Filmer in the wider context of English political thought from about 1600 to the death of the last Stuart monarch in 1714. I am, in addition, concerned to establish the status of patriarchalism within the western political tradition itself. This essay is not so much a study of the sources and subsequent influences of Filmer's patriarchal doctrine as it is an investigation of the theory of the familial basis of politics, with particular emphasis upon seventeenth-century England. As the best-known patriarchalist, Filmer is certainly one of the focal points; the origins and eventual development of his ideas are discussed, and the conceptions of other thinkers are frequently contrasted to his position. On the other hand, I have not attempted to dissect the whole of his thought. And while I have raised a number of questions about previous interpretations of Sir Robert, it is not my intention to provide a revisionist account of his writings. A *correct* understanding of Filmer is a secondary goal; of greater importance is an awareness of the intellectual tradition for which he has been the unacknowledged symbol for almost three hundred years. After his historical significance is established, there will be time enough for reappraisals of Sir Robert's actual theories. Thus, this essay comprises what is conventionally and loosely called the 'history of an idea', and the most obvious result of the study is the demonstration that this particular idea actually has a history.

Patriarchal doctrines can be found throughout the Stuart period and in all strata of thought, from well-ordered and self-conscious theories, through the lower level and often implicit rationalization and polemics of tractarians and controversialists, to the unstated prejudices of the inarticulate masses. Patriarchal assumptions had important places in the political theories of such thinkers as Hobbes, Locke, Sidney, and Sir William Temple; in a later age they were still sufficiently prominent to merit reconsiderations by Jeremy Bentham and by Rousseau on the Continent. In the pamphlets of less systematic writers—who were often motivated by theological controversies and political exigencies rather than by philosophic considerations—cruder versions of these same doctrines were utilized by royalists and puritans alike, were pitted against the assumed individualism of Hobbes and Locke, and were used by the enemies and advocates of Exclusion as well as the opponents and defenders of the 1688 Revolution.

Furthermore, patriarchal justifications of obedience to political authority were regularly and officially taught by the Church of England, which provided most people with their only formal and sustained contact with the world outside their particular households. This religious teaching, extending without interruption at least from the reign of Edward VI, consisted of a social and political interpretation of the duty to obey parents enjoined by the Decalogue; the simple requirement to 'Honour thy father and thy mother'[20] was expanded to include loyalty and obedience to the king and all magistrates, as well as to masters, teachers, and ministers. This reading of the Fifth Commandment appeared in a source that was common to all Englishmen, the catechism, which *everyone* had to learn. Catechistical instruction was often accompanied by elaborate explanations and numerous examples to illustrate the meanings of each part of the catechism; in the case of the Fifth Commandment, these embellishments were sometimes as vivid in their patriarchal details as the writings of political polemicists.

As these diverse manifestations of the theory suggest, a straightforward model of a single tradition of patriarchal political thought is deceptive in its simplicity. The patriarchal thesis has a complicated history, and the doctrine itself assumed various forms in seventeenth-century England. Some versions of patriarchalism will be seen to have had very little to do with either the defense of absolutism or the Adamite doctrines of Sir Robert Filmer. The larger theory will emerge as an exceedingly complex set of theses and outlooks that must be drawn together and distinguished from another and considerably more familiar explanation of political obligation, the social contract. Therefore, one of the recurring but unelaborated sub-themes of this study is the development, particularly in Stuart England, of contractual political philosophy and such related concepts as the state of nature, human freedom and equality, and government by consent.

The histories of the patriarchal and contractual accounts of politics are very much dependent upon one another. On one

[20] Exod. 20: 12.

level they were rival doctrines; in a more fundamental sense, however, they were complementary theories, for patriarchalism provided some of the presuppositions on which the contract rested. It is this relationship that must be demonstrated and ultimately disentangled. In the end, the patriarchal tradition will be seen to have had an importance that has been altogether unsuspected by subsequent ages. The aim of this 'history of an idea' will become not only to show that such a tradition existed but to suggest that its accommodation requires modification of some standard interpretations of Stuart political thought. Beyond this, I wish to suggest in this first chapter that attention to patriarchalism brings to light some previously unnoticed aspects of the nature of political philosophy itself and of the ways it can be examined.

### 3

It was Filmer's contention that kings were entitled to the absolute obedience of their subjects. Disobedience to one's ruler was contrary to God's law. That this was so, he reasoned, followed from the fact that all kings ruled as successors to the power God had given to Adam at the Creation. Sir Robert argued his case by explaining the political order in terms of familial symbols, which meant that political authority was identical with the rule of a father or patriarch over his family. In Filmer's terms, the most important features of paternal authority were that it was natural and initially unlimited. Restrictions on fatherly power were artificial and were defensible only to the extent that they did not contradict the natural source of fatherhood. Transferred to politics, this argument implied that government—and monarchy in particular—was a natural institution and that the burden of proof was on anyone who claimed that there were justifiable, enforceable limits to political authority. The theory was still unsupportable, for the applicability of the familial symbol to politics had not been validated. It was at this point that the power of Adam was invoked.

By tracing political sovereignty back to the Biblical account of Eden, Sir Robert implicitly claimed that the standards established by God at the very beginning of the world were the ones by which subsequent acts and institutions were to be judged. The patriarchal conception of political obligation was thus a *genetic* justification, for it defended the duty to obey in terms of the very origins of political society. Part of the controversy between patriarchalists and contractualists concerned the conditions that had prevailed at the beginnings of political organization and the question of how government actually arose. Contractual theorists adopted an alternative symbol in terms of which they perceived and attempted to explain the political world. The contract device suggested that politics was voluntary and conventional, rather than natural, and limitable both in extent and duration, rather than absolute. Contractual theorists asked the same genetic questions about governance as the patriarchalists, but their answers were vastly different. Like the paternal explanation, however, the contract theory relied upon an unstated premise that the nature of political society and the extent of subsequent political obligation were determined by the manner in which the state originated. Without some such notion, whether consciously held or not, there would have been no reason to appeal to a prior contract by which government was created. Since both the contractual and patriarchal theses rested upon vague and unrecapturable pasts that were mixtures of hypothetical reasoning, Biblical history, and crude anthropological assertions, there was no *prima facie* way of resolving the conflict between the two positions.

Ultimately, contractual notions came to rely more on logic and hypotheses than upon presumably factual history and moved away from genetic justifications altogether. At that point, the contractual–patriarchal dialogue necessarily broke down because the two theories no longer shared sufficient common ground to confront one another. Before this shift from genetic theories occurred, the seventeenth-century disputes over origins turned on such questions as whether God had granted both paternal *and* political authority to Adam and whether men who were naturally subjected to the authority of their fathers could nevertheless be *politically* free enough to establish their own governments.

This surrender of genetic arguments had a most interesting effect on the 'libertarian' theory that had been confronting patriarchalism. The reliance upon a contract was transformed into a derivation of obligation from individual consent, a notion that had long been implicit in the contract theory itself but had not been fully worked out. Consent theories rest upon the actions of the subject himself and not upon his duty to accept the political order agreed to by his ancestors. This distinction between contract and consent is not usually recognized, but that failure is probably due to our unfamiliarity with the genetic mode of argument and its implications. It will be seen in chapter thirteen that these problems were directly confronted by John Locke, who was especially disturbed by the genetic arguments entailed by Filmer's easy movement from God's grant of paternal right to Adam to the nature of monarchy in seventeenth-century England. His critique of Filmer led Locke to a rejection of the contractual defense of obligation. For Locke the contract, at the very most— and even then only in some cases—explained how political societies may have arisen, not why men had to obey them.

The origin of governance has always been recognized as one of the standard problems of political philosophy, and it is difficult to find serious political thinkers prior to the English Utilitarians who did not somehow attempt to show how political authority began. But it has never been clear what purpose these appeals to origins served or even if they were designed to accomplish the same things in all cases.[21] There has undoubtedly been something more at work than adherence to a convention, but just what or how much more remains an open question. It has not previously been noticed that this discussion of political origins played a crucial and distinctive role in the political thought of seventeenth-century England. In addition to providing an account—hypothetical, logical, or supposedly historical—of how government came into being, the treatment of this issue actually constituted a means of justifying political obligation. It was widely assumed during the period that there was a direct and discernable relationship between political duty and the way civil authority began.

Admittedly, the relationship could become extremely tenuous and complex, and there were always further questions that could be raised after the matter of origins had been settled. In addition,

[21] Donald J. Kreitzer, 'Problems of the Origin of Political Authority', *Philosophical Studies* (Maynooth), X (1960), 190–203, has isolated some of the questions that may be contained in the appeal to political origins, but he has done so in the context of Thomistic political philosophy and with the intention of clarifying the traditional Scholastic treatment of the problem. He does not deal with political obligation as such and fails to recognize the genetic doctrine as it is presented here. (See especially pp. 195–8 of Kreitzer's article.)

the problem of origins in general was often not distinguished
from the beginnings of a specific nation; it is not uncommon,
for instance, to find the Norman Conquest discussed in terms
that are actually more appropriate to a consideration of what
factors made government itself necessary. The genetic thesis, all
in all, presented a loose if not a sloppy conception of the political
world. Nonetheless, the appeal to origins was accepted in Stuart
England and was compatible with the intellectual climate in
which it flourished. An awareness of genetic political assumptions
is essential to an understanding of patriarchalism, in terms of
what it attempted and of how it related to the contract and consent theories.

4

The patriarchal doctrine was more than a defense of political
authority. When the various components and strands of the
theory are separated, it is possible to isolate three essentially
different types of patriarchal notions, but it should be stressed
that they are often found in concert—especially in Stuart
England—and were more closely related than this analytic separation might suggest. (1) In the first place, patriarchalism explained
the origins of the state and was a descriptive or 'anthropological'
thesis. (2) The patriarchal theory of obligation—which has been
briefly described above—attempted to move from these same
anthropological 'facts' to an entire political philosophy; I refer to
this version as a 'moral' theory. (3) Finally, there is the simple
assertion that political obedience is due to the king because of his
fatherly right; this doctrine—which is really the conclusion of
the moral theory without its elaborate reasoning—was regularly
and officially taught by the Church of England and may be regarded as an 'ideological' conception. An examination of these
different forms of patriarchalism in greater detail will illustrate
their differences and relationships. At this stage, it is necessary
to withhold criticism and to oversimplify for the sake of clarity.
Also, these categories—especially the second—are more abstracted models than they are representations of genuine theoretical statements. The various parts of this scheme are far more
consistent and self-contained than the views of the writers whose
works will be examined. Like all models, this set of distinctions

is designed to provide a frame of reference and to add rigor and unity to an otherwise unorganized and vague body of doctrine—in short, to provide a theoretical context in terms of which patriarchalism may be analyzed.

(1) *Anthropological patriarchalism.* As the designation anthropological suggests, this strand of the larger theory purported to be an historical account of the development and transformation of the primitive familial association into a wider and more perfected society. The head of this community increased or altered his authority over the members of his household as the need for different kinds of restraint became apparent. These changes occurred because of the population growth, territorial expansion, and external threats and aggression. This thesis was often not so much a political theory as it was a presumed description of the pre-political world.

By itself, this description did not entail a theory of political obligation or even provide the basis for one. What was missing was some larger and logically prior principle that could have shown the relationship of the earlier familial society to the nature of subsequent political organization. A teleological doctrine or acceptance of the genetic proposition that origins determine development would have served this purpose. Teleology, of course, would have incorporated this descriptive thesis into a normative system similar to that of Aristotle. But it would not have been the primeval family that was important for understanding the state so much as it would have been the emergent political order that determined the nature of the household. Central to a teleological view of the world is a conception of essence as the end result; it is the finished product that sheds light on the beginning rather than the source that shapes the outcome. Thus, filial obedience could not have provided a justification or explanation of political obligation. In terms of the distinctions among patriarchal theories that are being sketched here, teleological appeals to the family as the historical source of society are neutral anthropological descriptions and not moral assertions. In short, teleological notions do not *use* origins so much as they *account* for them, and origins themselves play no active role in the theory but acquire a meaning in terms of something else.

The addition of a genetic explanation of obligation to this derivation of political society from the household distinguishes the fuller patriarchal theory from these descriptive versions; this more elaborate doctrine will be examined below. Even when it was not utilized as the basis for a theory of obligation, the anthropological thesis often provided a more detailed picture of the state of nature than has generally been appreciated. Similarly, the meaning of 'individuals' or 'people' in much of the literature of the Stuart period can be clarified by recognizing that for many authors it was only the fathers of families who agreed to compacts of government. The men who faced one another in the pre-political condition with no formal authority above them were not necessarily discriminate individuals but were often the heads of independent families. Within their separate households, there was order and authority—even though many authors insisted that it was not *political* rule—and there was still a state of nature!

(2) *Moral patriarchalism.* The most important form assumed by patriarchal political thought was the justification of obedience to the state on the ground that political authority had originally belonged to fathers. This conception usually added a literal reading of the Bible to the anthropological thesis. The heads of independent families were presumed to have been the patriarchs named in the Old Testament, who were thought to have possessed monarchical power. Great emphasis was placed upon the Creation and Flood legends, and kingship was said to have begun with God's grant of a universal and unlimited monarchy to Adam and again to Noah. Both had ruled the entire world with coextensive and indistinguishable fatherly and political sovereignty, but it was the political title of Adam that became the primary point of departure. This theory defended the claims of divine right absolutism on the ground that absolute monarchy alone enjoyed God's sanction because it was the form of government He had specifically selected when He created man.

Insisting upon the reality of society and politics, moral patriarchalism held, in opposition to the contract theory, that social relations and political institutions were not voluntarily erected or otherwise established by men for their own convenience. Man had never been without society and government, and the constraints of social hierarchy were integral and perpetual parts of his existence. These same claims could be stated without drawing on Biblical support. What had to be demonstrated was that men had always lived in families and that familial and political rule were not separable, in short, that a man who was naturally bound to obey his father could never be sufficiently free to be the author of his own political obligation. In this *identification* of paternal and regal authority we can see the complete application of the familial symbols to politics, and it is this strict adherence to the metaphor that most significantly denotes the fullest version of the patriarchal theory of political obligation.

Behind this argument, of course, was the genetic insistence upon the relationship of origins to duty. But this preoccupation with origins did not always refer to the primeval beginnings of politics itself. What was often intended was the establishment of a specific state or set of political institutions, as Filmer's observations on the source of customary law indicate:

For every custom there was a time when it was no custom, and the first precedent we now have, had no precedent when it began. When every custom began, there was something else than custom that made it lawful, or else the beginnings of all customs were unlawful. Customs at first became lawful only by some superior power which did either command or consent unto their beginning. . . . From which we must necessarily infer that the Common Law itself, or common customs of this land, were originally the laws and commands of Kings at first unwritten.[22]

The implication of this view was that the authority possessed by kings who were responsible for the first institution of the common law descended intact to their legitimate successors. The reaction of Filmer's critics is equally instructive; as Pocock observes, they 'did not argue, on grounds of historical relativity, that sovereignty in Charles [II] must mean something quite unlike the sovereignty possessed by Melchizideck'. This can be seen in their having 'angrily denied the occurrence of a Norman Conquest', even though Filmer never used this notion in support of his own position. 'They did so', Pocock continues, 'because they unreservedly agreed that if William I in the eleventh century had ruled with absolute power, there was nothing to prevent Charles II in the

[22] Sir Robert Filmer, *Patriarcha: A Defence of the Natural Power of Kings against the Unnatural Liberty of the People* (written *c.* 1640), *Political Works*, pp. 106–7. This was not a unique claim by any means. Pocock quotes a very similar statement made in 1612 by Sir John Davies, Attorney General for Ireland (*Ancient Constitution*, pp. 32–3).

seventeenth from revoking every law and liberty ever granted by the kings of England.'[23]

The immediate constitutional task confronting the Exclusionists and defenders of the 1688 Revolution was not so much to discredit Filmer's thesis about the patriarchal nature and descent of regal authority as it was to show that no king of England had ever possessed as much power as was claimed for Charles II and James II. Other questions were certainly not ignored; indeed, Sir Robert's interpretations of Biblical passages and of the patriarchal theory in general were subjected to detailed criticisms. However, in terms of legal thought, these were secondary considerations. The debate was over political origins—in this case, the Norman origins of the state that became Stuart England—and there was no question but that obligation in the seventeenth century had to be understood as a result of those beginnings.

One further aspect of the patriarchal conception of obligation should be indicated—its naturalism.[24] Society and government were both regarded as natural rather than man-made phenomena; it therefore followed that obligation to obey the state was natural and not conventional. It was essential to the patriarchal thesis that obligation be understood as a part of the nature and order of the universe (or the dictates of God) if the natural authority of fathers was to have any bearing upon the power of kings. Even the critics of political patriarchalism were usually willing to admit that the right of fathers to control their children was an inherent and natural attribute of paternity. What they disputed was the assumption that the rights of monarchs could be inferred from this power.

(3) *Ideological Patriarchalism.* The third type of patriarchal political thought was the simple use of the fatherly image as the basis of political obligation without an elaborate, supporting set of historical and moral principles. The most interesting and frequently encountered form of this version of patriarchalism was the interpretation of the Fifth Commandment that was the offi-

---

[23] Pocock, *Ancient Constitution*, p. 189.

[24] I am using the term 'naturalism' in contrast to 'conventionalism', that is, to denote something that is presumed to inhere in 'the nature of things' rather than that which is artificially made. See the discussion of 'nature and convention' in K. R. Popper, *The Open Society and Its Enemies*, 4th ed., paperbound, 2 vols. (London, 1962), I, pp. 57–73.

cial teaching of the Church in the Catechism. This doctrine was not necessarily concerned with the origins of the state and political authority beyond their having been instituted and sanctioned by God. Parents, and especially fathers, were used as symbols for all persons vested with authority, including masters, teachers, and magistrates. The importance of these various powers was God's having commanded that they be obeyed so long as their orders were not contrary to divine law; the logical and historical sources of social and political status in familial relationships appeared only as incidental arguments. Therefore, the teachings of the Church supported political authority in general rather than a particular form of government, and obedience to the monarchy as well as to the Commonwealth was defended with the Fifth Commandment. Between 1649 and 1660 'King' was changed to 'magistrate' in many catechism books, but the general principle remained unaltered.

Catechistical instruction was almost impossible to escape in seventeenth-century England. It will be argued in chapter four that this derivation of political obligation from the duty to obey parents was the fundamental political view of the great masses of Stuart Englishmen who were never able to overcome this much of their childhood training. Some form of paternal authority was the only kind of status relationship with which most of these people were familiar. It is not at all difficult to conceive of their expanding this loyalty to their parents to encompass masters and employers and ultimately magistrates. The Church's interpretation of the Fifth Commandment was an ideological complement to the society in which the masses found themselves. Childhood was not something that was eventually outgrown; rather, it was enlarged to include the whole of one's life. And if it is kept in mind that the members of this rank-and-file class were usually illiterate and so were not familiar with other explanations of their relationship to the state, it is difficult to believe that they could have known or understood any doctrine other than the one taught by the Church.

Outside the Church and above the level of 'ordinary' people, this same interpretation of the duty to obey parents acquired an importance in polemic literature. Patriarchal political theorists regularly cited the Fifth Commandment in support of their positions, and very early in the seventeenth century Chief Justice

Coke included this doctrine in one of his major opinions. But less than ninety years later, Locke was to imply that the Fifth Commandment had nothing to do with political obligation. His sentiments were soon echoed by the outspoken Benjamin Hoadly, a self-proclaimed follower of Locke, against Charles Leslie, the non-juring Filmerian. To Hoadly, the doctrine was a mere metaphor with no literal meaning whatsoever. When a man who was to be named to an important Bishopric in the Church of England could so interpret the principle that scarcely fifty years earlier had been at the very center of his Church's conception of political obedience, the world had surely changed.

5

The organization of this book is essentially chronological. The three categories of patriarchal reasoning just discussed will serve as frameworks through which the historical materials can be interpreted. In this manner it will be possible to examine the development of the theory without giving undue emphasis to this abstract differentiation among its components. The next two chapters are a broad survey of familial doctrines in political philosophy in the period before 1603; chapter two deals with European thought from Plato to Bodin and Althusius, and chapter three analyzes the political theory of Tudor England. This discussion shows that while the familial symbol had played a significant role in political thinking, there was no patriarchal theory of obligation prior to 1603. It then becomes possible to appreciate the doctrinal and logical changes that would be required to support such a theory. Chapter four departs from the chronology and establishes the intellectual and social context of moral patriarchalism. Several reasons for the appearance of the theory are suggested, and the actual structure of the family in seventeenth-century England is briefly examined for its relationship to the political theory in which it played so important a symbolic role. The latter part of the chapter extends this discussion of social structure and examines the patriarchal political thought of the masses, the group on whom the Church's ideological instruction and the patriarchal nature of family life most heavily weighed. Except for two chapters at the end, the remainder of the essay should occasion no conceptual problems, for it presents patriarchalism as it can be found in political literature throughout the seventeenth century. The last two chapters deal with the place of the family in Hobbes's political philosophy and Locke's discussion of the familial origins of political authorty. These chapters have been placed together because they raise questions and require the use of methods that are different from those found in the rest of the book.

Hobbes and Locke were, after all, the unassailable giants not only of Stuart but of the whole of English political thought; their political writings were far more than mere polemic tracts. No matter what methodological biases toward the history of political philosophy one might harbor, he will hardly deny that the *Leviathan* and the *Two Treatises* demand more serious attention than most Stuart pamphlets. It is simply more important that they be read correctly than it is that Dudley Digges, John Maxwell, Henry Neville, or Charles Leslie, for instance, be properly understood. To have given Hobbes and Locke the attention they deserve in their proper historical sequence would have detracted both from the chronology and from the study of these thinkers themselves. But there is another and probably more important reason for saving them until the end of my study. All writers— no matter how great their philosophical prowess and no matter how much they are held to have 'transcended' their own historical periods—must eventually be read in relation to the circumstances and intellectual forces and prejudices by which they were surrounded. The thesis of this book is that the patriarchal political theory provided a part of that context for Hobbes and Locke. But since patriarchalism has not previously been recognized as significant, it has not been possible to appreciate its impact on Hobbes and Locke. Not until this background has been thoroughly documented and examined can they be studied in terms of it.

# II

## Patriarchal Political Thought from Plato to Bodin and Althusius

I

The relationship between the family and society as a whole—and between familial and political authority—is one of the leitmotives of social and political philosophy. The pseudo-Aristotelian treatise *Economics*, Hannah Arendt has observed, limited actual participating membership in the polis to 'the household heads, who have established themselves as "monarchs" at home before they join to constitute the public political realm of the city'.[1] During the debates over the franchise at the American Constitutional Convention, Colonel George Mason, a delegate from Virginia, suggested fatherhood as one of several possible alternatives to the property qualification; Mason's premise was that a man with children had as genuine a stake in the society as a land owner:

A Freehold is the qualification in England, & here it is imagined to be the only proper one. The true idea in his opinion was that every man having evidence of attachment to & permanent common interest with the Society ought to share in all its rights and privileges. Was this qualification restricted to Freeholders? Does no other property but land evidence a common interest in the proprieter? does nothing beside property mark a permanent attachment. Ought the merchant, the married man, the parent of a number of children whose fortunes are to be pursued in their own [country],

[1] Hannah Arendt, *Between Past and Future: Six Exercises in Political Thought* (New York, 1961), p. 117, citing *Economics*, 1343a 1–4.

be viewed as suspicious characters, and unworthy to be trusted with the common rights of their fellow Citizens.[2]

And as recently as November, 1963, when the city of Madrid, Spain, held its first municipal elections in nine years, the only persons eligible to vote for one-third of the council-men were the 'heads of resident families'.[3] These, of course, are isolated examples, but they are part of a persistent pre-occupation in political thinking. The most likely reason why the familial metaphor is invoked in politics is that fatherly authority and the hierachical relationships of the household are so obvious and inescapable. Fatherhood and kinship can always be used analogically to explain other kinds of status relationships, if only to demonstrate the differences between the family and other associations.

It was not until the seventeenth century that familial reasoning was used as a direct justification of political obligation. Up to that time, the household image was used for other purposes in political discourses: (1) to show the importance of the family to the preservation of the social order, (2) to demonstrate the origins and historical evolution of society, and (3) to determine membership in the political community. A broad survey of some of the most important and characteristic observations about the relationship between politics and the family in the period from ancient Athens to the accession of James I will be useful for several reasons: to call attention to the changing use and status of the metaphor; to indicate some of the important similarities and differences between seventeenth-century English patriarchal thought and the earlier notions that gave rise to it; and to provide some of the immediate intellectual background to the appearance and development of patriarchal theories of obligation in Stuart England, a problem that will be examined in greater detail in chapter four. The discussion is divided into two parts, (1) the continental tradition from Plato to Althusius, which is the subject of this chapter, and (2) English thought during the Tudor period, which is dealt with in chapter three.

[2] Max Farrand, ed., *The Records of the Federal Convention of 1787*, rev. ed., 4 vols. (New Haven, 1911–1937), II, 203. I owe this reference to Professor Gerald Pomper of Rutgers University.

[3] 'Monarchists Quit Madrid Campaign', *New York Times*, 29 October 1963.

2

The use of the family as a basis for society is illustrated in Plato's *Republic*. Even though he would have replaced the physical family with the community of wives and children, Plato was unwilling to surrender the traditional morality of the family in his ideal state. Every Guardian, Socrates insisted, 'must regard everyone who he meets as brother or sister, father or mother, son or daughter, grandchild or grandparent'. To which Glaucon replied:

> Very good; but here is a further point. Will you not require them, not merely to use these family terms, but to behave as a real family? Must they not show towards all whom they call 'father' the customary reverence, care and obedience due to a parent, if they look for any favour from gods or men, since to act otherwise is contrary to divine and human law? Should not all the citizens constantly reiterate in the hearing of the children from their earliest years such traditional maxims of conduct towards those whom they are taught to call father and their other kindred?

Socrates agreed and added, 'It would be absurd that terms of kinship should be on their lips without any action to correspond.'[4] In the *Statesman*, with the ideal replaced by the 'best possible', Plato went considerably further and specifically identified the governments of households and small political units. When the Stranger asked, 'Is there much difference between a large household and a small-sized city, so far as the exercise of authority over it is concerned?' the Young Socrates answered, 'None.' 'Well then,' the Stranger continued, 'our point is clearly made. One science covers all those several spheres, and we will not quarrel with a man who prefers one of the particular names for it; he can call it royal science, political science, or science of household management.' And the Young Socrates agreed, 'It makes no difference.'[5]

[4] Plato, *The Republic*, bk. v, 463, ed. and trans. F. M. Cornford (New York, 1945), pp. 164–5. For further discussion, see Ernest Barker, *Greek Political Theory: Plato and His Predecessors* (London, 1918), pp. 219–20 and 223 n.1.
[5] Plato, *Statesman*, 259b–c, trans. J. B. Skemp, in Plato, *Collected Dialogues*, ed. Edith Hamilton and Huntington Cairns (New York, 1961), p. 1022.

In his last dialogue, *The Laws*, Plato discussed the transformation of several independent households, each ruled only by 'custom and what is called *traditionary* law', into a genuine political society with fully developed legislation. In these non-political familial societies, he asked, 'do we not find that the oldest members rule, because their authority has come down to them from the father or the mother? The rest follow them and form one flock, like so many birds, and are thus under patriarchal control, the most justifiable of all types of royalty.' He then described the voluntary association of several of these households into larger communities and the eventual adoption of legislative institutions.[6] His treatment was brief, but Plato's understanding of the process of amalgamation differed very little from the notion that was generally accepted by seventeenth-century English thinkers.

Aristotle's account of the emergence of the state from the household in Book I of *The Politics* is quite well known. Transmitted by St. Thomas to the Scholastics, his analysis provided the basis for most discussions of the origins of the state after the thirteenth century. A number of Stuart patriarchalists, including Sir Robert Filmer, not recognizing the important distinctions between Aristotle's teleology and their own genetic doctrines, cited *The Politics* in defense of their justifications of political obligation on familial grounds. Basic to Aristotle's conception—as well as to that of seventeenth-century contractual theorists who regarded the family as the precursor of the political community—was an insistence upon the difference between paternal and political authority. Aristotle opened *The Politics* with a sharp criticism of Plato's identification of 'political science' and the 'science of household management' in the *Statesman*:

It is a mistake to believe that the 'statesman' [the *politikos*, who handles the affairs of a political association] is the same as the monarch of a kingdom, or the manager of a household, or the master of a number of slaves. Those who hold this view consider that each of these persons differ from the others not with a difference of kind, but [merely with a difference of degree, and] according to the number, or the paucity, of the persons with whom he deals. On this view a man who is concerned with few persons is a master: one who is concerned with more is the manager of a household: one who is

[6] Plato, *The Laws*, 680e–681b, trans. A. E. Taylor, in *Collected Dialogues*, pp. 1275–6.

B

concerned with still more is a 'statesman', or a monarch. This view abolishes any real difference between a large household and a small polis.[7]

A further difference between the household and polis, Aristotle contended, is that 'The authority of the statesman is exercised over men who are naturally free; that of the master over men who are [naturally] slaves; and again the authority generally exercised over a household by its head is that of a monarch (for all households are monarchically governed), . . .'.[8] In *The Nichomachean Ethics* yet another distinction was drawn between the state and the household, that the same kind of 'justice' could not prevail in both:

> The justice of a master and that of a father are not the same as the justice of citizens, though they are like it; for there can be no injustice in the unqualified sense, towards things that are one's own, but a man's chattel, and his child until it reaches a certain age and sets up for itself, are as it were part of himself, and no one chooses to hurt himself (for which reason there can be no injustice towards oneself). . . . Hence justice can no more truly be manifested towards a wife than towards children and chattels, for the former is household justice; but even this is different from political justice.[9]

Aristotle regarded the household as a natural community:

> there must necessarily be a union or pairing of those who cannot exist without one another. Male and female must unite for the reproduction of the species—not from deliberate intention, but from the natural impulse, which exists in animals generally as it also exists in plants, to leave behind them something of the same nature as themselves.

Through a series of physical expansions and moral transformations this nuclear family became the polis. The change began with the acquisition of slaves and servants as the family became a house-

[7] Aristotle, *The Politics*, I, i, 2, ed. and trans. Sir Ernest Barker (Oxford, 1948), p. 1. Brackets in Barker's text. See also III, iv, 11–13, p. 104.
[8] Ibid., I, vii, 1, p. 17. Brackets in Barker's text.
[9] Aristotle, *The Nichomachean Ethics*, V, vi, trans. Sir David Ross, World's Classics (London, 1954), p. 123. See also, *Politics*, I, xii, 1–3.

hold by the inescapable 'union of the naturally ruling element with the element which is naturally ruled, for the preservation of both'. When this took place, the unit began to approach the 'self-sufficiency' that epitomized political organization for Aristotle. The next step was the association of several households into a village, which was described as a 'colony or offshoot from a family'. In the last stage, the village became the polis, a genuine political order. The polis was initially ruled by a monarch because it had been 'formed of persons who were already monarchically governed'. Households were always monarchies, in which 'the eldest of the kin' ruled, 'just as villages, when they are offshoots from the household, are similarly governed in virtue of the kinship between their members'.[10]

By relating the state to the family in this manner, Aristotle fortified his view of the political order as a natural association that did not depend upon deliberate human actions. The insistence that the state was natural was to be a key element in the patriarchal attack on the conventionalism of the social contract theory, but it is very important to distinguish Aristotle's naturalism from that of seventeenth-century England. W. L. Newman observed in his edition of *The Politics* that having shown that the household was natural, if Aristotle could 'prove that the village [was] an outgrowth of the household, and the polis of the village, then the polis [would] be shown to be natural'.[11] However, this interpretation gives an unwarranted genetic cast to Aristotle's thought; moreover, his teleological metaphysics and his conception of the political unit as self-sufficient were capable of demonstrating that the state was natural regardless of its beginnings. The familial origins of the polis furnished logical and historical rather than moral supports for the theory. Besides, Aristotle believed that essence has nothing to do with origins but rests upon function.[12] Obedience in the pre-political family was probably not at all relevant to obligation in the polis, as indeed it could not have been in a teleological doctrine. Had Aristotle

[10] *Politics*, I, ii, 2 and 6, pp. 3 and 4. And see sect. 8 (p. 4): the state is more than the family and therefore higher because the polis is 'an association which may be said to have reached the full height of self-sufficiency'.

[11] Quoted by Barker in his notes to *Politics*, I, ii, 6, p. 4n.

[12] See *Politics*, I, ii, 8–10 (pp. 4–5, and especially n. 2 on p. 5); I, ii, 13 (p. 6); and III, ii, 2 (p. 96, and see Barker's note).

actually *derived* political obligation from familial authority, he
would have been saying that the earlier and therefore less complete form prescribed the nature of the final product. The strict
application of his teleological principle, on the other hand, would
have led to one of two conclusions, that the duties to obey in the
two spheres were unrelated or that political obligation, as the
final resultant of household obedience, actually determined the
essence of duty in the family. Either assertion would have been
out of place in the patriarchalism of seventeenth-century England.

3

The basic form of the Aristotelian notion was accepted by
Cicero, who asserted in his *De Officiis* that a common will and
feeling of fellowship were essential in a state even though it
had grown organically out of the natural association of the
family. The family, Cicero said, is 'the foundation of civil government, the nursery, as it were, of the state'.[13]

This understanding of political evolution was dominant from
the early Christian period to the Renaissance. Ernst Troeltsch
argues that the primitive church uniformly accepted the notion
that 'the monogamous family is the basis of Society and of the
State, which has itself been formed by the expansion of the
family'.[14] Nonetheless, whether governance was a part of man's
natural condition or a result of his fallen nature remained an un-
resolved issue. For instance, if the state were assumed to have

[13] Marcus Tullius Cicero, *De Officiis*, I, xvii, 54, trans. Walter Miller,
Loeb Classic Library (London, 1913), p. 57. The phrase *seminarium rei
publicae*, translated into 'seminary of the republic', was used a number
of times in Stuart England without reference to Cicero. On this same
passage, see also J. W. Gough, *The Social Contract: A Critical Study of
Its Development*, 2nd ed. (Oxford, 1957), p. 19.
  In *De Republica*, Scipio refused to 'go back to [the] primal constituents'
of the political system, saying, 'I shall not, for example, follow the usual
custom of scholars in this field, and begin with the first union of male and
female, with the propagation of offspring, and with the family relationships that ensue.' Cicero, *On the Commonwealth*, I, xxiv, ed. and trans.
George H. Sabine and Stanley B. Smith (Columbus, Ohio, 1929),
pp. 128–9.
[14] Ernst Troeltsch, *The Social Teaching of the Christian Church*, trans.
Olive Wyon, paperbound, 2 vols. (New York, 1960), I, 130.

resulted from the Fall, then it was necessarily related to the existence of evil in the world. If, on the other hand, it could be ascertained that some measure of order and coercion had existed in Paradise, then the state need not be regarded as altogether unholy. What was necessary in the second case was to determine how much authority God had initially established, what changes were brought about by the original sin, and where coercive political power fitted into the larger scheme. Given the belief in the familial origins of politics, the source of fatherly authority *vis-à-vis* the Fall should have assumed central importance. Troeltsch calls attention to two models:

> The family with its patriarchal dominion of men and its compulsory matrimonial right was, indeed, still regarded [by some] as a consequence of the Fall, like all law and all compulsion which had replaced the complete inner freedom of the Primitive State. Others, however, argued that the manner of Eve's creation proves that the subjection of woman is in the natural order of things; however, the overlordhip of man was only established when the curse was pronounced and Adam and Eve were driven out of Paradise.[15]

Even in terms of these two conceptions the *relationship* between the family and political rule does not seem to have been carefully or fully examined. How the family expanded into the state and whether the resultant political order was different in kind from its historical precursor are questions that were not answered simply by discovering whether or not paternal right existed before the Fall. The fatherly power might have been natural but not coercive. St. Augustine's treatment of these problems is instructive, for he drew an important but vague and incomplete distinction between the sociability of man, which was natural, and political and legal coercion, which was not. It was God's will, St. Augustine wrote, that men should 'associate with one another' and 'be bound together in harmony and peace' even before the Fall. Sin made this impossible and required the establishment of remedial political institutions that could restrain corrupted mankind. But the 'loving oversight of all the members of their household' by fathers was 'in accord with the natural order' that had existed in Paradise and was originally manifested in the natural bond between Adam and Eve. At the same time, St. Augustine

15 Ibid., I, 129.

accepted the family as 'the beginning or element of the city',[16] without really differentiating between the authority of a loving father and that of a legitimate magistrate. In these terms, it would have been difficult for him to account for the expansion of the family into the state without somehow demonstrating that this physical growth was accompanied by a moral transformation, which was the claim made by Aristotle. But St. Augustine was not at all clear on this point, and it is interesting to note the apparent absence from his writings of an explicit statement that familial society in Paradise was the prototype of political organization after the Fall.

A more cogent account of the relationship between the two kinds of power had, of course, been supplied by Aristotle. St. Thomas Aquinas returned to the Aristotelian notion that the prepolitical family was not a 'perfect' or 'self-sufficient' community and was therefore distinct from the state. After pointing out that men needed 'life's necessities' provided for them and were therefore required to live together, St. Thomas said:

There is indeed a certain sufficiency in the family of one household, so far as the elementary necessities of nutrition and procreation and such like are concerned. Similarly in one locality you may find all that is necessary for the fulness of life; and in a province we have an even better example, because in this case there is added the mutual assistance of allies against hostile attack. Whoever then rules a perfect community, be it a city or a province, is rightly called a king. The head of the household, on the other hand, is not called king but father. Even so there is a certain similarity about the two cases, kings are sometimes called the fathers of their people.[17]

In his *Commentary* on *The Politics*, St. Thomas paraphrased Aristotle's derivation of the state from familial society and repeated with approval that civil society is natural to man teleologically and because it 'is generated from the previously

---

[16] St. Augustine, *The City of God*, trans. Marcus Dods, Modern Library (New York, 1950), XIV, i, p. 441; XIX, xvi, pp. 694–5; and Herbert Deane, *The Political and Social Ideas of St. Augustine* (New York, 1963), p. 73.

[17] St. Thomas Aquinas, *De Regimine Principum*, I, i, *Selected Political Writings*, ed. A. P. d'Entreves, trans. J. G. Dawson (Oxford, 1948), p. 9.

mentioned societies [including the household], which are natural
. . .'.[18] Much of this was spelled out in greater detail in the *Summa
Theologica* where Aquinas related his Aristotelianism to man's
fall from Grace. He argued that political authority and the
hierarchies to which it gives rise are natural and that:

such dominion would have been found between man and man in the
state of innocence. . . . [M]an is naturally a social animal; and in consequence men would have lived in society, even in the state of
innocence. Now there could be no social life for many persons
living together unless one of their number were set in authority
to care for the common good.[19]

Aquinas showed, with Aristotle, that human associations were
joined together in a continuous, natural plenum that was structured both logically and historically from the household, through
the village and city communities, to the state. Government was a
part of the natural order and not the result of God's special
creation; it flowed from and therefore was perfectly compatible
with man's nature. Thus, naturalistic arguments could be used
to explain and to justify political authority. This Thomistic-
Aristotelian political naturalism was teleological and one of its
important theoretical consequences was the populist doctrine that
because the political order was an extension of human nature, the
ruler was not God's designated viceroy but was responsible to
the people. For it was their natural requirements that had given
rise to his authority.[20] But naturalism could also be used to support
an absolutist political theory, as Filmer and the patriarchalists
demonstrated in Stuart England. Patriarchal naturalism was
genetic rather than teleological and insisted that the development
of social institutions after the Creation could in no way further
extend nature. Doubtless, neither of these arguments occurred to

[18] St. Thomas Aquinas, *Commentary on the Politics*, I, i, 32, tran. Ernest
L. Fortin and Peter D. O'Neill, *Medieval Political Philosophy: A Source-
book*, ed. Ralph Lerner and Mushin Mahdi (New York, 1963), p. 309.
[19] St. Thomas Aquinas, *Summa Theologica*, I, 96, 4, *Political Writings*,
p. 105.
[20] See Walter Ullman, *Principles of Government and Politics in the Middle
Ages* (London, 1961), pp. 22 and 239–67; Ullmann, *The Individual and
Society in the Middle Ages* (Baltimore, 1966), ch. iii; and Charles H.
McIlwain, *The Growth of Political Thought in the West from the Greeks
to the End of the Middle Ages* (New York, 1932), pp. 153–5.

St. Thomas or even to his immediate followers; it remained for later thinkers to work out the full implications of this Aristotelianism in response to competing doctrines and specific political situations.

Medieval disputes between secular and clerical authorities gave impetus to the use of the origins in political argument. Numerous authors attempted to discover the relationship of the political order to the Church by showing how governance began. Accordingly, brief examinations of the supposed origins of the state appeared in political tracts with some frequency after St. Thomas.[21] The organic and necessary growth of the family into the perfected political order was the standard account,[22] for the general practice was simply to follow Aristotle. Marsilius of Padua's *Defender of the Peace* (1324) is representative. The 'first and smallest combination of human beings, wherefrom the other combinations emerged', Marsilius wrote, 'was that of male and female, as the foremost of the philosophers says in the *Politics*'. As the number of children increased, this family expanded into 'many households', several of which together were 'called a village or hamlet, and this was the first community, as is also written in the above-cited treatise'. With the gradual enlargement and duplication of these societies, Marsilius continued, 'men's experiences became greater, . . . [and] the parts of communities were more fully differentiated'. Finally, human reason and experience developed 'the things which are necessary for living and for living well', and the 'perfect community, called the state', was established.[23]

The same evolutionary doctrine had been advanced by Aegudius Romanus; he also suggested that the political realm began with the voluntary association of individuals and did not specify whether the two modes were complementary or alternatives.[24] This patriarchalism does not appear to have moved beyond the

---

[21] Ewart Lewis, *Medieval Political Ideas*, 2 vols. (London, 1954), I, 157.

[22] See Otto Gierke, *Political Theories of the Middle Ages*, trans. Frederic Maitland, paperbound (Boston, 1958), pp. 89 and 186, n.302; and Guenter Lewy, *Constitutionalism and Statecraft during the Golden Age of Spain* (Geneva, 1960), pp. 37 and 38.

[23] Marsilius of Padua, *The Defender of the Peace*, I, iii, 3–5, trans. Alan Gewirth, paperbound (New York, 1967), pp. 10–12.

[24] Aegidius Romanus, *De Regimine Principum* (1285), III, i, 6, as cited in Gough, *Social Contract*, pp. 42–3.

anthropological thesis about the origins of the state. The moral patriarchal theory was probably totally absent from medieval political thought, for no thinkers seem to have utilized the image of paternal authority as a direct justification of political obligation. At the very most, it might be said that the familial origins of the state could have been employed as a naturalistic defense of obligation. But this notion would still have required the introduction of an additional and determinative category, naturalism, rather than a direct appeal to familial source of political power.[25]

The secularized political thought of the Renaissance gradually abandoned even the limited Thomistic patriarchalism of Marsilius and moved toward a more voluntaristic explanation of political origins. Plato, it will be recalled, had combined voluntarism with a patriarchal theory in *The Laws*, but this was not the case with Machiavelli who either viewed the pre-political world as lacking even familial organization or felt that the question was not worth very much attention. 'At the beginning of the world the inhabitants were few in number,' he wrote in the *Discourses*, 'and lived for a time dispersed, like beasts. As the human race increased, the necessity for uniting themselves for defence made itself felt; the better to attain this object, they chose the strongest and most courageous from amongst themselves and placed him at their head, promising to obey him.'[26] Machiavelli said nothing more about the origins of government or the pre-political condition of man.

The fatherly image was used by Erasmus in his description of a monarch, but the purpose was to show that a king should be gentle rather than to provide a patriarchal basis for his authority. Nonetheless, Erasmus altered the traditional Aristotelian theory

[25] The authority of the Pope—to say nothing of the very etymology of his title—is an altogether different matter. At least two late medieval authors, Dante and Augustinus Triumphus, justified obedience to the Pope on patriarchal grounds; and some Popes and their supporters claimed that temporal rulers were virtual sons to the Pontiff and therefore had no rights against him. (Michael Wilks, *The Problem of Sovereignty in the Later Middle Ages* [Cambridge, 1963], pp. 145, 159, 160, 280, 286–7, and 337.)
[26] Niccolo Machiavelli, *Discourses on the First Ten Books of Titus Livius*, I, ii, trans. Christian E. Detmold, *The Prince and the Discourses*, ed. Max Lerner, Modern Library (New York, 1940), p. 112.

by denying that familial and political power were inherently distinct; he called a kingdom 'a great family' and suggested that a monarch was a father to his people. Notions such as these were to occupy central positions in the patriarchal political theories of the next century. Erasmus wrote:

The good prince ought to have the same attitude toward his subjects, as a good *paterfamilias* toward his household—for what else is a kingdom but a great family? What is the king if not the father to a great multitude? He is superior, but yet of the same stock—a man, a freeman over free men, not untamed beasts, as Aristotle justly comments, and this is what those poets of remotest antiquity meant when they applied to Jupiter—to whom they assign supreme authority of the whole world and gods, as they say—these words . . . 'father of gods and men'. We have been taught by Christ our teacher that God is the unquestioned prince of all the world, and we call him 'Father'. . . . As a *paterfamilias* thinks whatever increase of wealth has fallen to any of his house is [the same as if it had been] to his own private goods, so he who has the true attribute of a prince considers the possessions of his subjects to represent his own wealth. Them he holds bound over to him through love, so that they have nothing to fear at all from the prince for either their lives or their possessions.

It seems clear that these remarks were not intended to shed light on the origins of the state, for a few pages later Erasmus stated, 'In the very early times, the kings were selected through the choice of the people because of their outstanding qualities, which were called "heroic" as being all but divine and superhuman.' He urged rulers to 'remember their beginnings, and realize that they are not really princes if they lack that quality which first made princes'.[27]

Although the Thomistic-Aristotelian derivation of the state from the family was central to the Scholastics and is found in much of the writing of the Counter-Reformation, Juan de Mariana, Luis de Molina, Francisco Suarez, Francisco de Vitoria, and Domingo de Soto—all Spanish Jesuits—traced the political order to the expansion of the natural society of husband, wife,

[27] Desiderius Erasmus, *The Education of a Christian Prince* (1516), ed. and trans. Lester K. Born (New York, 1936), pp. 170–1 and 173. Brackets in Born's text.

and children. Molina, for instance, combined this doctrine with voluntarism as the immediate source of the state but insisted that agreement was only the formal means by which men acceded to the divine and natural ordination of governance.[28] The same conception of familial expansion can be found in lay French thought as well, particularly in the writings of Lambert Daneau, Louis Le Roy, and Pierre de Belloy.[29] None of these authors, however, advanced a patriarchal justification of political obligation; in fact, they saw the familial association as a picture of pre-political life and did not attempt to relate these origins to the nature of the political community itself. But in Jean Bodin's *Six Livres De la République* (1576) and the *Politica Methodice Digesta* of Johannes Althusius (1604) the household and paternal authority were accorded prominent places.

### 4

For Bodin and Althusius the family was the elemental social unit as well as the logical and historical source for more complex associations. In his first definition of a 'commonweale' Bodin called it 'a lawfull government of many families, and of that which unto them in common belongeth, with a puissant soveraigntie'.[30] Thus, there could be no commonweale unless there were families, but a family could stand by itself without being a part of some larger community. One household—no matter how large it grew or how extensive its territory became—could never be a commonweale, for a commonweale had to be a union of at least three families. Bodin defined the family as 'the right government of many subjects or persons under the obedience of one and

[28] See Gough, *Social Contract*, pp. 61–2 and 68–9; Lewy, *Constitutionalism*, p. 43; and Bernice Hamilton, *Political Thought in Sixteenth-Century Spain* (Oxford, 1963), pp. 31–5.

[29] Gough, *Social Contract*, pp. 57–8; J. W. Allen, *A History of Political Thought in the Sixteenth Century* (London, 1928), pp. 379 and 384; and William F. Church, *Constitutional Thought in Sixteenth Century France* (Cambridge, Mass., 1941), pp. 8 and 223. Also relevant is Otto Gierke, *Natural Law and the Theory of Society, 1500–1800*, ed. and trans. Ernest Barker, paperbound (Boston, 1957), p. 269, nn. 1 and 2.

[30] Jean Bodin, *The Six Bookes of a Commonweale*, I, i, trans. Richard Knolles (London, 1606), facsimile reprint, ed. Kenneth McRae, Harvard Political Classics (Cambridge, Mass., 1962), p. 1.

the same head of the family; and of such things as are unto them proper'.[31] This unit was ruled by a father, whose power alone of all the authority in the world was natural. 'The right and power to commaund,' Bodin wrote, 'is not by nature given to any beside the Father, who is the true Image of the great and Almighty God the Father of all things . . .'. Each father is 'by nature bound to nourish his children, according to his abilities, and to instruct them in all civilitie and vertue'; and the child, in return, is bound to his father, 'unto whom next unto God he is beholden for his life, and for whatsoever els[e] he hath in this world'.

Criticizing the distinction between political and domestic power in Book I of Aristotle's *Politics*, Bodin said that as the family 'is the true seminarie and beginning of every Commonweale, [it is] also a principal member thereof'. The error of Aristotle was 'without any probable cause, to have divided the Oeconomicall government from the Politicall and a Citie from a Familie'; this distinction can no more be maintained, Bodin concluded, than 'if we should pull the members from the bodie: or go about to build a Citie without houses'. The only distinction that Bodin was willing to acknowledge between a family and a commonweale was that familial authority extended to the private possessions and interests of all the members of the household, whereas political rule was concerned only with those things that were of common or public interest to all the constituent families of a commonweale. Aristotle, on the contrary, had likened fatherly power to monarchical rule over inferiors and stressed the egalitarian and participatory aspects of politics. For Bodin the commonweale originated in conquest and military alliance between a number of independent families which had previously been ruled by a patriarch with the 'power of life and death over his wife and children'.[32]

Bodin's conception of citizenship was built directly on this familial basis. The political order he envisaged was apparently a community of patriarchs or familial heads, for in his first discussion of citizenship he wrote:

[31] Ibid., I, vi, p. 46; I, ii, pp. 8–11; and I, iv, pp. 20–8.
[32] Ibid., I, ii, pp. 8 and 12, and I, vi, pp. 47–8. See also III, vii, where Bodin accepted the more traditional Aristotelian notion that the commonweale was the result of the expansion of the household into more inclusive and complex forms of association.

Now when the maister of the Familie goeth out of his owne house where he commaundeth, to entreat and trafficke with other heads of Families, of that [which] concerneth them all in generall, he then loseth the title of master, head, and lord, to be a companion equall and fellowlike with others, leaving his familie to enter into a Citie, and his domesticall affaires to entreat of publick; and in stead of a lord calleth himselfe a Citizen, which is no other in proper tearmes than *A free subject holding of the soveraigntie of another man.* For before there was either Citie or citizen, or any forme of a Commonweale amongst men, everie master of a familie was a maister in his owne house. . . .

The freedom of the person for whom citizenship was claimed was the crucial part of this definition. When he repeated this argument on the next page of the *République*, Bodin distinguished slaves from citizens and attempted to show how the bondage of slaves was different from the indebtedness of wives and children. He appealed to common practice rather than to an inherent difference between the two kinds of status; instead of clarifying the question, he tended to confuse it. The 'definition of a Citizen', he reiterated, is 'no other thing' than

*A free subject holding of the soveraigntie of another man. A free* subject, I say for albeit that a slave be much more subject unto the commaund of the highest authoritie than a free man; yet so it is, that al[l] people have alwayes with their common consent agreed, That a slave is no Citizen, and in questions of right is accounted no bodie; which cannot truely be said of mens wives and children, who are free from all servitude and bondage; albeit that their rights and liberties, and power to dispose of their owne goods, be from them in some sort cut off by the domesticall power: in sort that a man may say, that everie Citizen is a subject, some small part of his libertie being diminished by the majestie of him to whome he oweth obeyance.[33]

What Bodin seems to have been saying, when these two passages are considered together, is that only those persons who are not *politically* subjugated to someone else are eligible for citizenship in the commonweale. The subjection of slaves is political; therefore slaves have never been counted as citizens. Wives and children, on the other hand, are politically free, although the

[33] Ibid., I, vi, quotations from pp. 47 and 48.

exercise of their freedom is limited by the power of their patriarchal superiors. Political authority turns out, after all, to be distinguishable from domestic power and Aristotle's refusal to treat the two kinds of rule as the same was justified.

The patriarchalism of Althusius may be dealt with somewhat more briefly, for it is similar to Bodin's in several important respects. According to Althusius, social and political life were part of man's nature; even though the relationships involved were contractual, they could not be avoided and were therefore natural. These relationships grow out of families, which Althusius regarded as 'the seedbed of all private and public associational life'. Thus, it was a mistake to discuss the family and politics separately. Nonetheless, Althusius felt that the economic (or domestic) and political realms could be differentiated, for 'the skill of attending to household goods, of supplying, increasing, and conserving the goods of the family, is entirely economic, and as such is correctly eliminated from politics'. But 'altogether different' from this economic *purpose* of the family, he continued, is the *nature* of the 'association among spouses and kinsmen, which is entirely political' and has to do with 'governing and preserving of association' itself. Althusius designated this kind of association 'symbiotic', and within this more limited framework, he distinguished the family as a simple and 'private association' from the complex and public association of the 'polity'.[34]

In what had become the standard manner, Althusius discussed the expansion of nuclear families into villages, hamlets, and cities. The process began when the heads of a number of presumably neighboring households joined together into a 'collegium', which was a voluntary but still private association. Althusius quoted Book One, Chapter Six of the *République* and apparently agreed with Bodin's conception of the supra-familial order as communities of patriarchs. 'The public association exists,' Althusius said, 'when many private associations [including

[34] Johannes Althusius, *The Politics... An Abridged Translation of the Third Edition of Politica Methodice Digesta* (1614; originally published in 1604), ed. and trans. Frederick S. Carney (Boston, 1964), chs. ii–iii (combined by Carney), pp. 22–7. Althusius called this political order 'the universal and major public association'. 'It is a polity in the fullest sense,' he said, 'an imperium, realm, commonwealth, and people united in one body by the agreement of many symbiotic associations and particular bodies, and brought together under one right.' (Ibid., ch. ix, p. 61.)

families and collegia] are linked together for the purpose of establishing an inclusive political order' or 'community'. Membership in this community belonged to the constituent groups, not to individuals:

> The members of a community are private and diverse associations of families and collegia, not the individual members of private associations. These persons, by their coming together, now become not spouses, kinsmen, and colleagues, but citizens of the same community. Thus passing from the private symbiotic relationships, they unite in the one body of a community.

Thus, Althusius concluded that the family and the other private associations to which it gave rise were the logical as well as the historical precurors of the universal political realm.[35]

By maintaining the distinction beween private and public associations and by insisting that the household be seen as an economic organization and as a 'symbiotic' association, Althusius avoided the difficulties that were found in Bodin's account of the relationship between the familial and political orders. But even with these confusions eliminated, patriarchalism did not provide Althusius with a way of justifying political obligation; it was an historical and neutral description of the beginnings of political authority. The theory of Althusius, with a few notable exceptions, is very close to Aristotle's, and there is no suggestion in Althusius's doctrine of the possibility of deriving obligation from the familial origins of politics. The fact that the state was preceded by the household explains why functioning membership in the political community was limited to the heads of families, but it does not provide reasons why those patriarchs were bound to obey their political rulers. In order to move in this direction, it would have been necessary to add some further theory to the historical patriarchalism. Bodin's criticism of Aristotle seems to have contained an implicit recognition of this need, but nothing in the *République* suggests that Bodin would have been willing to accept a patriarchal defense of political duty. His denial of political naturalism was also a rejection of patriarchalism. Similarly, Althusius's conception of the political community as a voluntary association seriously undermined the

---

[35] Ibid., chs. iv, p. 28; v–vi, pp. 34–5; and ix, p. 61.

main thrust of the moral patriarchal theory. The combination of doctrines and interests that made possible a patriarchal theory of political obligation seems to have been peculiar to the England of the seventeenth century, and the immediate origins of that combination are to be found in the writings of Tudor political thinkers.

# III

## Patriarchalism in Tudor Political Thought

### I

Unlike the rest of Europe, England produced very little genuine political theory during the first half of the sixteenth century;[1] what there was rarely included examinations of the origins of the political order,[2] a problem that was central to the patriarchal justification of political obligation as well as to the descriptive, Aristotelian acount of the transformation of the pre-political family into the *societa perfecta*. Accordingly, patriarchal political theories were seldom advanced by early Tudor thinkers.

In the absence of a significant volume of theoretical literature, it is difficult to be certain, but prescription appears to have been the most widely accepted basis of legitimacy. Obedience was due to the reigning king simply because he was in power. This conception of sovereignty helps explain why origins was not one of the questions that occupied English political writers before the Reformation: an examination of origins would have served no purpose. As late as 1540, statements about the beginnings of political power would not have contributed to an understanding of political obligation because, as J. W. Allen has observed, there was still a 'general refusal to admit that any case [could] be made for a right of rebellion'.[3] Without either a theory of rebellion or the perceived possibility of resistance, there would be no

[1] See Christopher Morris, *Political Thought in England: Tyndale to Hooker*, Home University Library (London, 1953), pp. ix and 4.
[2] Franklin le Van Baumer, *The Early Tudor Theory of Kingship* (New Haven, 1942), p. 92; and Allen, *Sixteenth Century*, p. 126.
[3] Allen, *Sixteenth Century*, p. 131.

need for a theory of obedience; the fact that men usually obey the state does not get translated into a moral or ideological statement of their political duty until disobedience threatens to or actually becomes more than marginal.

So long as men are not disobeying or talking about disobeying in significant numbers, there is little likelihood that other men will write documents that attempt to demonstrate the illegitimacy of such actions or proposals. Once the process starts, however, the entire question of political obedience becomes an intellectual as well as a social problem. Justifications, defenses, and rationalizations are provided for behavior; and the nature of political life itself can become a fitting subject for speculation.

In the England of Henry VIII, however, there was not yet a firmly established tradition of political debate. Among the most important reasons for this absence is the fact that king and parliament were consolidated in their rejection of Rome. Consequently, neither side had to assert its rights against the other. This religious alliance, the existence of a certain trust, and a general failure even to raise the question 'of the king's relation to law dictated', according to Baumer, 'that neither a theory of divine-right monarchy nor parliamentary sovereignty should have been propounded by Henrician Englishmen'.[4] In short, there was no point in resisting and no conscious need for theories of resistance. The result was an apparent satisfaction with the *status quo* that did not call for an examination of origins, for there was no reason to ask how an unpopular condition had come into being.

This is not to suggest that patriarchalism was altogether absent from the political doctrines of pre-Elizabethan England. The Fifth Commandment was used to compel obedience to political authority in the *King's Book*, a summary statement of Anglican principles written in 1543. It was claimed of the Decalogue duty to honor parents:

And by this commandment also subjects be bound not to withdraw their said fealty, truth, love, and obedience towards their princes for any cause whatsoever it be, ne [*sic*] do any thing towards the hindrance or hurt thereof, nor of his estate.

And furthermore by this commandment they be bound to obey

---

[4] Baumer, *Early Tudor Theory*, p. 126.

also all the laws, proclamations, precepts, and commandments, made by their princes and governors, except they be against the commandments of God. And likewise they be bound to obey all such as be in authority under their prince, as far as he will have them obeyed.[5]

But in his now classic account of Christian duties published in 1528, William Tyndale had carefully avoided subsuming political authority under parental power when he discussed the meaning of the first precept of the Second Table.[6] Parents, he said, are entitled to the obedience of their children because God has made them His substitutes and agents:

And as He made thee through them, so hath He cast thee under the power and authority of them, to obey and serve them in His stead; saying, 'Honour thy father and mother' (Exod. xx). Which is not to be understood in bowing the knee, and putting off the cap only, but that thou love them with all thine heart; and fear and dread them, and wait on their commandments; and seek their worship, pleasure, will and profit in all things; and give thy life for them, counting them worthy of all honour; remembering that thou art their good and possession, and that thou owest unto them thine own self, and all thou art able, yea, and more than thou art able to do.

Understand also, that whatsoever thou doest unto them, be it good or bad, thou doest unto God. When thou pleasest them, thou pleasest God; when thou displeasest them, thou displeasest God; when they are angry with thee, God is angry with thee; neither is it possible for thee to come to the favour of God again, no, though all the angels of heaven pray for thee, until thou have submitted thyself unto thy father and mother again.[7]

Tyndale did not claim this same measure of divine right for magistrates, at least not in his discussion of the family. He

[5] *A Necessary Doctrine and Erudition for any Christian Man; Set Forth by the King's Majesty of England* (1543), ed. by T. A. Lacey as *The King's Book or A Necessary Doctrine* ... [etc.] (London, 1932), p. 104.

[6] This somewhat cumbersome phrase has been used rather than Fifth Commandment to avoid confusion, for Tyndale regarded this as the Fourth Commandment, as the Roman Catholic and Lutheran Churches still do.

[7] William Tyndale, *The Obedience of a Christian Man* (1528), ed. Richard Lovett, Christian Classics Series (London, n.d.), p. 78.

assumed that the duties owed to parents, husbands, masters, and political superiors were related, for he often shifted his argument from one to the other and back again, always providing a separate Biblical sanction for each (with magistracy firmly rooted in the Epistle to the Romans). Of these relations he wrote, 'Such obedience unto father and mother, master, husband, emperor, king, lords and rulers, requireth God of all nations, yea, of the very Turks and infidels.' Resistance was never justified, not even to correct wrong–doing: 'Neither may the inferior person avenge himself upon the superior, or violently resist him, for whatsoever wrong it be. If he do, he is condemned in the deed-doing', for vengeance, Tyndale concluded, belongs specifically and exclusively to God.[8]

An interesting instance in which patriarchal doctrines were not used is Thomas Elyot's charming *The Boke Named the Governour* (1531), a belated contribution to the medieval *speculum* literature. Elyot's failure to employ patriarchalism is noteworthy because many of his arguments and conclusions were to be regularly incorporated into the paternalistic political tracts of the next century. Attacking democracy and aristocracy, Elyot insisted that the government of one man is best; the second chapter of the *Governour* was entitled 'That one soverayne governour ought to be in a publyke weale. And what damage hath happened, when a multitude hath hadde equall auctoritie without any soveraigne'. Elyot said of monarchy:

that manner of governance is best approved, and hath longest continued, and is most ancient. For who can denye, but that all thyng in heven and earth is governed by one god, by one perpetual ordre, by one providence? One sonne ruleth over the day, & one Moone over the nyght.

Elyot then pointed to the government of bees and to God's having selected single persons to rule over Israel as evidence for the natural and divine sanctions of kingship.[9] The use of analogy by Elyot and his view of the universe as a structured, orderly whole in which such inferences would be valid were not rhetorical

[8] Ibid., pp. 87 and 88.
[9] Thomas Elyot, *The Boke Named Governour Devised by Thomas Elyot Knyght* (1531; London, 1544), sigs. 6–7; chapter title in black letter.

flourishes but were parts of a traditional way of perceiving the world.[10] As Christopher Morris has remarked, Elyot's 'universe is the conventional medieval universe, and more than one of his paragraphs could be used as a *locus classicus* for the idea of "the Great Chain of Being" '.[11] Missing from Elyot's defense of monarchy, however, was the obvious analogy—so commonly encountered in the seventeenth century—of the family, with its single, patriarchal head. Also absent from the *Governour* were attempts to defend political authority and to develop a conception of political obligation through the use of specific Biblical injunctions to obey temporal rulers. Of course, it must be kept in mind that unlike Tyndale, Elyot had not written a treatise on human duty but a handbook for rulers.

The derivation by Tyndale of political authority from the book of Romans is instructive, for that practice was very much in keeping with the Reformation conception of government as a remedial institution especially created by God to suppress the evil effects of sin. Use of a patriarchal–familial theory of obligation, on the other hand, would have necessitated acceptance of the political nautralism of St. Thomas; for in this case, the duty to obey the state would have been inherent in man's very nature rather than a specific result of his Fall. While it does not follow that the author of the *King's Book* was a self-conscious naturalist, the *implications* of his position placed him in a political tradition that was quite different from that in which Tyndale stood.

The contrasting understandings of the nature and purpose of society and government implicit in naturalism and special creation were ultimately irreconcilable, as the differences between the Augustinian and Thomistic views of the political world indicate. However, neither view entailed a particular substantive account of political obligation. Special creation, when interpreted through Romans 13, ended inescapably in political absolutism; but with a shift from God to man as the creator, the notion that the political order was an artifact supported the doctrine of limited government associated with social contract theories. In

[10] For examinations of both these ideas see Greenleaf, *Order, Empiricism, and Politics*, ch. ii; and E. M. W. Tillyard, *The Elizabethan World Picture*, paperbound (London, 1963).

[11] Morris, *Tyndale to Hooker*, p. 24.

much the same way, the naturalism of St. Thomas led Scholastics
to populist conclusions, but in the hands of Filmer, a similar
naturalistic argument ended in the divine right of kings. Before
Filmer could make his claims, the ground had to be prepared for
him; naturalistic, patriarchal conceptions had to supplement
or replace the conventional defenses of unlimited governmental
authority.

The beginnings of this replacement can be found in Bishop
John Hooper's commentary on the thirteenth chapter of Romans.
In what seems to have been the earliest instance of such a coupling in England (1551), Hooper unhesitatingly equated the duties
of children with those of subjects. He did not draw any inferences
from this argument but merely used the Fifth Commandment as
a means of extending his comments on the obedience owed to
rulers: 'Feare is due unto GOD, the kyng, to parentes, to all
others [by] whome we be holpe in bodie or soule, and so is
honour due likewyse. Therefore sayeth the lawe, feare GOD,
honoure the kynge, honoure father and mother.'[12] Hooper insisted that all monarchs were entitled to the passive obedience[13]
of their subjects; the magistrate was to be disobeyed only when his
commands violated God's law, for 'then we must obey more god
then men'.[14] However, Hooper did not provide a standard from
which subjects would be able to determine when they were
absolved of their political duties. The absence of such a standard

[12] John Hooper, *Godly and Most Necessary Annotations in ye. xiii Chap-
tyer to the Romaynes* (Worcester, 1551), sig. Di$^v$; original text in black
letter.
[13] This doctrine holds, in effect, that there are some cases in which the
subject may refuse to obey the magistrates, but he must be fully prepared
to pay the penalty for his disobedience. Strictly speaking, this is a theory
of passive *dis*obedience, and it must be distinguished from the more severe
doctrine of non-resistance with which it is often confused. Non-resistance
does not allow the subject the right to disobey even for reasons of conscience. This latter theory asserts that God alone is the judge of the
sovereign's actions and motives and that the ruler must be obeyed even
when his commands are contrary to the word of God. In such a case, the
sin is the ruler's not the subject's. Very few political thinkers adopted this
extreme doctrine; Filmer and Hobbes are probably the best examples.
Nonetheless, the term non-resistance is frequently used to describe what
are actually theories of passive obedience.
[14] Hooper, *Godly and Most Necessary*, sigs. Biv and Bv; original text in
black letter.

was a serious omission in all Christian thought of this period, for it made even this limited right of resistance paradoxical if not self-defeating. The theoretical result was either an anarchic situation in which every man judged for himself when divine law was being ignored or a despotic condition in which some person authoritatively made such a judgment for the community as a whole. This was not quite so serious a problem in Hooper's writings, for even if the subject could have known when his obligation ceased, he was prohibited from using force. 'Yet rather shuld a man suffer deathe,' Hooper proclaimed, 'then to defende hym selfe by force and vilente resystinge of the superyour powers, as Christ, his Apostles and the prophets dyd.'[15]

Bishop John Poynet's important *Short Treatise of Politique Power*, published in 1556, five years after Hooper's *Annotations*, is a most instructive example of the extremely limited use of familial reasoning in support of political authority in the early Tudor period. Poynet said that only because of the advantages of living under benevolent rulers, people 'used in times past to call such good Governours, Fathers: and gave them no lesse honour, than children owed to their Parents'.[16] Like so many of his English predecessors and contemporaries, Bishop Poynet paid very little attention to the origins of the political order, but he did attempt to deduce the existence of government from an unhistorical grant to the community by God. And while he did not even mention the Fifth Commandment, there can be no doubt that as an Anglican Bishop he would not have hesitated to proclaim the political implications of Exodus 20: 12 had his task been an explication of that passage. What is significant about Poynet's *Treatise* is that it at least revealed a willingness to use the paternal metaphor in a political discussion.

2

Had the patriarchal theory of political obligation been more than a burgeoning concept by the mid-sixteenth century, it could have proved embarrassing to the defenders of absolute monarchy

[15] Ibid.
[16] J[ohn] P[oynet], *A Short Treatise of Politique Power* (1556; [London], 1639), p. 45.

during the reigns of Queens Mary and Elizabeth, for its insistence upon the inherent inferiority of women would have seriously undercut the legitimacy of those Queens. An anti-feminist doctrine was developed by John Knox in his attack on what he called 'the Monstrous Regiment of Women', but monarchist authors during the reign of Queen Elizabeth failed to come to grips with Knox's inherent patriarchalism. Writing in 1558 from the safety of Geneva specifically against the two papists Queens, Mary of England and Mary of Scotland, Knox paraded all the reasoning and Biblical passages used in the next century by Filmer in asserting the God-given superiority of Adam over Eve and by the authors of family obedience books to demonstrate the power of husbands over their wives.

Knox did not expand his views into a patriarchal political theory, for his argument was basically a negative attempt to show the moral, logical, and legal inability of women to rule men. His conclusion was that the evils befalling England and Scotland were God's punishments to those nations for having allowed women to usurp authority. Knox's prime purpose was to protect Protestantism; the Roman Catholicism of the Queens, therefore, was treated as an additional cause of God's wrath as well as one of its manifestations. Basing most of his argument upon two Biblical passages—one from the Old and one from the New Testament—that subordinated women to their husbands,[17] Knox maintained that no woman could ever rule, for 'the immutable decree of God . . . hath subjected her to one membre of the congregation, that is to her husband'. For this reason, 'the holie ghost concludeth, that she may never rule nor bear empire above men. For she that is subject to one may never be preferred to many. . . .' Knox allowed only one exception to his denial of the possibility of legitimate government by women, and that was the rule of Deborah, the Judge. But no inferences could be drawn from the fact that Israel had once been under the rule of a woman, especially not in support of the titles of the usurping Queens Mary. For 'Deborah or any godlie woman' (a description that obviously precluded Roman Catholics) cannot be shown to have gained her title by 'birth or blood'.

---

[17] Gen. 3: 16. '. . . and thy desire *shall be* to thy husband, and he shall rule over thee'. I Cor. 11: 8. 'For the man is not of the woman; but the woman of the man.'

Neither yet [he continued,] did they claime it by right or inheritance; but God in his singular priviledge, favor, and grace, exempted Deborah from the common malediction given to women in that behalf: and *aginst* nature he made her prudent in counsel, strong in courage, happie in regiment, and a blessed mother and deliverer to his people.

And she ruled '*not as princes used to command*', but as one who has ' special revelation from God'.[18]

For John Aylmer, Elizabeth's self-proclaimed supporter against Knox, the immediate task was not to break new ground but to defend the title of his Queen. Insisting upon the divine right of kings, Aylmer said that no man may question God's wisdom in sending a Queen to rule. In response to Knox's implicit patriarchalism, he argued that 'a woman maye rule as a magistrate, yet obey as a wife'.[19] Aylmer based this conclusion on the similar position of a son who is his father's political sovereign, such as David or Saul, and the difference between the authority of a father and that of a husband:

for the childe is the fathers subjecte, and the Father the childes ruler, as Aristotle saithe (whom you [Knox] so muche urge) and his rule is ... kynglike over his childe. But the husbandes is ... civill, then if the childe by nature a subject, maye be by lawe a heade, yea the heade of his father, and his father his subjecte: Whie may not the woman be the husbandes inferiour in matters of wedlock, and his head in the guiding of the commonwealth.[20]

This attempt to distinguish between 'kynglike' and 'civill' authority, unsuccessful though it may have been, was an early forerunner of the anti-patriarchal distinction between political and economic power. Also, Aylmer's statement is the closest that an apologist for Queen Elizabeth came to appreciating the possible conflict between the claims of a patriarchal theory of obligation and the presence of a woman as the head of state. Aylmer was not altogether satisfied with his feminist arguments, for he

---

[18] [John Knox], *The First Blast of the Trumpet against the Monstrous Regiment of Women* ([Geneva], 1558), folios 16–16ᵛ, 42 and 44.
[19] [John Aylmer], *An Harborowe for Faithfull and Trewe Subjects* ('Strasborowe' [London?], 1559), sig. Cl; citing Job 36: 23.
[20] Ibid., sig. C4ᵛ. (Ellipses indicate omission of Greek.)

went on to say that because the English government was mixed, the rule of a Queen could not be dangerous. Any attempt at tyranny by the Queen would be checked by the other two estates with which she shared power.[21]

The treatment of this issue in Alexander Nowell's *Catechism* of 1563 is also quite interesting. Discussing the Fifth Commandment, Nowell said that while its words seem to refer 'only to parents by nature', they actually have to be understood as including

all those to whom any authority is given, as magistrates, ministers of the church, school masters; finally, all they that have any ornament, either of reverent age, or of wit, wisdom, or learning, worship, or wealthy state, or otherwise be our superiors, are contained *under the name of fathers;* because the authority both of them and *fathers* came out of one fountain.

That 'one fountain', he continued, is:

The holy decree of the laws of God, to which they are become worshipful and honourable as well as natural parents. From thence they all, whether they be parents, princes, magistrates, or other superiors, whatsoever they be, have all their power and authority; because by these it has pleased God to rule and govern the world.[22]

It is noteworthy that Nowell emphasized the 'father' of his text while England was under the government of a woman. His total disregard of the 'mother' of the Fifth Commandment invites comparison with Filmer. In Filmer's case, the omission served a polemic purpose, but for Nowell it meant the loss of a valuable opportunity to make his doctrine more relevant to contemporary political circumstances. If further support were needed, he might easily have employed the latter portion of Isaiah's proclamation of the restoration of Israel: 'And kings shall be thy nursing fathers, and their queens thy nursing mothers,'[23] a text that was to pro-

[21] Ibid., sigs. H3–H4. See also Corinne C. Weston, 'The Theory of Mixed Monarchy Under Charles I and After', *The English Historical Review*, LXXV (1960), 427.

[22] Alexander Nowell, *A Catechism Written in Latin* (1563), trans. Thomas Norton (1570), ed. G. E. Corrie (Cambridge, 1853), pp. 130–1. Emphasis added.

[23] Isa. 49: 23.

vide the point of departure for several sermons delivered before Queens Mary and Anne between 1689 and 1714. (Interestingly enough, no sermons that used this passage as a text seem to have survived from the Elizabethan period.)

One final aspect of this passage that should not go unnoticed is Nowell's brief but evident use of genetic reasoning in his statement that the authority of fathers and all other superiors originally 'came out of one fountain'. But his position was still quite short of a self-conscious appeal to origins to substantiate a major political point. Two factors that contributed to the rise of genetic political conceptions in this period were the 'discovery' of Aristotle's *Politics* and the existence of genuine political controversies. Aristotle may have become known to some Elizabethan writers through Bodin, for English political thinkers appear to have been unaware of *The Politics* until very near the end of the sixteenth century. Of the controversies, the most significant was the dispute over the succession to the throne after Elizabeth.

### 3

The succession debate produced two tracts in which political origins were examined in ways that foreshadowed the writings of patriarchalists and their critics. The tracts were written by Robert Parsons, opponent of the succession of James I and the leading Jesuit in England, and his antagonist Sir John Hayward. Both works were reprinted in the early 1680s as contributions to the Exclusion Controversy. Parsons' book, *A Conference about the Next Succession* (1594), was pseudonymously issued under the name of R. Doleman. It purported to be a denial of the principle of hereditary succession and an impartial examination of the alleged titles of all the claimants to the English throne. In fact, the *Conference* was an apologia for Philip of Spain and his daughter, the only claims it took seriously. For present purposes, the most important aspect of this tract is the author's circuitous and not quite Thomistic derivation of the family and society from the same natural source, human sociability. Of all the creatures, Parsons said, 'only man is borne feble [*sic*] and naked, not able to provide [for] or defende himselfe in many yeares, but only by the healp of others, which is a token that he is borne to live in company and to be holpen by others . . .'. Therefore, man has been endowed with a

natural instinct to society, . . . that is the fountaine of al[l] the rest, that enseweth in a common wealth . . .: for of this come familyes, villages, townes, castles, cyties, and common wealth, al[l] which Aristotle in his books before named [*Politics* and *Ethics*], doth prove to be of nature, for that this first inclination to live together (where-of all those other things do spring) is of nature, as hath been declared.

On this same basis, Parsons reasoned that magistracy too was natural, for he regarded men as unable to live together in peace unless there was some authority, without which one man 'would consume and devour the other'.[24]

No specific *form* of government had the sanction of God and nature, according to Parsons, but political authority in general did. This argument became commonplace among seventeenth-century critics of absolutism who did not want to deny the God-sanctioned and natural origins of governance itself. To Parsons, this conclusion was the only one that could be drawn from an awareness of the numerous and diverse political arrangements that had been adopted by various nations at different times. Still, he felt that monarchy was superior to all other types of government and that it best conformed to nature. In addition, monarchy had the advantages of unity and convenience.[25] But this was monarchy with a difference, for Parsons believed in the right of the people to discipline evil kings. In fact, one of the implications of his position was that the people were superior to the king, a conclusion he avoided stating directly.[26] It was precisely be-cause popular sovereignty was implicit in his teachings that Parsons was reviled in the absolutist literature of the next century and why he was often treated as a symbol of the link between Rome and the hateful populist doctrine.

Hayward's criticism, prompted more by the need to defend the title of King James than by the desire to answer Parsons' theoretical assertions, was more in sympathy with the Jesuit than

[24] R. Doleman [Robert Parsons], *A Conference about the Next Succession to the Crowne of Ingland* ('Printed at N.,' 1594), pp. 5 and 7.
[25] Ibid., pp. 9–17; cf. p. 3.
[26] See ibid., pp. 134–6.

with the King on fundamental issues.[27] The main points to be established against Parsons were the principle of hereditary succession and the divine ordination of monarchy, but Hayward was not particularly successful in either matter. He claimed that primogenitive succession to government was ordained by God but did not support his position with statements about the patriarchal nature of kingship—which certainly would have helped to explain the origin of the rule. Instead, Hayward simply wrote that 'the succession of children, is one of the primarie precepts of nature . . .'.[28] In response to Parsons' assertion that if a particular governmental form had been sanctioned by God, it would have been found everywhere, Hayward weakly answered that all governments were originally monarchies and indicated that there was a natural tendency for them to revert to that form.[29] He did not explain how they could have changed from monarchies in the first place.

The very limited use that Hayward made of patriachal doctrines is especially pertinent. He believed that the state was essentially a family and attempted to show, analogically, that monarchy was natural:

The whole worlde is noethinge but a greate state; a state is no other than a greate familie; and a familie is no other than a greate bodye. As one GOD ruleth the worlde, one maister the familie, as all the members of one bodye receiveth both sence and motion from one heade, which is the seate and tower both of the understanding and of the will: so it seemeth no lesse naturall, that one state should be governed by one commaunder.[30]

Sir John failed to claim either that Adam had been a patriarchal monarch (or even that he had been a king apart from his patriarchal right, for that matter) or that the nature of fatherly authority was inherently political. Both arguments would have strengthened his case, but he implicitly rejected them, saying that 'politicke' government began with the usurpation of Nimrod; before that, there had been only domestic or 'oeconomical [rule],

[27] See Allen, *Sixteenth Century*, p. 260.
[28] [John Hayward], *An Answer to the First Part of a Certaine Conference, Concerning Succession* (London, 1603), sigs, C4–D1.
[29] Ibid., sigs. B2$^V$–B4$^V$.
[30] Ibid., sig. B4.

according as men were sorted in families: for so *Moses* hath written'. The first person 'who established government over many families, was *Nimrod* the sonne of *Cush* . . .'.[31]

Hayward destroyed his own argument by refusing to admit these two points, for it is difficult to understand how he could have thought that monarchy was especially ordained by God while simultaneously believing that there was no 'government' in the world until after the Deluge.

The first Englishman who showed more than superficial familiarity with Aristotle's derivation of the entire social order from the primitive household was Sir Thomas Smith, one of the leading diplomats of Elizabethan England. Smith saw in the household the first commonwealth, which he regarded as a private aristocracy. After acknowledging his debt to Aristotle, he said:

So in the house and familie is the first and more naturall (but private) appearances of one of the best kindes of a common wealth, that is called *Aristocratia* where a few and best doe governe, and where not one alwaies: but sometimes and in some thing one, and sometime and in some thing another doth beare the rule. . . . The house I call here the man, the woman, their children, their servaunts bond and free, and all other things, which are reckoned in their possession, as long as all these remaine togeather one, yet this cannot be called *Aristocratice*, but *Metaphorice*, for it is but an house, and a little sparke resembling as it were that government.[32]

The government of the household transcended these private bounds through sheer expansion; in the process, the private, metaphorical aristocracy became a monarchy. When a household grew too large for efficient rule, and the children married and desired partial independence, they were sent out by their parents 'to roote towards the making of a new stocke, and thereupon another house or familie'. Eventually, this multiplication of households became 'a streete or village', and they in turn 'joyned togeather [into] a citie or borough'. When 'by common and mutual consent for their conservation', several of these units were ruled 'by that one and first father of them all, it was called a nation

31 Ibid., sig. E3: citing Gen. 10: 5.
32 Sir Thomas Smith, *De Republica Anglorum: A Discourse on the Commonwealth of England* (1583), ed. L. Alston (Cambridge, 1906), I, xi, p. 23.

or kingdome'. This development, Smith reasoned, was the 'most natural beginning and source ... of all civill societies', which were originally held together by the natural inclination of men to obey their ancestors: 'For so long as the great grandfather was alive and was able to rule, it was unnaturall for any of his sonnes or offspring to strive with him for the superioritie, or to go about to governe or any wise to dishonour him from whom he had received life and being.'[33]

Sir Thomas did not explain how this natural obedience was to be reconciled with the 'common and mutual consent' or what this consent was. He simply went on to describe the transformation of the natural paternal monarchy into a filial aristocracy. Upon the death of the patriarchal king, the 'heads of families' met together to determine:

how to demeane and order their matters, best for the conservation of themselves, and each of their families, generally and particularly. Thus a few being heades and the chiefe of their families, equall in birth and nobilitia, and not much different in riches, governed their owne houses and the descendentes of them particularly, and consulted in common upon publike causes, agreeing also upon certaine lawes and orders to be kept amongst them. So the best, chiefest, and strongest did rule. ...[34]

Smith employed no Biblical references and said nothing about primogeniture; in fact, he implicitly rejected the primogenitive principle by describing the familial chiefs as 'equall in birth and nobilitia'. Sir Thomas's patriarchalism, of course, was limited to the simple descriptive or anthropological thesis about the origin and early history of the state. But even this discussion was quite different from the treatment of the same problem by many of his predecessors.

An even greater departure from previous writers and a more interesting use of Aristotle is found in the important tenth chapter of Book I of Richard Hooker's *Laws of Ecclesiastical Polity* (1593). Hooker assumed the existence of some form of the state of nature (although he never used the term), derived the origin and rise of lawful government from consent, and

---

[33] Ibid., I, xii, p. 24.
[34] Ibid., I, xiii, pp. 25–26.

distinguished between the private government of the household and the public rule of society.

Government arose, Hooker contended, because man was incapable of satisfying his natural needs without assistance; 'there fore to supply those defects and imperfections which are in us living single and solely by ourselves, we are naturally induced to seek communion and fellowship with others. This was the cause of men's uniting themselves at first in politic societies. . . .'[35] Men voluntarily established 'some form of government public, and . . . yield[ed] themselves thereunto' in order to remove the 'mutual grievances, injuries, and wrongs' they suffered without it. The greatest of these difficulties was traceable to the natural tendency of men to favor themselves in cases of conflict, especially when there was no superior authority to restrain them. It eventually became obvious, Hooker continued, 'that strifes and troubles would be endless, except they gave their common consent all be ordered by some whom they should agree upon'. Patriarchal authority existed only within families; its political significance was limited to having predisposed men to monarchical government:

To Fathers, within their private families, Nature hath given a supreme power; for which cause we see throughout the world, even from the foundation thereof, all men have ever been taken as lords and lawful kings in their own houses. Howbeit, over a whole grand multitude, having no such dependency upon any one, and consisting of so many families as every politic society in the world doth, impossible it is that any should have complete lawful power but by consent of men, or immediate appointment of God; because not having the natural superiority of fathers, their power must needs be either usurped, and then unlawful; or, lawful, then either granted or consented unto by them over whom they exercise the same, or else given extraordinarily from God, unto whom all the world is subject. It is no improbable opinion, therefore, which the arch-philosopher was of, that as the chiefest person in every household was always as it were a king, so when numbers of households joined themselves in civil societies together, kings were the first kind of governors amongst them. Which is also (as it seemeth) the reason why the name of Father continued still in them, who of fathers

[35] Richard Hooker, *The Laws of Ecclesiastical Polity*, I, x, *The Works of Mr. Richard Hooker, Containing Eight Books of the Laws of Ecclesiastical Polity and Several Other Treatises*, 2 vols. (Oxford, 1843), I, 198.

were made rulers; as also the ancient custom of governors to do as Melchizedek, and being kings to exercise the office of priests, which fathers did at the first, grew perhaps by the same occasion. . . .[36]

Hooker did not deal with the expansion of one household into a familial community, the series of events that for Smith marked the transition from private to public governance. In one sense, this omission removed a part of the burden of literal history from Hooker's doctrine. Whether or not he would have been satisfied with this consequence is quite another matter, as is evidenced by his use of specific examples.

More important omissions are Hooker's failure either to explain who was qualified to consent (to say nothing of the status of those who were unwilling to comply and how the consent was obtained) or to reconcile the life men enjoyed in families before the establishment of government with his earlier statements that they lived alone and therefore found it necessary to submit themselves to society. These questions were to exercise both the advocates and critics of the patriarchal theory of political obligation during the seventeenth century.

[36] Ibid., p. 200–1; citing Aristotle, *Politics*.

C

# IV

## The Stuart Family: As a Political Symbol and a Social Institution

The two preceding chapters have shown that the family was an established and frequently employed category in political philosophy prior to the seventeenth century. It would certainly not be an exaggeration to speak of a familial tradition in pre-modern political thought. I have shown that the various manifestations of this familial notion did not assume a single form, for the tradition consisted of several distinct and perhaps contradictory strands. Moreover, the family was never consciously recognized as a standard category in political argument and did not acquire an overtly important status in the centuries before the Stuart period. It is nevertheless true that the patriarchal–familial conception had become the chief view of political origins by this time. What is more, this doctrine at least implied—if it did not actually require—an understanding of the movement from family to state that determined political attitudes in ways that were initially unappreciated. Basic to all this was an implicit failure to distinguish between the political and social realms of human experience— an unavoidable failure that reflected an ability to distinguish, in twentieth-century terms, between state and society. W. G. Runciman has recently suggested that this distinction is relatively new, for it raises issues that 'could become meaningful only after the emergence of the modern idea of the State as such'.[1] The sudden appearance of patriarchal political theories in seventeenth-century

[1] W. G. Runciman, *Social Science and Political Theory* (Cambridge, 1963), p. 25.

England can, I think, be understood as a direct result of the early development of this new differentiation. The assertion that social and political matters were not identical and the corresponding claim that politics could be comprehended in its own terms (or at least in terms that were separable from those pertaining to the rest of society) was a direct challenge to European culture's own self-image.

What happened, very simply, was that the contractual theory of political obligation—with its insistence that the political order was conventional as demonstrated by its origins—contradicted the traditional view that human relationships were the natural outgrowths of the familial association and its paternal authority. The patriarchal doctrine, in response, was tranformed from a vaguely articulated societal theory into an intentional political ideology. Patriarchalism thus answered and corrected the erroneous non-naturalism of the contractualists. In effect, arguments that derived political power and organization from a voluntary contract were criticized by calling attention to the widely held and previously unchallenged belief that the source lay in the family.

We should be very clear about what was being claimed in this controversy and what issues were at stake. The voluntarist theory presupposed that the parties to the original compact were sufficiently free to have established a political authority over themselves; the usual purpose of state of nature arguments was to validate this doctrine of natural, original freedom. Because government was conventionally instituted, it was subject to the control and direction of its originators and their successors. Political obligation could thus be seen as something artificial. And consent theorists ultimately argued that each man must be the personal author of his own obligation. Patriarchalists asserted, on the other side, that since everyone but Adam had been the natural subject of his father, no one was ever free enough to have established a government. The political order was coterminous with the family, and great states and empires resulted from nothing more complex than the enlargements of households. Political authority was therefore natural, not conventional; men had not created the state and were powerless to change or control it.

The rejoinders open to contractualists did not include a denial of the patriarchal account of the historical origins of the state, for there was no reason to doubt that familial associations were the organizational precursors of all status relationships. What was necessary was that this history—which was, of course, the anthropological patriarchal thesis—be assimilated to the voluntarist or populist conception of political obligation. Contractual writers eventually insisted upon the inherent difference between familial and political rule. Only in these terms was it possible to accept the historical and anthropological aspects of patriarchalism while simultaneously denying that subjection to one's father was itself the absence of political freedom. Obviously, contractual apologists did not recognize all at once where their positions were leading them, just as patriarchalists did not initially realize that the whole of their perception of society and governance was under attack. In fact, it was probably the contractualists' assault that first made proponents of patriarchalism recognize that they even had a particular social and political outlook that they needed to and could defend.

The possibility of including within the contract thesis either natural familial authority or political freedom shows the separation between state and society that was implicit in the compact doctrine. The patriarchal answer to contractualism can thus be seen as having missed the point that actually divided the opposing theories. Filmer and the other patriarchalists said, in effect, that if advocates of the state of nature would go back to the beginnings of government, they would see that their explanation was totally incorrect. Men have always been born into families and *therefore* were never free. But the contractual theorists had already rejected the main thrust of this argument; the conclusion following the 'therefore' was, in their view, a *non sequitur*. In these terms, the debate between the contractual and patriarchal explanations of political authority never really took place, for the two theories argued past each other.

The differences between these conceptions of politics were, in actuality, not at all this clear. There were ambivalences on both sides; portions of the rival doctrines were put together in strange and often inconsistent ways. Nonetheless, the intentional assertion of political patriarchalism must finally be understood as the bringing to the level of consciousness of a series of related attitudes and assumptions that had previously been implicitly held and imperfectly understood. These notions had not really been challenged before and therefore had not been fully articulated. The irony is that the careful and self-conscious working out and enunciation of this view signaled the beginnings of its demise rather than its validity, for it is now clear that the social and political presumptions to which patriarchalism belonged were even then losing their relevance. A normative social or political theory is regarded as acceptable by a given culture or historical period not so much because of its 'truth' as because of its persuasive force. Successful persuasion is largely the result of the doctrine's ability to 'fit into' a culture and to incorporate and rely upon the principles that are widely accepted or taken for granted. In a culture that was beginning to make a fundamental distinction between political and social authority, a theory such as patriarchalism that presupposed their identity was bound to become outmoded, irrelevant, and therefore unacceptable.

A further reason for the appearance of patriarchal political doctrines is the new role the family occupied after and because of the Reformation. The demise of religious chastity and the growing clerical denunciation of virginity as an ideal led, in the writings of English Protestants, to a moral elevation of the status of families and to an increased urging of marriage and the raising of children.[2] Also, the familial head, in this same period, began to perform some of the tasks that had previously belonged to the priesthood. 'Fatherhood', Michael Walzer observes, 'was transformed into a religious office, with its duties and its obligation prescribed in the Word.'[3] As the authority of priests was reduced, that of lay household heads was correspondingly elevated. According to Christopher Hill, fathers began to be looked upon 'as intermediaries between the central government and their own servants and dependants, no less than between the latter and God'.[4] And, as I shall show later in this chapter, the widely held view of the family and fatherly authority in Stuart England was that householders ruled their dependants with absolute authority.

[2] Richard B. Schlatter, *Social Ideas of Religious Leaders, 1660–1688* (Oxford, 1940), pp. 10–12, and Charles H. George and Katherine George, *The Protestant Mind of the English Reformation* (Princeton, 1961), pp. 265–9.

[3] Michael Walzer, *The Revolution of the Saints: A Study in the Origins of Radical Politics* (Cambridge, Mass., 1965), p. 49; see also p. 55.

[4] Christopher Hill, *Society and Puritanism in Pre-Revolutionary England*, 2nd ed., paperbound (New York, 1967), p. 446.

These changes suggest that the family's existence and its functions in society were made more important by the Reformation and that the patriarchal authority of the father began to
loom larger in the minds of sixteenth- and seventeenth-century
Englishmen. Accordingly, the possibility of transferring the
familial image to politics and of using fatherhood to explain
political power became more obvious. In other words, the household was made available for political debate by having attention
directed toward it. Furthermore, once perceived, the natural,
communal relationship of the family became an ideal alternative
to the individualism and the conventional account of social relationships implicit in the Reformation's particularistic notions of
salvation through personal grace or faith.

The modes of historical thought prevalent in the late Tudor
and early Stuart periods were yet a third set of factors that contributed to the appearance of patriarchalism as a full-scale conception of political obligation. I have previously indicated that
the patriarchal theory was an instance of genetic political thinking
and that this way of discussing political obligation made it possible
to defend the duty to obey contemporary rulers by appealing to
the familial origins of governance. This genetic conception contained an implicit view of history and change. In principle, at
least, a genetic theory is committed to the rejection of change as a
source of normative standards; for a preoccupation with origins
—to expand some of the arguments advanced in chapter one—
must assert that the only viable standard and source of all political values is the beginning of the political order. This does not
mean that a genetic method of justification denies the existence
of change and is unaware of or refuses to recognize time. Quite
the contrary, for one of the main points of a critical genetic
theory is to show that modern conditions are in fact distinguishable from their beginnings and that this alteration is bad. The
passage of time is not, of course, identical to change, for it is
possible for a principle or standard or institution to persist unaltered from its origins to some later age while other parts of
the world decay, develop, or merely undergo random changes.
Some alterations are neither good nor bad; they simply occur and
can be accounted for or ignored without departing from the
established norms. What is important is that the norms themselves
retain their original form and content. Thus, a genetic political

philosophy would assert that while there are social and political changes that become evident through the passage of time, there are not and cannot be normative changes as well. Any presumed change in standards would be criticized as based upon faulty perception, bad judgment, or an incorrect understanding of the nature of political principles.

Once the distinction between political behavior and the standards by which that behavior is judged is accepted, the genetic doctrine can be seen as far less astounding than it might have appeared at first. All that is being claimed is that there are knowable, unchanging, absolute principles to which politics ought to conform. What *is* astounding about political geneticism, and especially its use in the patriarchal theory, is that belief that these invariable criteria of judging came into existence or were validated at a particular and identifiable historical time. Such a view is dependent upon an imprecise historical awareness, for it tends to see time as undifferentiated chronology since the beginning. Recognition or acceptance of an orderly process of change as anything other than a departure from that original standard should have implied that the rules governing social change can also be applied to political principles, a view that was alien to political thinkers who reasoned from genetic principles. This intellectual ambivalence could have persisted unnoticed until an historical sense was developed that was capable of pointing it out.

The sense of the past at the end of the Tudor period could not have supported an attack on the implicit anti-historicalism of the genetic doctrine, for historical studies were just beginning to emerge from the methodological indifference of the Middle Ages. Medieval Christianity undoubtedly inhibited the development of a genuine historical consciousness, for the pre-Reformation Church was preoccupied with eschatology and post-historic redemption. The historical process was viewed essentially as an interlude between the Fall and the Redemption; it was not something with a meaning that ought to be understood.[5] Medieval historiography, as F. Smith Fussner points out, was largely static and committed to the belief 'that chronological change did not reflect fundamental historical change'.[6] The past was conceived

[5] See J. G. A. Pocock, '"The Onely Politician": Machiavelli, Harrington, and Felix Raab', *Historical Studies: Australia and New Zealand*, XII (1966), 275 and refs.

of as little more than a random assemblage of events. It simply
would not have made sense before the late fifteenth century to
claim that historical occurrences were anything other than mere
chronology. Indeed, the conscious need to develop a specific
way of analyzing the past—that is, the attempt to work out
rules of historiography—seems to go back in the early modern
period no further than to the contemporaries of Machiavelli
and Guicciardini.[7] In France, according to Julian Franklin, the
'standard view' at the time of Bodin was of 'an endless series
of vicissitudes in history—productive, to be sure, of novelties
and regulated in their oscillation by some law or providence,
but not necessarily progressive'.[8] The task confronting Bodin,
Machiavelli, and Guicciardini was to discover the principles
or laws according to which historical change took place. In the
previous age—which had regarded such change as insignificant
—it would have been pointless to search for these rules, and it
it unlikely that it would have occurred to many to do so. Translated into normative terms, the quest after the laws of history was
a search for standards in terms of which all events could be seen
and evaluated.

Any attempt to reconstruct historical understanding in this
early stage of its development is bound to run into difficulties, for
there was no clear distinction drawn between three different
kinds of historical interests: (1) the methodological principles
that should be applied by historians to determine the authenticity
and worth of documents and other types of evidence, (2) the
causal laws according to which everything presumably took place,
and (3) the moral or normative standards by which various past
events were to be legitimated and rejected. Perhaps this lack of
differentiation is to be expected in an age when men had not yet
fully learned to distinguish between the inviolable 'laws of nature'
that explained the behavior of physical objects and those normative 'laws of nature' that prescribed desirable behavior for men.
Nonetheless, the resultant confusion in historical thought in this

---

[6] F. Smith Fussner, *The Historical Revolution: English Historical Writing
and Thought, 1580–1640* (London, 1962), p. 299.
[7] Felix Gilbert, *Machiavelli and Guicciardini: Politics and History in Sixteenth-Century Florence* (Princeton, 1965), chs. v-vii.
[8] Julian H. Franklin, *Jean Bodin and the Sixteenth-Century Revolution in
the Methodology of Law and History* (New York, 1963), p. 119, n. 9.

period is not usually noted. Among its consequences is the fact that any controversy over historical method would probably be inseparable from simultaneous disputes about what actually took place and why and whether it was right or wrong.

The debate over the English past had just begun early in the Stuart period, and it showed precisely this conjunction of historiography, causality, and evaluation. As historical methods were improved, it became possible to discredit a rival statement of the actual facts. And if the facts were wrong, the prescriptive implications drawn from them would certainly have to be rejected, for the problem was not just to discover the nation's history but to determine the political significance of that past as well.[9] The question at issue was the historical source of the rights of Englishmen. Did they stem from the 'feudal law' which was established by a specific ruler, or were they the products of an immemorial law or 'ancient constitution' that virtually inhered in the nature of the world? If the former, and if these rights were due to royal grace, their retention depended upon the willingness of successive rulers; they could be contracted or even eliminated by the king with total impunity. Perhaps more significantly, these rights could not be used against the sovereign nor to support the alleged authority of the people to control their government.

Quite the contrary was true of rights rooted in an immemorial law, for they would have been at least equivalent if not superior to the power of any king. Not only were the rights an absolute bulwark against the political order, they were one of the very foundations from which government derived its legitimacy. Since the appeal to an 'ancient constitution' could be upset by a demonstration that the various liberties of the English people had been instituted at an identifiable historical time, studies of the nation's past were of great significance, and it became important to discover England's origins. Thus, partisans on both sides of the debate thought it worthwhile to trace England back as far as Adam and the sons of Noah in some cases or at least to the Trojans and Germanic tribes. This controversy was not properly

[9] The growth of historical consciousness is brilliantly discussed by J. G. A. Pocock, *The Ancient Constitution*, upon which the next few sentences are based. Even though there are considerable differences in emphasis, my indebtedness to Pocock should be apparent to anyone who is familiar with his book.

understood and finally resolved until the eighteenth century,[10] but its immediate importance is that it helped to make inquiring into the past and into political origins an acceptable mode of dealing with normative political problems.

At least two further attitudes toward the past contributed to the context within which a genetic political theory could flourish. There was, in the first place, the reliance upon Biblical literalism and the belief that God, as the author of all moral standards, had fully revealed his designs at the Creation. This view was gaining back some of its old, Augustinian prominence since the Reformation redirected attention to the Old Testament and to man's fall from grace and the consequences of sin. If governance was created by God, this line of reasoning seems to have suggested, then its purpose and essence can most clearly be seen at the time of its establishment and in the surrounding circumstances. In the second place, there was a belief that the world was deteriorating and progressively falling away from its once ennobled status, that a situation had been reached in which men found, in the words of John Donne's *Anatomie of the World*, 'all coherence gone'. According to this doctrine, which enjoyed its greatest popularity from about 1570 to 1635,[11] decay and disorder were inescapable; they could be seen in man's fallen nature and moral corruption, in the imperfections of nature, and in the cosmos itself. Questions about the order and harmony that were missing and whether they could ever be recaptured required analyses of earlier ages. And these analyses too helped to entrench the practice of taking standards from a specific and long-past historical moment. The conception of corruption was very close to Biblical literalism, for the lost golden age that was the measure of perfection was life in Eden before the fall. In a man-centered universe in which all parts were organically related, human sin could cause decay throughout.

[10] See Isaac Kramnick, *Bolingbroke and His Circle: The Politics of Nostalgia in the Age of Walpole* (Cambridge, Mass., 1968), pp. 128–36 and 177–81, and the same author's 'Augustan Politics and English Historiography: The Debate on the English Past, 1730–35', *History and Theory*, VI (1967), 33–56, esp. 34–8.

[11] Victor Harris, *All Coherence Gone* (Chicago, 1949), pp. 3–4. For recent discussions, see Christopher Hill, *Intellectual Origins of the English Revolution* (Oxford, 1965), pp. 11–15, and W. H. Greenleaf, *Order, Empiricism and Politics* (Oxford, 1964), pp. 26–32.

None of these notions was necessarily genetic, but by looking backward for the source and justification of principles, they made it possible to inquire into the origins of whatever was being examined or urged as a suitable practice. For it was always possible to ask what validated the establishment of this practice. These 'pre-origins' could themselves be subjected to the same treatment until one theoretically came to rest at the beginning of all things. What was created was that bugbear of the intellectual historian—a 'frame of mind' or 'common practice', in this case, of looking into the past in order to understand and prescribe for the present.

Like the inability to distinguish between state and society, however, the historical attitudes that permitted genetic accounts of political obligation to come into being were soon to be replaced by other conceptions of the relations between the present and the past. With the disappearance of genetic political thinking, patriarchalism would lose another of the crucial components of the seventeenth-century mind that had supported it. These changes, of course, are the end of the story; what we encounter here at its beginning are several factors whose confluence sometime around 1600 makes it possible to understand why the family became a central category in English political thought during the Stuart period.

These factors may be summarized as follows: (1) The family had been the implicitly accepted source of society's origins in Europe for almost 2,000 years. When one of its main implications, the inseparability of state and society, was challenged by the contract theory, the working out of an answer helped to elevate patriarchalism from a relatively unappreciated political theory to a fully rationalized doctrine. (2) Religious and conceptual changes in English society after the Reformation called attention to the family and altered the way it was perceived as well as its actual role in society. Through this new awareness, the household became more relevant to political discourse, and this new symbolization perhaps provided some added insight into the kinds of relationship that were being alleged as the prototype of all social ties. (3) A growing but still crude historical understanding and a tendency to look into the past for the normative principles that underlay the present made it possible to dispense with the teleology that had previously been associated with the tracing of political origins back to a primitive family. The teleology was replaced by a genetic doctrine in which contemporary political obligation came to be understood in terms of those origins. In short, it was possible to hold that because political power was merely an extension of natural and absolute paternal authority, the obligation of the subject to obey his sovereign was identical to the unquestioning obedience a child owed its father.

2

The remainder of this chapter is devoted to an analysis of the Stuart family itself as a means of shedding more specific light on the image of politics that was projected by resort to the patriarchal theory. In addition, the role of the family in the development of political attitudes will be examined. It will be suggested that the seventeenth-century English family was indeed an authoritarian institution that was well suited to be the basis of an absolutist political doctrine and, furthermore, that for the vast majority of Englishmen in this period, the patriarchal justification of the duty to obey the state was an accurate translation of their regular experiences into political terms.

The analysis of the family requires knowledge of its actual structure as well as of contemporary attitudes toward it. We are particularly fortunate in both areas, for the evidence about attitudes is plentiful, and social structural information is rapidly becoming available. Seventeenth-century Englishmen seem to have been quite eager to write at length about family relationships, the obligations and rights of the various stations in the hierarchy, and the claims that members of the household might legitimately make upon one another. The family obedience book was a popular literary form throughout the century. Domestic relations were the topic of many sermons and pamphlets, and the subject was regularly discussed in large theological treatises. On the social structural side, much information has recently been discovered concerning the composition of familial groups, the ages of their members, and the numbers of servants and children; in some cases, it has been possible to correlate this numerical data with the occupation or social status of the head of the household. Taken together, this literary evidence and the facts about the structure of the household provide a clearer and fuller picture of the family in Stuart England than has previously existed and give us great insight into the use of this social institution as a political symbol as well as its role in the forming of political attitudes. These two sources of information are generally compatible with each other, which make it possible to infer some valuable conclusions about family life in the period.[12]

It may be said without hesitation that for the overwhelming majority of Stuart Englishmen, the family was indeed an authoritarian institution in which great power was concentrated in its patriarchal head. It is no exaggeration to state that virtually all social relationships—not merely those between fathers and children and magistrates and subjects—were regarded as patriarchal or familial in essence. The family was looked upon as the basis of the entire social order in seventeenth-century England. The Stuart family, it must be remembered, was not merely the nuclear association of husband, wife, and children. It included masters and servants (or apprentices) as well and was referred to as the 'household' as often as it was called the 'family'. A 'well ordered family', Robert Abbot, a London pastor, wrote in 1653, is one that has 'an orderly head, and orderly members having mutuall and fit relations. . . . *Orderly members* are those that depend upon the head, whether [they are] wife, children, or servants.'[13] And the general presumption seems to have been that the whole of society was a community of these households. It was only as a member of a family that one acquired any meaning or status in society, for it was *through* the family that an individual came into contact with the outside world.

It was in the family that an individual acquired his rudimentary discipline and education, learned a trade, and received his basic training as a Christian. And so long as a person occupied an inferior status within a household—as a child, servant, apprentice, or even as a wife—and was subordinated to the head, his social identity was altogether vicarious. The family was represented

---

[12] For fuller development and more ample documentation of the following argument, see my 'Patriarchalism, Politics and Mass Attitudes in Stuart England', *Historical Journal*, XII (1969), 413–41, of which the present discussion is a bald summary.

[13] Robert Abbot, *A Christian Family Builded by God: or, Directions for Governors of Familys* (London, 1653), p. 5.

to the larger community by its head[14]—its patriarch, as it were—and those whom he commanded were 'subsumed' in his social life.[15] Thus, the father-master of each family was both its link with society as a whole and its authority, and his status was universally recognized. Citizenship was generally the preserve of male familial heads, and even then it was limited to members of the upper echelons of society, but lower-class household rulers were still considerably closer to being considered persons than were their social peers who were still in service and lacked families of their own.

Before a man achieved social status—if he ever did—he would have spent a great many years in various positions of patriarchal subordination, passing successively from the rule of his father to that of a master, an employer, a landlord, and perhaps a magistrate. If he were high enough in the social scale to receive a formal education, he was also subject to the control of his teacher. The authority of ministers, which touched everyone in the population, was a further part of this same larger pattern. There is nothing particularly striking about these various forms of subordination in themselves. What is significant is that the relationships they comprised—master and servant, teacher and student, employer and worker, landlord and tenant, clergyman and congregant, and magistrate and subject—were all understood as identical to the relationship of father and children. This patriarchalism was not just the characteristic understanding of social status that was shared by those who commented on the family and its implications; as we shall see later in this chapter, it was supported by an official and regularly taught ideology that corresponded to, justified, and rationalized life as it was actually experienced by the illiterate and inarticulate masses of seventeenth-century Englishmen. Servants and apprentices who lived-in were literally members of the households where they worked

---

[14] See Hill, *Society and Puritanism*, pp. 470–1, for the representational role of the familial head.

[15] 'Subsumed' is Peter Laslett's term for the process by which 'boys and girls were caught up . . . into the personalities of their fathers and masters'. The same kind of relationship existed 'between the great household in a village community and the ring of smaller households ranged about it, sited on the landlord's estate, engaged for the most part in working his land.' (Laslett, *The World we have lost*, 2nd ed. [London, 1971], p. 21.)

and owed their masters and employers the same filial obedience that children did their parents.

Statements to this effect from books on the governance of households are easily duplicated. In their famous *Godly Forme of Household Government*, John Dod and Robert Cleaver wrote, 'The householder is called *Pater Familias*, that is, a father of a familie, because he should have a fatherly care over his servants, as if they were his children.' All 'godly servants', they further said, 'may in a few words learne what dutie they owe their masters, mistresses, and dames: namely to love them, and to be affectionated towards them, as a dutifull child is towards his father . . .'.[16] Thomas Cobbet, in a similar tract, urged his 'Courteous Reader' to 'remember . . . that under the notion of children, in this discourse, are understood, all such as are in the relation of children, whether Adult persons, or children in Age'.[17]

It was generally agreed that fathers and masters should be motivated by love and concern for the welfare of their charges, that they should be fair and reasonable in their demands, and that they should use gentleness and persuasion to get their bidding done. But it was also agreed that the patriarch, at least in principle, was the final and absolute authority in his own family. His commands were not to be resisted and could be enforced with stern punishment.

Insight into the nature of servitude is provided by the comments of William Fleetwood, who was to be made Bishop of Ely by George I. Fleetwood, in 1705, attempted to justify to servants the apparent discomforts and deprivations they suffered by pointing out the advantages of their lowly status. In the process, he inadvertently provided a contemporary estimate of the ways in

---

[16] John Dod and Robert Cleaver, *A Godly Form of Household Government, for the Ordering of Private Families* (1598), reprinted (London, 1630), sigs. Z5 and Aa5. Original text of first passage in italics.

For an analysis of this literary genre see Chiliton L. Powell, *English Domestic Relations, 1487–1653* (New York, 1917), pp. 101–46 and 234–242.

[17] Thomas Cobbet, *A Fruitfull and Usefull Discourse Touching the Honour Due from Children to Parents* (London, 1656), Epistle, sig. A2ᵛ. Original text in italics.

For further examples, see my 'Patriarchalism, Politics and Mass Attitudes in Stuart England', esp. pp. 415–18.

which servants were insulated from the society in which they lived; his observations are also worth quoting in full:

[Servants] are only concerned in *one* matter, to do the work that lies before them, whilst others have a *world* of things to look on, and look after. *They* have their Masters only to please; their Masters, may be, are to court and humour all they deal with: They, generally speaking, have themselves alone to provide for; Their Masters have Wives and Children, and Relations. Whatsoever scarcity or dearness happens, *they* find but little Alteration; Whatever publick mischiefs oppress a Nation, they feel but little of them: Changes of Government affect them not, that, may be, quite undoe and overthrow their Masters; they contribute little to the supporting the Publick, pay no Rates, nor Taxes; lose no gainful Employments, suffer nothing by the Malice, or Insolence of Parties, undergo no Odium, Calumny, or Slander; in a word, they are less distress'd and straitned, suffer less hardships and misfortunes than any sort of People else, above them. These are Conveniences that generally attend Servants of the lowest Condition; and which they would do well to reflect on, now and then, as well as to keep them more easie, as to make them the more thankful, and that they might the better discern the kindness of Gods Providence, in ordering matters so, that, with these Advantages, their Condition, however mean and low it is to all apperances, is yet upon the square, for ease and happiness of Mind, with that of many of their Masters.[18]

### 3

Many people were caught up in this orientation. Seventeenth- and early eighteenth-century listings of the inhabitants of local communities collected by the Cambridge Group for the History of Population and Social Structure[19] indicate that as many as one-fifth to one-third of the families in a village might have had

---

[18] William Fleetwood, *The Relative Duties of Parents, Husbands, Masters* (London, 1705), p. 385–6.

[19] The Cambridge Group was founded in 1964. For a description of its work, see Peter Laslett, 'Historical and Regional Variations in Great Britain', in *Quantitative Ecological Analysis in the Social Sciences*, ed. Mattei Dogan and Stein Rokkan (Cambridge, Mass., 1969), pp. 507–18; Laslett, *The World we have lost*, 2nd ed., General Note, pp. 254–7; and E. A. Wrigley, ed., *An Introduction to English Historical Demography*

servants. In a study of one hundred English communities from 1574 to 1821, Peter Laslett found that 28.5 per cent of the households had servants.[20] In the seventeenth century, these servants typically accounted for 10 per cent to 15 per cent of the population; for the period from 1574 to 1821, the figure is 13.4 per cent. Children still living in their parental homes constituted approximately another third of the population (42.6 per cent for Laslett's one hundred communities). There is, of course, wide variation among the villages for which records exist. Moreover, since there are relatively few communities for which these calculations can be made, it is impossible to generalize to the whole of England. At best, we may note the similarities and persistent patterns in towns and hamlets for which there is information. It can at least be observed that the structure of authority in these communities should not have been unlike that in the rest of the country. There were significant numbers of children and servants who had to be disciplined, and they were undoubtedly trained according to the patriarchal principles. We may note also that the household or family was still in the seventeenth century—as it was throughout the pre-industrial period—the primary unit of

---

(London, 1966). The listings of inhabitants are census-type surveys of all the members of a community arranged according to their households. They were drawn up for various reasons, including governmental and church directives and, apparently, personal fancy. The amount of information they contain varies; some state little more than the name of the head of each household, but others provide the full names, ages, marital status, and other vital information for each person. The Cambridge Group recently issued a collective volume based on these data for England and other countries: see *Household and Family in past time*, ed. Peter Laslett and Richard Wall (Cambridge, 1972). For earlier and somewhat preliminary statements see the following works by Laslett: 'The Study of Social Structure from Listings of Inhabitants', in Wrigley, ed., *Introduction*, pp. 160–208; and with John Harrison, 'Clayworth and Cogenhoe', *Historical Essays 1600–1750 Presented to David Ogg*, ed. H. E. Bell and R. L. Ollard (London, 1963), pp. 157–84.

The following discussion is based upon Laslett's published work, conversations with him, and unpublished material generously placed at my disposal by the Cambridge Group in the summer of 1967. Neither Mr. Laslett nor any of his colleagues is responsible for the use I have made of these findings.

[20] See Laslett, 'Mean household size in England since the sixteenth century', ch. 4 of *Household and Family*, ed. Laslett and Wall, pp. 148–152, for this and the next references.

production and economic activity in society. It was partially because familial authority was the exclusive source of regulation and discipline that the family so readily became a model of political authority.

When we turn to the actual size of the household, the data becomes much more abundant and consistent. It can be said with little hesitancy that at least 45 per cent and probably a larger proportion of Stuart Englishmen lived in large households, that is, those with six or more persons.[21] *On the average*, each family contained two or more persons of inferior status, for the typical or 'normal' household consisted of only one conjugal family and its dependants. Upon marriage, children moved out of their parents' homes and set up their own families; resident grandparents, in-laws, and married or unmarried siblings of the parents were unusual in traditional English households, except, perhaps, in the larger manor houses and homes of the nobility.[22] Married servants were extremely rare, for marriage marked the individual's emergence into society and his readiness to establish a household of his own. The relative independence of the status of householder and family head was incompatible with the subordination of servants and apprentices.

Until they married, individuals owed a filial obedience to their masters and fathers. Thus, there were numerous, large groups of servants and children regularly living together in mutual subordination to the heads of their households. They would have varied from young children barely able to comprehend their lowly status to servants in their early to late twenties and in some cases older.[23] Servants, of course, were someone's children; they

[21] Laslett's figure is 53 per cent for the 1574–1821 period. Ibid., p. 136.

[22] The point cannot be too strongly emphasized that the household of traditional English society typically consisted of the nuclear family and its servants, contrary to a still lingering supposition of an extended household consisting of all sorts of resident kin. See Laslett, 'Introduction' (ch. 1) to *Household and Family*, ed. Laslett and Wall; it is indicated that some localities in Europe, never England, were marked by the presence, but rarely the predominance, of complex households.

[23] On the age at first marriage, variations in the average, and explanations of these fluctuations see E. A. Wrigley's fascinating article, 'Family Limitation in Pre-Industrial England', *Economic History Review*, 2nd ser., XIX (1966), 82–109, esp. 82–90; and the same author's *Population and History*, World University Library (New York, 1969), pp. 116–19 and index, 'Marriage, age at', *s.v.*

usually entered service between the ages of ten and fifteen—and occasionally younger. The discipline they received from their masters was merely an extension of their earlier training under their natural fathers. It goes almost without saying that the size of the family and servant group increased as the relative social status of the head of the household improved. The more prosperous and prominent members of the community, those who would have needed large groups of servants and could afford to provide for them, had the largest households.

With so many people living as inferiors in large families, there was a need for governance of some sort. Children who became servants were not really educated in a formal sense. But they had to be restrained—to be taught respect for their superiors and to be made conscious of the duties of their stations—because they were assigned tasks that had to be done. There is no evidence to indicate that the general training they were given departed significantly from the authoritarian, patriarchal discipline prescribed by the literature on the household. The patriarchal structure of society was firmly impressed upon the servant, whose life was a series of movements from his own lowly beginnings to a servile position in the home of one of his social betters and then back to his menial origins to bear children who would join the procession. From the perspective of both the master and the servant, the actual physical household and the attitudes toward it were part of one self-contained and consistent whole.

The preceding account of the Stuart family is undoubtedly exaggerated, for it provides a picture of a rigidly authoritarian institution. Disobedience and rejection of fatherly authority were not uncommon.[24] What is more, the English family and the whole of English society were changing in the seventeenth century. Women were acquiring an identity and perhaps even a significance of their own;[25] contractual reciprocity rather than the mere assumption of status was beginning to color attitudes toward and understandings of servitude, just as the growth of rationalism and its faith in man and the powers of education were

[24] See my 'Patriarchalism, Politics and Mass Attitudes in Stuart England', pp. 419–20, for examples.
[25] See Keith Thomas, 'Women in the Civil War Sects', *Past and Present*, 13 (April, 1958), 42–62.

working away at the roots of a status-oriented society.[26] The opening up of the American continent as a refuge for younger sons as well as for the unsuccessful and lower elements of society certainly had its effects. Colonization undoubtedly tended to drain off persons who would otherwise have remained in the ranks of the submissive; at the same time, London was growing at a rate that far exceeded the surplus of births over deaths, and many of these new inhabitants—who, it has been estimated, averaged approximately 8,000 per year between 1650 and 1750[27]—would have remained in subservient ranks had they stayed in the countryside. These things can all be seen in the Stuart period, but their fruition was still at least one hundred and fifty years off. The structure and essence of family life do not seem to have altered materially between 1600 and 1714. Locke's rejection of absolute fatherly authority at the end of the century and a growing emphasis upon contractual reciprocity[28] were symptomatic of what was coming rather than images of what had already taken place.

## 4

The reasons why people will accept the political regimes under which they live are numerous and varied; they include social structural inducements and symbolic reinforcements as well as political beliefs and attitudes themselves. The propensity of an individual to accept political authority as a result of the impact of these factors on him is often manifested in unconscious and seemingly unmotivated behavior. Obeying one's government is

[26] See, for instance, E. A. Wrigley, 'A Simple Model of London's Importance in Changing English Society and Economy, 1650–1750', *Past and Present*, 37 (July, 1967), 44–70, esp. 51 and 67, where it is suggested that this transition from 'traditional' to 'rational' relationships was in part due to the 'steady spread' of London's urban environment.

[27] Ibid., p. 46. 'Given the mortality conditions of the day,' Wrigley adds, 'any large group of twenty-year-olds coming into London would represent the survivors of a birth population at least half as large again. Some 12,000 births, therefore, in the rest of England and elsewhere were earmarked, as it were, each year [on the average] to make it possible for London's population to grow as it did during this period.' (p. 47.)

[28] See Walzer, *Revolution of the Saints*, pp. 202–3, and the discussion in section 6 of this chapter.

generally not a thought-out action. Except in times of revolution and unusual political stress, obedience is a learned and habituated response—something one does as a result of his political 'socialization' and which he may not realize he is doing. It is possible in these terms to account for the political behavior of the self-conscious and reflective part of the population as well as of the inarticulate masses. In the rest of this chapter I shall be concerned with the latent political attitudes of these masses in Stuart England.

As we have seen, the individual was confronted with a patriarchally ruled family and society from birth; until a man became the head of his own household, he was successively in the status of a filial inferior to his father, his master, and his employer. Servants and apprentices who lived-in were literally members of the household where they worked and owed their masters and employers the same filial obedience that parents could expect from their children. These familial experiences must have played a central role in the political socialization process in Stuart England, but in the absence of specific information, we are forced to be mildly speculative. We know that large numbers of persons experienced this symbolic and structural patriarchalism at crucial periods in the development of their cultural and political awarenesses. A consciousness that already knew and understood the family and fatherhood was extended to include the political order and magistracy. Children who previously had no conception whatever of politics were introduced to the state and told that it was identical to the household. It made no difference that the king was not one's literal or biological father; neither was his master!

This conception of politics was part of an ideology that complemented and justified the patriarchally ordered society of Stuart England. What is more, it was a doctrine taught to all seventeenth-century Englishmen, and it came from the most reliable of all sources, the Church. A central element in the philosophical and polemic partriarchal theories was the derivation of political duty from the obligation to 'Honour thy father and thy mother' prescribed by the Fifth Commandment. This interpretation was also an official doctrine of the Church of England. In fact, the Church's position was that the Fifth Commandment placed upon the individual the obligation to obey all who were in authority over him. The child–parent relationship was thus seen as standing for the relation between subjects and magistrates, servants and masters, students and teachers, laymen and clergy, wives and husbands, and youths and elders. A traditional array of Biblical citations designed to show that God was the author of each form of subordination was always included in these exegetic readings of the Fifth Commandment. All the groups that were somewhat uncomfortably associated in the Anglican Church taught this doctrine. Even the dissenting clergy did not disagree about the implications of the Fifth Commandment. There were no significant variations of opinion about the meaning of the duty to obey parents among the sects during the entire Stuart period.

The importance of the Church and of religious teaching in general for the extremely Bible-conscious and God-fearing seventeenth century is obvious. The Church was most likely the only official agency encountered by the overwhelming majority of the population. Laslett remarks, 'It is true to say that the ordinary person, especially the female, never went to a gathering larger than could assemble in an ordinary house except when going to church.'[29] The exceedingly low rate of literacy in Stuart England makes the influence of the Church more readily apparent, especially if it is kept in mind that literacy was lowest among the very classes of people with whose latent political ideas I am now concerned.[30] The man who did not know books and therefore could not argue from external sources had little opportunity to challenge what was heard from the pulpit. In addition, there was strikingly little variation in the treatment of similar topics by different clergymen (except, of course, on matters of doctrine over which the diverse sects disagreed). The impact of this intellectual monopoly upon the formation and development of rank-and-file

[29] Laslett, *The World we have lost*, pp. 8–9.

[30] On the relatively unknown subject of literacy in the Stuart period, see Roger Schofield, 'The Measurement of Literacy in Pre-Industrial England', in *Literacy in Traditional Society*, ed. Jack Goody (Cambridge, 1968), pp. 311–25; Lawrence Stone, 'Literacy and Education in England, 1640–1900', *Past and Present*, 42 (February, 1969), 63–139; and my 'Patriarchalism, Politics and Mass Attitudes in Stuart England', esp. pp. 421–2. The beginning point for any analysis of literacy and society remains Jack Goody and Ian Watt, 'The Consequences of Literacy', *Comparative Studies in Society and History*, V (1962–3), 304–45. The Cambridge Group has in preparation a collective volume on literacy to be edited by Roger Schofield.

or vulgar beliefs could only have been profound—especially when it is remembered that it was an ideological complement to the society in which these beliefs were formed.

The most likely material upon which to base a study of the theological influence upon vulgar attitudes toward political obligation is not, as might be supposed, the great volume of sermons that have survived. It is, rather, the teaching of the much neglected catechism book, which is an excellent source from which to infer something about the content of mass education. The catechism is a series of questions and answers designed to demonstrate the basic tenets of the faith through explications of its primary documents—the Apostles' Creed, the Ten Commandments, and the Lord's Prayer—with an explanation of the Sacraments appended. It is certain that few members of the Anglican communion were able to avoid instruction in the catechism during the Stuart period. Knowledge of the catechism was required for confirmation, and there was virtually no end to the clerical statements attesting to the importance of proper catechistic instruction.

The Catechism of the Church of England was drawn up in approximately its present form in 1549, presumably by Cranmer and Ridley, and underwent a number of slight modifications until 1661 when it was separated from the Confirmation service in the readoption of the Book of Common Prayer. The clergy are specifically enjoined to teach the catechism regularly by the Prayer Book Rubric preceding the catechism and by Canon LIX of 1604, which says in part:

Every Parson, Vicar, or Curate, upon every Sunday and Holy-day, before Evening Prayer, shall, for half an hour or more, examine and instruct the youth and ignorant persons of his parish in the Ten Commandments, the Articles of the Belief, and in the Lord's Prayer: and shall diligently hear, instruct, and teach them the Catechism, set forth in the Book of Common Prayer. And all fathers, mothers, masters, and mistresses, shall cause their children, servants, and apprentices, which have not learned the Catechism, to come to the Church, at the time appointed, obediently to hear and to be ordered by the Minister, until they have learned the same.

Excommunication was the penalty prescribed for continual failure either of the clergy to teach the catechism or of adults to send their wards for instruction.[31] It is doubtful that this punishment was frequently used; persuasion and threats were probably sufficient.

Diligent attention to the catechism was almost invariably inspected for in regular diocesan visitations. An examination of over one hundred different visitation articles of the Elizabethan and Stuart periods has revealed that while the specific phrasing and the kinds of questions asked varied, there was not one instance in which the teaching of the catechism was omitted.[32] It is difficult, on the other hand, to determine how thoroughly and conscientiously catechizing was carried out. Examples of neglect and expressions of discontent with the teaching of the catechism can be found throughout the period. There was clearly a gap of some measure between the official requirements of the Church and the results that were actually achieved.[33] But to generalize from these cases of neglect to the whole of seventeenth-century England would certainly be unwarranted, for there are also many examples of ministers who taught the catechism regularly and faithfully, and there is no reason to suppose that catechizing was unduly neglected.

5

Learning the catechism did not consist solely in memorizing questions and answers; the catechumen was also to understand the principles of Christianity. Many conscientious clergymen wrote supplements to the established catechism to explain Church doctrines. These augumentations usually consisted of

[31] J. V. Ballard, ed., *Constitutions and Canons Ecclesiastical, 1604* (London, 1934), pp. 62 and 64.

[32] The visitation articles examined were in the libraries of the British Museum and Cambridge University. An attempt was made to see articles from at least three dioceses for each decade and two or more sets of articles from each bishopric for the entire period. Because of the general disruption of the Civil War and the abolition of the episcopacy in 1646, no visitation articles were found for the years 1650–60 and very few for the period from 1641 to 1649.

[33] For examples of neglect and statements of dissatisfaction see J. H. Overton, *Life in the English Church, 1660–1714* (London, 1885), pp. 175–8.

subsidiary questions and answers and Biblical illustrations and were written in exposition of the Prayer Book Catechism. Some of them, however, were altogether new works, designed, as Richard Baxter said of his own, 'For those that are past the common small Catechisms, and which grow to a more rooted *Faith*, and to the fuller *understanding* of all that is commonly needful to a safe, holy, comfortable and profitable life.'[34]

Many of these supplementary catechism books originated in the instruction that children received, for the minister frequently included additional materials in his lessons. The writing of these explanatory books was so popular in the early part of the seventeenth century that King James I is reputed to have said that 'every mother's son in these days thinks himself fitted to compose a catechism'.[35] Occasionally, and especially after 1661, these aids to learning and teaching acquired some of the characteristics of polemic and propaganda, particularly in their discussions of the Sacraments. The year 1661 also witnessed the beginnings of an even greater increase in the number of catechistic expositions. The reasons for this sudden attention is the reinstitution of the Book of Common Prayer, with its catechism, the consequent proscription of the Long Parliament's Calvinistic Directory, and the relegation to unofficial status of the *Shorter Catechism* of the Westminster Assembly of Divines that had been in use since 1648.

The Assembly's Catechism has been described by Alexander Mitchell, a sympathetic commentator, as 'thoroughly Calvinistic and Puritan'. Because its authors minimized the essential differences between Anglo-Scottish Calvinism and Anglicanism on matters 'relating to the mere organization of Christians as an external community', Mitchell continues, the Catechism of the Westminster Assembly achieved a popularity within the Church of England (even among enthusiastic conformists) that lasted throughout the seventeenth century.[36] Like the Church of England's, the Assembly's *Shorter Catechism* contains no supplemen-

[34] Richard Baxter, *The Catechizing of Families: A Teacher of Householders How to Teach Their Households* (London, 1683), title page.
[35] Quoted without reference in Edmund A. Knox, *Pastors and Teachers: Six Lectures on Pastoral Theology* (London, 1902), p. 108.
[36] Alexander Mitchell, ed., *Catechisms of the Second Reformation* (London, 1886), Introduction, pp. xxvii–xxix.

tary questions or helps to learning. The decisions to omit material
of this nature were virtual invitations to the prospective authors
of expository works. With minor modifications, the *Shorter
Catechism* is still officially used by the Presbyterian Church. But
in England between 1661 and 1689—aside from its having been
adopted by some dissenters—it was merely the most popular of
several expositions of the Creed, Decalogue, Lord's Prayer, and
Sacraments that were offered as helps for the mastery of the
Prayer Book Catechism.

The discussion of the Ten Commandments in the Anglican
Prayer Book Catechism is characteristically brief. None of the
commandments is specifically interpreted; the catechumen merely
recites all ten in order and is then asked, 'What doest thou
chiefly learn by these Commandments?' He answers, 'I learn
two things: my duty towards God and my duty towards my
neighbour', a distinction that corresponds to the traditional
interpretation of the division of the decalogue into Two Tables.
After stating his duty toward God, the catechumen continues:

My duty towards my neighbour is to love him as myself, and to
do to all men as I would they should do unto me: to love, honour,
and succour my father and mother: to honour and obey the King
and all that are put in authority under him: to submit myself to all
my governors, teachers, spiritual pastors and masters: to order myself
lowly and reverently to all my betters: to hurt nobody by word nor
deed: to be true and just in all my dealings: to bear no malice nor
hatred in my heart: to keep my hands from picking and stealing,
and my tongue from evil-speaking, lying, and slandering; to keep
my body in temperance, soberness, and chastity: not to covet nor
desire other men's goods; but to learn and labour truly to get mine
own living, and to do my duty in that state of life unto which it
shall please God to call me.[37]

The *Shorter Catechism* of the Westminster Assembly was, by
contrast, quite full; each commandment was dealt with separately
and in some detail. The discussion of the Fifth Commandment
stressed the rights and duties of station:

[37] Catechism of the Church of England (1549, etc.), reprinted in Phillip
Schaff, *A History of the Creeds of Christendom*, 3 vols. (London, 1878),
III, 519–20.

Q[uestion] 64. *What is required in the fifth Commandment?*

A[nswer]. The fifth Commandment requireth the preserving the honour, and performing the duties, belonging to every one in their severall places and relations, as Superiors, Inferiors, or Equals.

Q. 65. *What is forbidden in the fifth Commandment?*

A. The fifth Commandment forbiddeth the neglecting of, or doing anything against, the honour and duty which belongeth in their severall places and relations.[38]

On this particular point, there was no difference between the two catechisms. Indeed, the Assembly's version was nothing more than an elucidation of what was implicit in the Prayer Book Catechism. And, it might be added, it was a much needed amplification for the child who was to learn and understand and not merely memorize the catechism. This same interpretation can be found in every Tudor and Stuart gloss upon the official text; whenever the Decalogue was discussed, political duty was extracted from the Fifth Commandment. Of course, the extent of that duty, the clarity with which it was set forth, the inclusion of the corresponding duties of superiors, and the number of relationships that were incorporated into this Commandment were all subject to individual variation. What is important, however, is that the Fifth Commandment was assigned the task of justifying government—a task that had largely been the preserve of the thirteenth chapter of Romans during the Middle Ages. In the catechism books, Romans 13 was one of the Biblical citations used in support of the political extension of Exodus 20: 12.[39]

John Poynet's *Catechismus Brevis,* a book that all schoolmasters were ordered to use in the name of King Edward VI, provides an interpretation of the Fifth Commandment that is representative of the treatment found throughout the period. In addition to obliging men to 'love, feare, and reverence' their natural parents, Poynet said, the Fifth Commandment 'byndeth us also most humbly, and with most natural affection to obei the magistrate:

[38] Westminster Assembly of Divines, *The Shorter Catechism* (1644), reprinted in Mitchell, *Second Reformation*, pp. 22–3.

[39] Romans 13 did not disappear as an independent justifier of (political) authority; it continued to provide texts for sermons throughout the period. But the coupling of Romans 13 with the duty to obey parents as an arguments for obedience was very much a product of the sixteenth and seventeenth centuries.

to reverence the Minyesters of the church, oure Scholemasters, with al oure elders, and betters'.[40] An anonymous catechism published in 1614 defined the father and mother of the Fifth Commandment as 'Our naturall Parentes, the fathers of our Countrie, or of our houses, the aged, and our fathers in Christ'.[41] Several others described political rulers as fathers. Robert Ram, in 1655, saw those to whom obedience was due as '1. Our naturall Parentes, Fathers and Mothers in the flesh. 2. Our Civil Parents, Magistrates, Governours, and all in Authority. [and] 3. Our spiritual Parents, Pastors, Ministers, and Teachers.'[42] The very important *Whole Duty of Man*, which was described in its Preface as 'a short and plain direction to the very meanest readers',[43] provided this interpretation of the Fifth Commandment:

. . . here it will be necessary to consider several sorts of Parents, according to which the duty to them is to be measured. Those are these three, the Civil, the Spiritual, the Natural.

The Civil Parent is he whom God hath established the Supreme Magistrate, who by a just right possesses the Throne of a nation. This is the common father of all those that are under his authority.[44]

The number of catechisms quoted could be greatly increased, but the result would seldom be more than a tiresome repetition of words such as those employed by Humphrey Brailsford to explain the Fifth Commandment in 1689. His inclusion of the rights of inferiors is worth noting:

These words, Father and Mother, include all superiours, as well as a Civil Parent (the King and His Magistrates, a Master, a Mistress, or an Husband) and an Ecclesiastical Parent (the Bishop and Ministers) as the natural Parent that begat and bore thee: to all these

---

[40] [John Poynet], *A Short Catechism, or Playne Instruction* (London, 1553), fol. vi^v. Original text in black letter. (This work, a translation of the *Catechismus Brevis*, is also known as *King Edward's Catechism*.)

[41] *Short Questions and Answeres, Contayning the Summe of Christian Religion* (London, 1614), sigs. B2^v–B3. Original text in black letter.

[42] Robert Ram, *The Countrymens Catechisme: or, A Helpe for House-holders* (London, 1655), p. 39.

[43] [Richard Allestree], *The Whole Duty of Man Laid Down in a Plain and Familiar Way* (1658; London, 1842), Preface, p. xxvii.

[44] Ibid., Sermon XIV, sets 1 and 2, p. 231.

I owe Revereance and Obediance, Service and Maintenance, Love and Honour.

...And I must have from my Natural Father, Maintenance, Education, Instruction, Correcting and Blessing: From my King, Justice, Reforming Abuses in Religions, Encouragement to the Good, Punishment to the Bad: From my Husband, Love, Direction, Maintenance and Protection: From my Master (or Mistress) Instruction, Food, Correction, Wages: From my Minister, a Good Example and wholsome Administration of Spiritual Things.[45]

The position of the Nonconformist was no different, even after the granting of toleration. John Flavell wrote in explanation of the assembly's *Shorter Catechism* in 1692, 'All Superiours and Inferiours are concerned in it [the Fifth Commandment]: Especially (1) Political Fathers and their Children; that is Kings and Subjects: Mark 11. 10 ... (2) Spiritual Fathers and their Children; that is Ministers and their People: I *Cor.* 4. 15 ... (3) Natural Parents and their Children; *Ephes.* 6. 1 ... (4) All Civil Superiours and Inferiours, as Husbands and Wives, Masters and Servants: *Ephes.* v. 22 ... and *Ephes,* 6. 5.'[46]

6

There should be no question that Englishmen of all backgrounds were taught very early in their lives that they had to obey the king because God ordered it when He gave the Fifth Commandment to Moses. While it is impossible to determine the full significance of this fact, it does seem reasonable to speculate that ordinary members of Stuart society—to the extent that the problem was one on which they were capable of reasoning—would have been inclined to explain their political obligation by referring to the divine duty to obey their mothers and fathers. A response based on the contract, on the other hand, would not have been compatible with the experiences of the masses. There was certainly a contractual tradition of which these people were

---

[45] [Humphrey Brailsford], *The Poor Man's Help* (London, 1689), p. 40.

[46] John Flavell, *An Exposition of the Assemblies Catechism* (London, 1692), pp. 133–4.

For further examples, see my 'Patriarchalism, Politics and Mass Attitudes in Stuart England', pp. 428–33.

aware; it existed along side of and within the patriarchal explanation of social rank. However, it is unlikely that ordinary Englishmen understood this tradition in terms of the factors that the twentieth century attributes to the contract device in political theory: limits on authority and the source for personal rights and claims. The contract seems to have been used more as a formal explanation of how people entered relationships than as a definition of the nature and content of those stations. This was certainly the case with servitude. It is unlikely that many people would have learned a new doctrine—or acquired the ability to place a new interpretation on a familiar one—after leaving the households of their masters and after their learning and socialization were largely completed. Moreover, there were few inducements for them to do so.

The insistence that one must obey his master or pay his rent because he has promised or contracted to do so and, correspondingly, that he is entitled to certain stated rights or privileges that his master or landlord has agreed to respect or provide are seldom encountered by themselves in the seventeenth-century literature on the household. Instead, we find Richard Steele telling the husbandmen in his 'Countrey Congregation' as late as 1681 that landlords are their patriarchal superiors:

> The Eighth Temptation of the Husbandman is, *Slavish fear of Man*. It is true, he must keep a due Reverence for the Magistrate, for he is the Minister of God; and therefore to contemn him secretly, or disdain him openly, is no little crime. And a just fear and respect he must have for his Landlord, or the Gentlemen his Neighbour, because God hath placed them above him, and he hath learnt that by *the Father* he ought to honour, is meant all his Superiours; and himself expects the like from his children and servants.[47]

The limits on and duties of superiors accordingly flowed from the nature of fatherhood rather than from a prior and conditional agreement.

[47] Richard Steele, *The Husbandmans Calling: Shewing the Excellencies, Temptations, Graces, Duties, &c. of the Christian Husbandman*, 3rd ed. (London, 1681), p. 104. See also Thomas Cobbet, *A Fruitfull and Usefull Discourse Touching the Honour Due from Children to Parents* (London, 1656), pp. 1–2.

To combine these doctrines in this manner was, of course, paradoxical. Patriarchalism, at its base, treated status as natural and supported authority and duty without reciprocity. The contract emphasized the conventional sources of status and ultimately led to limits on authority and the reciprocity of rights and duties. These were precisely the terms in which these theories confronted each other as rival accounts of political obligation, but it should not be surprising that the inconsistency of using them together was unnoticed in the less philosophic literature on the household. The recognition, working out, and eventual elimination of inconsistencies is an intellectual activity that belongs to political philosophy. The abilities and interests required by this activity are not congruent with unreflective behavior; nor are they generally characteristic of the kind of mind that would devote itself to detailed analyses of social relationships. When this specific inconsistency was noticed by thinkers who appreciated its implications for political life, attempts were made to resolve the issue in favor of one or the other position.

In strictly social and non-philosophic terms, it remained for Bishop William Fleetwood in 1705 to recognize what had long been implicit. Fleetwood saw not just the household but the whole of society as sets of contractual and reciprocal relationships. 'I take it for a Rule, and granted', he wrote, 'that there is no Relation in the World, either Natural, or Civil and agreed upon, but there is a Reciprocal duty obliging each Party.' 'I only mention this', the Bishop continued, 'to make it very evident that the Obligation of Children to love, honour, respect and obey their Parents, is founded originally upon the Parents love and care of *them*, and to shew that no one can require any thing from another as a Duty, to whom he does not always *owe* something, by way of Duty.' On this basis, Fleetwood explained all status:

> There is no thing more certain, than that Superiours are oblig'd as much in Reason, and Justice, and by Gods Commands, to discharge what they owe to their Inferiours, as Inferiours are to discharge what they owe to their Superiours. For every Relation being built, and depending upon a Contract, either suppos'd in Nature and Reason, or actually agreed upon and made betwixt the Parties related, upon what terms they found it convenient; it must needs be, that each Party is oblig'd to perform his part of that Contract upon which the Relation stands: For Justice and Reason know no

# V

# The Emergence of the Patriarchal Theory of Obligation in the Early Seventeenth Century

## I

When the familial symbol is analyzed as a contribution to rational and philosophic political discourse, it becomes more than an ideological expression of the social structure of the society. Political symbolization on this conscious level is genuine intellectual persuasion rather than the mere dogmatic supplementing of status inducements to obey. The persons at whom a rational political doctrine is directed are at least theoretically capable of rejecting it; they must be *shown* that the argument is 'correct', that it is preferable to alternative theories, and that it fits into their lives and therefore ought to be embraced and followed. Ironically, the patriarchal symbol appealed for its meaning to a range of experiences that corresponded to the lives of the rank-and-file members of society (who, because of their low status and lack of education, were 'immune' to political philosophizing) and to the childhoods of the men whose political loyalties it sought. The persons to whom the patriarchal theory of political obligation was directed were themselves either patriarchs in their own households or adults who had long ago outgrown the habits of servitude and subordination. They were being asked to transfer their childhood experiences to the political realm and to see themselves *vis-à-vis* political authority as they had once been in relation to their fathers and masters and as their own servants now presumably saw them.

D

There is something paradoxical in the willingness of a master to reassume a subordinate status and in his ability to do so without surrendering his present familial headship. This situation is not so difficult to understand if two things are kept in mind. First, it was the *authority* of the householders that was appealed to, not the *subsumption* of their children and servants. Second, the conception of the world as a continuous and logical plenum—the 'great chain of being' notion—was very much a part of this kind of thinking. While servitude is undoubtedly a social consequence of authority, no one seems to have been conscious of this possible status conflict and to have recognized just how much was actually being asked of subjects. Even if these problems had been appreciated, the chain-of-being thesis would have made it possible to be both the master in one's own household and a servant in another, 'higher' one. This view of the world as an interrelated and consistent unit disguised some of the harsher political implications of the patriarchal theory.

The doctrine of cosmological continuity was closely related to the state/society question discussed in chapter four. The failure to distinguish between political and other kinds of phenomena was a part of the insistence that the world is a self-contained whole and that what applies on one 'sphere' or 'level' is validly transferable to the others. The contrary belief that 'politics' has its own logic and standards was a denial of this interrelatedness— or at least a demand that the nature of the cosmic unity be redetermined. The breakdown of this unified world view is, of course, one of the hallmarks of the emergence of the modern age; and the patriarchal theory, to the extent that it presupposed the chain of being, was a remnant of the middle ages, one of the remnants that was to be discarded soon after its nature was discovered.

2

On the conscious doctrinal level, a genuinely moral patriarchal theory did not develop in England until the appearance of a truly absolutist political theory and practice, for it was only in defense of absolutism that patriarchalism assumed its full dimensions. Both the theory and the practice of absolutism came to England with James I. In his youth, James had been nurtured on the populism of his teacher, George Buchanan, but the King had rejected that much of his education even before he came to the English throne. James's statements about the nature of kingly power are replete with fatherly images, but they do not contain a clearly defined patriarchal doctrine. While the King frequently argued from the role of the father as the head of his family to his own status as head of his kingdom, his usage was analogical; he never actually *identified* regal and paternal power. A good king, James said, is always concerned with the 'wellfare and peace of his people; and as their naturall father and kindly Master, thinketh his greatest contentment standeth in their prosperitie'. But, he continued, with a very interesting and unique modification of the same fatherly image, 'an usurping Tyran' acts toward his people 'as a step-father and an uncouth hireling'.[1]

In his best-known and most theoretical work, *The Trew Law of Free Monarchies* (1598), King James coupled this notion with the claim that upon suceeding to his throne, a king *becomes* the father of his subjects: 'By the Law of Nature the King becomes a naturall Father to all his Leiges at his Coronation: And as the Father by his fatherly duty is bound to care for the nourishing, education, and vertuous government of his children; even so is the king bound to care for all his subjects.'[2] In only one instance did James use the familial image to demonstrate the duty that subjects owed to their ruler; comparing political obligation with filial duty, he insisted that as children could not rise up against their fathers even when their acts were wicked or foolish, so subjects could not resist their rulers:

... if the children may upon any pretext that can be imagined, lawfully rise up against their Father, cut him off, & choose any other whom they please in his roome; and if the body for the weale of it, may for any infirmitie that can be in the head, strike it off, then I cannot deny that the people may rebell, controll, and displace, or cut off their king at their owne pleasure, and upon respects moving them. And whether these similitudes represent better the office of a King, or the offices of Masters or Deacons of crafts, or Doctors in

[1] James I, *Basilikon Doron* (1599), *Political Works of James I*, ed. Charles H. McIlwain (Cambridge, Mass., 1918), p. 19.
[2] James I, *The Trew Law of Free Monarchies* (1598), *Political Works*, p. 55.

Physicke (which jolly comparisons are used by such writers as maintaine the contrary position) I leave it also to the readers discretion.[3]

The authority and status of a king for James were unrelated to the monarch's being a father of his people or having derived his position from the power of a patriarch. In fact, the King appears to have rejected *jus paternum* as one of the historical sources of government. In his 1609 speech to Parliament, the British Solomon observed that 'in the first originall of Kings, . . . some had their beginning by Conquest, and some by election of the people',[4] which was an implicit denial of patriarchal origins. By and large, James argued from the nature of monarchy and did not attempt to derive that nature from anything more specific than God's grant. The claim of divine ordination was supported by Biblical injunctions to obey temporal rulers and a few examples of kinship taken from the monarchy of the Hebrews. Even in his use of the Hebrew monarchy, King James was more interested in the power and authority of Saul than he was in the fact that the government had been directly instituted by God.[5]

Although patriarchalism as such did not appear in his own political writings, James was aware of the doctrine and was responsible for spreading the ideological version of the theory among his subjects. In 1615 the King ordered publication of a patriarchal tract, an anonymous pamphlet entitled *God and the King*, presumably written by Richard Mocket, Warden of All Souls, Oxford. James ordered that the book be studied in all the schools and universities and that it be purchased by all householders in England and Scotland. This command was strengthened in Scotland in 1616 by acts of both the Privy Council and the General Assembly, and it has been asserted that *God and the King* 'had in consequence an enormous sale'.[6] but the extent of this success has been questioned.[7] Charles II had the work re-

---

[3] Ibid., pp. 65–6.
[4] James I, *A Speach to the Lords and Commons . . . Anno 1609*, *Political Works*, p. 309.
[5] See *Trew Law*, pp. 55–60, where James quoted and discussed the classic description of a king by Samuel as he warned the Hebrews of the oppressions they would have to endure under a monarch (I Sam. 8: 11–18).
[6] *DNB*, 'Mocket, Richard', *s.v.*
[7] David H. Willson, *King James VI and I*, paperbound (London, 1963), p. 295.

published early in his reign, and the title page of the reprint proudly heralded the book as 'Formerly compiled and reprinted by the especial Command of King JAMES (of blessed memory;) and now commanded to be reprinted and published by his Majesties Subjects in their Duty and Allegiance'.[8]

*God and the King* is a tiresome tract on political obligation; it was written as a conversation between the familiar 'well met' friends of seventeenth-century dialogues and opened with an unyielding insistence upon the political meaning of the Fifth Commandment:

*Theodidactus.* You are well met friend Philalethes; your countenance and gesture import that your thoughts are much busied: what may be the occasion of these Meditations?

*Philalethes.* Somewhat I heard this Evening-Prayer from our Pastor in his Catechistical Expositions upon the fifth Commandment, Honor thy Father, and thy Mother: who taught that under these pious and reverent appellations of Father and Mother are comprised not onely our natural Parents, but likewise all higher Powers; and especially such as have Soveraign Authority, as the Kings and Princes of the Earth.

*Theodidactus.* Is this Doctrine so strange unto you as to make your muse thereat?

*Philalethes.* God forbid; for I am well assured of the truth thereof, both out of the Word of God, and from the Light of Reason. The sacred Scriptures do stile Kings and Princes the nursing Fathers of the Church [Isa. 49:23], and therefore the nursing Fathers also of the Common-weal: these two Societies having so mutual a dependance, that the welfare of the one is the prosperity of the other.

And the Evidence of Reason teacheth, that there is a stronger and higher bond of Duty between Children and the Father of their Countrey, than the Fathers of private Families. These [latter] procure the good onely of a few, and not without the assistance and protection of the other, who are the common Foster-fathers of thousands of Families, of whole Nations and Kingdoms, that they may live under them an honest and peaceable life.[9]

[8] [Richard Mocket], *God and the King* (1615; reprinted, London, 1663), title page.
[9] *Ibid.*, pp. 1–2. Philalethes portion of original text in italics.

The monarchical authority defended in *God and the King* was thorough-going divine right absolutism. The frontispiece to the Restoration reprint was as graphic a representation of divine right as possible (surpassing even the plate of the Royal Martyr that adorned the *Eikon Basilike*). It showed Charles II, in his long-haired magnificence, having the crown placed on his head by two cherubs. Floating above within a flaming sun and ringed by a cloud was the Hebrew for 'God', and surmounting the whole, the battle-worn proverb, 'BY MEE KINGS RAIGNE'. The dialogue reasserted the people's inability to resist or punish their king who was answerable to God only. As Philalethes summed up his position: 'Our Soveraign Lord King JAMES, receiving his Authority onely from God, hath no Superior to chastise and punish him but God alone.' The Papal power of deposition was discredited on the same grounds: that only God was capable of disciplining a king for whatever reason.[10]

The significance of this tract, of course, is its use of the Fifth Commandment as the starting point for a discourse concerning obedience to the king. The pervasive character of at least this portion of the teaching of the catechism book could not have been more dramatically documented; the political ideology of the catechism would certainly have been re-enforced by whatever attention *God and the King* received. Mocket went even further than the authors of most catechism books and claimed that the Fifth Commandment pertained more to political than to familial obedience. Theodidactus concluded the dialogue by comparing the subservience of children and subjects:

But the duty of Subjects in obedience unto their Soveraign, is grounded upon the Law of Nature; beginning with our first beginning. For as we are born *Sons*, so we are born *Subjects*; his Sons, from whose loyns; his *Subjects*, in whose Dominions we are born. The same duties of Subjects are also enjoyned by the Moral Law, and particularly (as you shewed in the very entrance unto this our Conference) in the fifth Commandment, *Honor thy Father and thy Mother:* where, as we are required to honor the *Fathers* of private Families, so much more the *Father* of our Countrey and the whole Kingdom.[11]

[10] Ibid., pp. 16 and 27–8.
[11] Ibid., p. 35.

3

Some nine years before the publication of *God and the King*, in 1606, the same interpretation of the Fifth Commandment had been placed in a much more specifically political and legal setting by Chief Justice Coke in the important case of *Postnati*. He did not rely upon the Fifth Commandment as much as Mocket later would, but Coke did demonstrate that catechistical instruction was not necessarily forgotten after confirmation. Combining the law of nature, Paul's Epistle to the Romans, and the patriarchalism of the Fifth Commandment into a single basis of obligation, the Chief Justice said:

> The law of Nature is that which God at the Time of Creation of the Nature of Man infused into his Heart, for his Preservation and Direction; and this is *Lex Eterna*, the Moral Law, called also the Law of Nature. And by this Law, written with the Finger of God in the Heart of Man, were the People of God a long Time governed, before the Law was written by *Moses*, who was the first Reporter or Writer of Law in the World. The Apostle in the second Chapter to the *Romans*, saith *Cum enim gentes quae legem non habent naturaliter ea quae leges sunt faciunt*. And this is within that Command of the Moral Law, *Honora Patrem*, which doubtless doth extend to him that is *pater patriae*.[12]

The sentiments expressed by Coke were echoed by Arthur Lord Capel, Baron of Hadham, before he went under the executioner's blade in 1649; he justified his obedience to Charles I on the basis of God's command to obey parents. It was because he kept the Fifth Commandment, Capel said, that he was going to his death:

> I die, I take it, for maintaining the fifth Commandment, enjoin'd by God himself, which enjoins Reverence and Obedience to Parents. All Divines, on all hands, tho' they contradict one another in many several Opinions, yet most Divines do acknowledge that here is intended Magistracy and Order; and certainly I have obeyed that Magistracy and that Order under which I have liv'd, which I was bound to obey; and truly, I do say very confidently, that I do die

---

[12] Edward Coke, *Postnati*, Calvin's Case, VII *Coke Reports* 12 (1606); text from London printing of 1727. The Biblical passage is from Rom. 2: 14.

here for keeping, for obeying that fifth Commandment given by God himself, and written by his own Finger.[13]

A patriarchal reading of Genesis was set forth in the opening pages of the celebrated *Convocation Book of 1606*, a volume of proposed additions to the Church canon. Drawn up under the leadership of John Overall, who was later elevated to the Bishopric of Norwich, and approved by both houses of Convocation in 1606, the book was, in part, an attempt to add an official body of political principles to Anglican doctrines. James refused to approve the work, because he felt that it 'dipped too deep into what all kings reserve among the *arcana imperii*'. Deprived of the King's assent, the new canons were without official status and remained in manuscript until 1690 when William Sancroft, the non-juring Archbishop of Canterbury, had them published.[14]

'To him that shall duly read the Scripture,' the *Convocation Book* asserted, 'it will be plain and evident' that before the Flood the authority that God gave to Adam and other familial heads to rule over their wives and children in their capacities as husbands and fathers was '*protestas regia*' and 'had no superior authority, or power, over, or above it on earth'.[15] It followed that there had never been a state of nature and that power was not originally in the people; these notions were directly contrary to the Bible:

If any man shall therefore affirm that men at the first, without all good education, or civility, ran up and down in woods, and fields, as wild creatures, resting themselves in caves and dens, acknowledging no superiority one over another, until they were taught by experience the necessity of government; and that thereupon they chose some amongst themselves to order and rule the rest, giving them power and authority so to do; and that consequently all civil power, jurisdiction, and authority, was first

---

[13] Arthur Capel, Scaffold Paper (1649), in *The Dying Speeches and Behaviour of the Several State Prisoners that Have Been Executed in the Last 300 Years* (London, 1720), p. 166.

[14] James's comments are printed in the introduction to John Overall, *The Convocation Book of 1606* (written in 1606, first published in 1690), Library of Anglo-Catholic Theology (Oxford, 1844), p. 8.

[15] *Convocation Book*, ch. ii, pp. 2–3. Brackets in the 1844 printing have been eliminated from this and succeeding passages for clarity.

derived from the people, and disordered multitude; or either is originally still in them, or else is deduced by their consents naturally from them; and is not God's ordinance originally descending from Him, and depending upon Him, he doth greatly err.[16]

Because the historical charms of the social contract theory were untenable, the entire doctrine had to fall. The *Convocation Book* thus provides the earliest example in England of the substitution of the patriarchal account of political origins for the anthropological underpinnings of populism. The argument is clearly a genetic one, and there is not the slightest suggestion in Overall's text that the defense of his own case required anything more than a refutation of the contractual theory of the origins of the political order. The reference point was the Old Testament; after demonstrating that the theory of natural political freedom was incompatible with Scripture, Overall's task was simply to extract the true story from Genesis.

He began, however, not with Adam but with Noah, saying, 'Touching this patriarchal, or in effect, regal government of Noah, there is more expressed in the Scriptures, than there was before the flood, of the power and authority of Adam, or of any of the chief fathers and rulers that were descended from him. . . .' Noah had a large family and for many years after the flood 'was the patriarch, or chief governor over them; ruling and ordering them, by virtue of that superiority, power, and authority which was given unto him by Almighty God, and was also warranted by the laws of nature and reason'. His patrimonial domain was so vast that Noah 'lawfully distributed the whole world unto his . . . three sons, and their posterity'. These sons thereby became 'three great princes', and their sons '(of whom about seventy are named) were the heads and governors of the families and nations that descended from them, according to their tongues, in their several cities'.[17]

Overall's argument stopped at this point, and there was no attempt to demonstrate that the nature of monarchy in the seventeenth century was dictated by its patriarchal origins. Overall's

[16] Ibid., Canon II, p. 3. Original text in black letter. J. W. Allen says that the mention of 'caves and dens' was a clear reference to George Buchanan (*English Political Thought 1603–1660*, vol. I, 1603–1644 [London, 1938], p. 104, n.2).

[17] Ibid., ch. vi, p. 7.

conclusions were that governmental authority is absolute and exists by divine right, but he did not relate the Biblical history to the substantive political claims of the *Convocation Book*. Overall himself undoubtedly saw no need to establish such a relationship, and this failure can probably be attributed to his implicit reliance upon the genetic mode of political argument. Once it had been shown how political authority originated and what form it initially took, there was no need to explain why this discussion of origins was relevant. Like the authors of catechism books, the members of the 1606 Convocation could extract an ideological claim from the Fifth Commandment without fear of contradiction or the need for detailed analysis. They relied instead on consensus and said, 'It is generally agreed upon that obedience to kings and civil magistrates is prescribed to all subjects in the fifth commandment, where we are enjoined to "honour our parents". Whereby it followeth, that subjection of inferiors unto their Kings and governors, is grounded upon the very law of nature.'[18]

4

The *Convocation Book* is a remarkable document; it was agreed upon by the assembled houses of Convocation of the Church of England and was not the political thinking of an

[18] Ibid, ch. xvi, p. 23.

This interpretation of the Fifth Commandment was quite common, even by 1606. The extensiveness of this doctrine is indicated by the title of a work published in 1609 by Robert Pricke, preacher at Denham, Suffolk: *The Doctrine of Superioritie, and of Subjection, Contained in the Fifth Commandment of the Holy Law of Almightie God* (London, 1609). An anonymous reissue in 1616 was entitled *The Doctrine of Subjection to God and the King, Gathered Out of the 5. Commandement: Fit for All the Kings Subjects to Read, Wherein They May Learne True Obedience* (London, 1616). The Fifth Commandment, Pricke said, extends to 'all such as are in stead of Parents, not onely in regard of superiority, but also for that they are to provide for the good and benefite of their inferiours, both in soule and bodie. For so wise and merciful is the Lord, that as hee hath appoynted naturall Parents to begette and bring foorth children, and thereby to give them simplie a beeinge in this life: so hath hee ordayned other persons (As it were Parents) to tender and give them a well and happy being.' (Sig. B3ᵛ, both eds.) An introduction by Stephen Egerton combined the Fifth Commandment and Romans 13 into a single basis for authority, but otherwise the titles of this book are of greater interest than the text.

isolated or unique individual. Although its use of the patriarchal theory was relatively limited, the position of the *Convocation Book* exceeds that of Sir John Hayward, who, only a few years earlier, had not used a moral or historical patriarchalism against the populism of Parsons.

Richard Field's massive *Of the Church* (1606), a book that was written about the same time the Convocation was meeting, was much more detailed in its exposition of Adam's patriarchal–political authority. Echoing Hooker, Field saw political and spiritual rule united in primitive fatherhood and regarded Adam as a priest and king. Adam's authority was evident in Eve's inferior status, and after the Fall, God made Adam 'a King to rule in the little World of his owne Family', as well as a priest over it. It was natural to Field that Adam should have been given this kingly power over his family. 'For when there were no more in the World but the first man whom God made out of the earth, the first woman that was made of man, and the children which GOD had given them, who could be fitter to rule and direct, than the man for whose sake the woman was created, and out of whose loynes the children came?'[19]

To George Carelton, Bishop of Chichester, writing in 1610, there was no difference between a family and a kingdom. 'And what is a King by nature,' he asked, 'but the father of a great family? and what is the father of a familie by nature, but a little King?'[20] Carleton wrote to answer the Papal arguments against James I's Oath of Allegiance. He sought first to discredit the populist theory of governmental origins 'because some of the Pope flatterers of late, as others also, to open a wide gappe to rebellions, have written that the power of government by the law of nature is in the multitude'. The error of this doctrine, the Bishop believed, could be seen by examining the true origins of government:

The first principalitie that was set up to rule many families, was a kingdome; as the first simply was in the government of a family: so before there could be a commonwealth, there must be a citie, or the collection of many families into the lawful right of one societie;

[19] Richard Field, *Of the Church* (1606), 2nd ed. (Oxford, 1623), p. 410.
[20] George Carleton, *Jurisdiction Regall, Episcopall, Papall* (London, 1610), p. 12.

and before there could be a citie, there must be particular houses
and families: so that the first government that was in the world
among men, was the government of a family, it is absurd to thinke
and impossible to proove, that the power of government was in the
multitude.

This familial origin of government demonstrates that 'the first
government of the states by the lawe of nature, was by Kings'.
Like Field and Hooker, Carleton believed that kingship, priesthood, and paternal authority were originally one. In an interesting
and important use of origins to demonstrate the nature of successive political arrangements, he argued that the monarch of
England in 1610 had the power of intervention in Church
affairs because '*Kings in the time of Law of nature, had all the
power Ecclesiasticall, both of order and Jurisdiction.*' James could
appoint Bishops and generally oversee the Church because Moses,
'who had the place of a King in [the Hebrew] government', had
appointed Aaron to be the High Priest.[21]

5

John Selden, the noted jurist, regarded families as the first
states. In his *Titles of Honour* (1614), he accepted the anthropological patriarchal thesis, saying, 'Communities of life, and
Civill Societie, beginning first in particular Families, under the
Oeconomique rule (representing what is now a commonwealth)
had, in its state, the Husband, Father, and Master, as King.'[22]
But in the second edition of the same work (published in 1631),

---

[21] Ibid., pp. 12, 11, and 17–18.
[22] John Selden, *Titles of Honour* (London, 1614), p. 2. The parenthetical
remark in this passage suggests that Selden had implicitly appreciated the
difference between 'Oeconomique rule' and the political authority of the
commonwealth, but the subject was not pursued. However, Selden did say
that while the familial origins of government demonstrated that 'Monarchie is ancienter than any State', this fact was of no consequence to the
seventeenth century, for 'what we now call a Kingdome . . . cannot but presuppose a popular State or Democracie' (Ibid., p. 5). Once again, this
was all that Selden said on the subject; he did not, for instance, discuss
how this tranformation from familial monarchies to popular kingdoms
came about.

all discussion of families and original patriachal power was deleted. Instead, Selden merely asserted that there had been monarchies in the world before the Flood, as against the view that Nimrod was the first king. However, he reached this conclusion without examining the origin or nature of any of these governments.[23] In fact, he no longer seemed interested in the historical foundations of government at all.

In his *Mare Clausum*, which was originally written at the request of King James in 1618 against Grotius' *Mare Liberum*, but not published until 1636 when it was revised, Selden repeated his earlier anthropological notion and went far beyond the first edition of *Titles of Honour*. While developing his argument that the seas, like land, were private property, Selden found it necessary to determine the origin of private ownership in general. His treatment was confused (as Filmer was quick to point out), for he acknowledged that Adam had held the world alone but also implied that there had once been genuine communal ownership. One of the instances of private lordship to which he pointed was God's grant of the world to Noah and his three sons. He then used this same grant as an instance of communistic dominion, presumably because when they were given the world, Noah and his sons were the only qualified owners then alive.[24]

Selden recognized that he had embraced these two positions, for he said, 'Neither the Law Natural nor Divine . . . hath expressly commanded or forbidden, but permitted both; that is to say, a common enjoinment, as well as a private dominion or possession of the things of this life.' This system of communal ownership lasted until the cataclysmic confusion of tongues at Babel, when private possession was reinstituted through mutual

---

[23] Selden, *Titles of Honour*, 2nd ed. (London, 1631), pp. 4–7.
[24] John Selden, *Mare Clausum* (1636), translated by Marchmont Nedham as *Of the Dominion, or, Ownership of the Sea* (London, 1652), pp. 17–20. Filmer's criticism is in *Patriarcha*, pp. 63–6.
Selden confused communal ownership with the parceling out of the whole among all eligible persons. His first mention of Noah and his sons indicated that each was given so much dominion that their combined possessions extended over the entire world. This is certainly not the same as saying that each of the four had equal rights of access to and use of every part of the whole world, which is what communality must entail.

consent.[25] 'But in this division of Bounds, and Territories,' he continued, 'there intervened, as it were, a consent of the whole bodie or universalities of mankind (by the mediation of something like a compact, which might binde their posteritie) for quitting of the common interest or antient right in those things that were made over thus by distribution to particular Proprietors.'[26] This notion of a 'compact which might binde their posteritie' brought Selden much closer to the moral patriarchal theory than he probably realized, for he was acknowledging that people could be required to fulfill agreements made by their ancestors.

As Filmer was to appreciate, the derivation of any obligation or duty from an ancestral contract was a denial of the fundamental tenet of populism: because the 'people' had freely and voluntarily created political authority, they were entitled to control it. Binding a man to the institutions established by his predecessors, Filmer claimed, was an admission of the superior powers and rights of fathers.[27] Selden himself was not very far from Filmer's position, for he concluded his discussion of property with the observation that private ownership arose out of a compact that was 'in full force and virtue transmitted to posteritie by the Father, who had the power of distributing possessions after the Flood'.[28] Selden's argument here is the first overt instance in English thought of what could be called a 'concession' to patriarchalism, that is, a positive use of the patriarchal theory by a contractual author.[29]

---

[25] Even then, 'common enjoinment' did not disappear completely, for Selden said that there was still a general community property in 'wilde-Beasts, Fishes, Birds and the like . . . [which] becom theirs who catch them' (Selden, *Mare Clausum*, p. 22). Cf. Richard Schlatter, *Private Property: The History of an Idea* (London, 1951), p. 131. Locke used fish as an example of property that is held in common (*Two Treatises*, II, 30).

[26] Selden, *Mare Clausum*, pp. 20–1.

[27] See Sir Robert Filmer, *The Anarchy of a Limited or Mixed Monarchy* (1648), *Political Works*, p. 287, and Ch. VII below.

[28] Selden, *Mare Clausum*, pp. 20–1 and 23.

[29] Even greater 'concessions' to patriarchalism can be found in Hugo Grotius' *De Jure Belli ac Pacis Libri Tres* (1625), II, v, 23; conveniently translated by Donald W. Kelsey as *The Law of War and Peace*, Classics of International Law (New York, 1925), p. 253.

# VI

## Patriarchalism in the Puritan Revolution

### I

In 1640 John Swan, an otherwise undistinguished Anglican
divine, published a book entitled *Redde Debitum: or, A Discourse
in Defence of Three Chiefe Fatherhoods*. Swan's fatherhoods
were natural paternity, magistracy, and priesthood; paternity
was used as the basis for a general discussion of obedience to constituted authority. Swan did not rest his case immediately upon
the Fifth Commandment but relied instead upon the first half
of Proverbs 30:11: '*There is* a generation *that* curseth their
father. . . .' This text *plus* the Fifth Commandment, Swan contended, extends not merely to natural parents who beget children
but includes 'several sorts of other parents. . . . They are not
onely our parents who give us a beeing,' he wrote, 'but such also
as give us a safe and well-being. Our naturall parents give us the
first: Our political parents give us the second: And from our
spiritual parents we receive the third or last which is the perfection of all the rest.'[1] This tract was altogether unoriginal, and
the greater part of Swan's efforts was devoted to the priesthood,
But the title of this book suggests that the paternal image had become an established symbol in Stuart thought by 1640.

When Henry Parker attacked Charles I's 'Answers' to Parliament's 'Nineteen Propositions' in 1642, he insisted that the
figurative fatherhood of monarchs had nothing to do with
political obligation:

[1] John Swan, *Redde Debitum: or, A Discourse in Defence of Three Chiefe
Fatherhoods* (London, 1640), pp. 5–6.

so the King is a Father to his People, taken singly, but not universally; for the father is more worthy than the son in nature, and the
son is wholly a debtor to his father, and can by no merit transcend
his dutie, nor challenge any thing as due from his father; for the
father doth all his offices meritoriously, freely, and unexactly. Yet
this holds not in the relation betwixt King & Subject, for its more
due in policie, and more strictly to be challenged, that the King
should make happy the People, than the People make glorious the
King.[2]

Parker, who has been credited with having 'advanced for the
first time in English history a theory of Parliamentary
sovereignty',[3] was immediately answered by apologists for King
Charles. The most important of Parker's royalist critics were Sir
John Spelman, son of the antiquary, and Dudley Digges the
younger, both of whom were at Oxford with the King. Spelman
and Digges, as well as other writers, used patriarchal arguments
against Parker. Their criticisms consisted largely of the Biblical–
historical claim that the origin of governance was God's bestowal
of fatherly power upon Adam, Noah, and the Hebrew patriarchs.
The validity of such arguments, of course, depended upon the
usually unstated genetic premise that if the people were not the
*source* of political authority, they certainly could not judge its
legitimate exercise.

   'Domesticall government is the very Image and modell of
Sovereignty in a Common-weale', Spelman asserted[4] against the
assumedly unqualified populism of Henry Parker.[5] Government
began with God's direct grants of authority to Adam and the
Patriarchs in their capacities as fathers:

   I shall observe that even in *Adam*, and after the Patriarchs,
*Noah, Abraham, Jacob*, and others, the common Fathers of Man-

---

[2] [Henry Parker], *Observations upon Some of His Majesties Late Answers
and Expresses* ([London, 1642]), pp. 18–19. See also his anonymously published *Jus Populi: or, A Discourse Wherein Clear Satisfaction is Given*
(London, 1644), p. 28: '... Princes are not to be called Fathers of their
Subjects, except taken *divisim*: but are meer servants to the people taken
*collectim*.'

[3] Margaret A. Judson, 'Henry Parker and the Theory of Parliamentary
Sovereignty', *Essays in History and Political Theory in Honor of Charles
Howard McIlwain* (Cambridge, Mass., 1936), p. 138.

[4] [John Spelman], *A View of a Printed Book* (Oxford, 1642), p. 9.

[5] See [Parker], *Observations*, esp. p. 1.

kind, Regall Government was instituted by GOD himself, without any Election of the people; GOD created mankinde, *ex uno, ut esset inter homines non Democratia, sed Regnum:* after which the Elders, or Fathers of Families successively, had by making war and executing sentence of death upon offenders:[6] And from these original Stock-fathers, Kingdoms and Monarchies, I suppose for the most part, have had their beginning, without popular Election, in this first commencement, and therefore I would have our Kings style continued, Carolus Dei gratia, rather then [*sic*] *Carolus electione populi.*[7]

It was not necessary, Spelman said, to enter into a detailed refutation of the populist doctrine, since everyone was familiar with its papal origins. 'But were we shie of *Jesuitisme*, as well as of *Popery*, we would not with so little examination receive opinion which we know had their first hatchings in the Schoole of the Jesuite.'[8] Spelman was not willing to abandon the theory so easily, for with proper modification, the doctrine could be effectively used in support of royal absolutism. The difficulty was not with the principle of consent itself but that it was 'mightily misapplyed by the *Observator*' (i.e., Parker), who said that because power had originally come from the people, it could be taken back. Spelman replaced this concept with the almost Hobbesian theory of an irrevocable contract, but he did not provide a theoretical context for his view, merely asserting, 'I should rather think if Regall power were originally conveyed from the people, they by conveying it over, have divested themselves of it.'[9] What Spelman was saying, of course, was that even if political authority had originally been established by popular agreement, this consent did not determine the relationship between the government and the people. Still, this concession to historical claims of the contract theory was an important departure from his previous

[6] See Gen. 14: 14 (Abraham as the commander of his family in warfare) and Gen. 38: 24 (Judah condemning Tamar to death for whoredom). These examples were used by Filmer (*Patriarcha*, p. 58).
[7] [Spelman], *A View*, p. 13.
[8] [John Spelman], *Certain Considerations upon the Duties Both of Princes and People* (Oxford, 1642), p. 2. (Cf. Filmer, *Patriarcha*, p. 53, verbal parallel: 'This tenet [populism] was first hatched in the Schools for good Divinity, and hath been fostered by succeeding Papists.')
[9] [Spelman], *A View*, p. 14.

derivation of monarchy from 'these original . . . Stock-fathers without popular election'.[10]

Dudley Digges was one of the most perceptive and careful thinkers writing in defense of Charles I during the Civil War period. His sensible moderation and skillful combining of populism and consent with patriarchalism entitled him to a greater fame than he had been accorded. Digges contributed three pamphlets to the Parker Controversy, but it was in the last one, *The Un-lawfulnesse of Subjects Taking up Arms against Their Soveraigne in What Case Soever* (1643), that he made his most important points. Nevertheless, the two earlier tracts are worth consulting for a fuller picture of their author's views. Digges was no more consistent than Spelman, but these inconsistencies enabled him to embrace the seemingly incompatible consent and patri-archal explanations of obligation. Early in *The Unlawfulnesse* he denied the applicability of the patriarchal origins of government to discussions of politics in his own time:

For though it be most true, that paternall authority was regall, and therefore this of Gods immediate constitution, and founded in nature, yet it is not much pertinent to the present decision, nor can it concern moderne controversies betweene Rulers and People. Be-cause it is most evident, no King at this day (and much lesse other Governours) holds his Crowne by that title, since severall paternall powers in every State are given up, and united in one common father, who cannot pretend a more immediate kindred to Adam, then [*sic*] all the rest of mankinde.[11]

Despite these protestations of irrelevance, Digges reached vastly different conclusions and did not refrain from discussing the state of nature and the regality of primitive 'paternall authority'. Parker's conception of the pre-political world, he said,

presents us with I know not what rude multitudes, living without lawes, without government, till such time, as out of the sense of their sufferings, which evidently proceeded from this want, they were

---

10 When he presented the whole of his political anthropology in *Cer-taine Considerations*, which was not specifically directed against Parker, Spelman's acceptance of Hobbes-like doctrines was more apparent, but the wider context was still missing. See esp. pp. 2 and 3.

11 [Dudley Digges], *The Unlawfulnesse of Subjects Taking up Armes against Their Soveraigne in What Case Soever* (1643; n.p., 1647), pp. 14–15.

forced to fly to such remedies [i.e., the establishement of government through their freely given consent]. However this fancy might pass for currant among such heathen Politicians as were ignorant of the originall of the world, & dreamed that the first men were bred as Insects, out of the mud of the earth . . .; yet we, who are satisfied with the history of the creation, cannot imagine, that Anarchy was before a regulated Government, and that God who had digested one *Chaos* into order, should leave the most noble creatures in a worse confusion.[12]

Instead, Digges believed, men have always and naturally been born subject to their fathers and therefore lacked the inherent power necessary to make them the authors of government.[13] This subjection was not a *denial* of natural human freedom, but such freedom existed only within the confines of fatherly authority. 'It is true, if we look upon the Priviledges of Nature, (*abstracting from paternall dominion*) Freedome is the birth-righte of mankinde, and equally common to every one . . .'[14] Digges was elucidating what a great many of his contemporaries assumed but merely implied or left unsaid. His complaints about the failure of state-of-nature theorists to consider the existence of familial rule were generally valid; few writers indicated that they had taken account of an already existing family structure in their explanations of consent. By making this point explicit and accepting it himself, Digges became one of the first writers who clearly grasped the implications of the distinction between political and other kinds of relationships. And it was this distinction that was eventually to be so important in the theoretical overthrow of political patriarchalism.

After limiting the scope of natural freedom to what could be 'abstracted' from paternal rule, Digges said that a genuinely non-political condition did not afford sufficient protection of life or private possessions. Therefore, men saw that they had little choice but to 'reduce themselves into a civill unitie, by placing over them one head, and by making his will the will of them all, to the end there might bee no gap left open by schisme to return

---

[12] [Dudley Digges], *An Answer to a Printed Book, Intituled Observations upon Some of His Majesties Late Answers and Expresses* (Oxford, 1642), p. 4.

[13] [Dudley Digges], *A Review of the Observations* (Oxford, 1643), pp. 3–4.

[14] Digges, *Unlawfulnesse*, p. 2. Emphasis added.

to their former confusion'. He further stipulated that an unavoidable result of the establishment of a 'civill unitie' was the
obligation of every person to remain loyal and not to revert to his
natural freedom; in short, the compact was irrevocable, just as it
had been for Spelman. The 'former confusion' from which
men had escaped was not a condition of individualist anarchy
but a patriarchal order in which all fathers were 'naturall princes'
and 'every family was a kingdome'. In the early days of the world,
Digges wrote, 'a Commonwealth was lodged in a Cottage,'[15]
and the patriarchs lived so long and fathered so many children
that they 'might people a Nation out of their own loynes, and
be saluted *Pater Patriae* without a metaphor; the same being their
subjects and their children'.[16]

Whatever its previous association with natural fatherhood,
kingship no longer coincided with paternity. Nonetheless, it still
retained the characteristics of paternal authority. In an important
and curious union of consent with patriachalism, Digges said that
the 'King hath paternall powers from the consent of the people'.
By 'people' he probably meant the primitive fathers whom he
had described earlier as 'natural princes', for he further wrote:

It was our owne act which united all particular paternal powers in
Him [the king], and that these are truly transferred, and now really
in Him is very evident, because else we should be bound to obey
our Fathers commands, before those of the King. For divine precept
stands in full force, *Honor thy Father, &c.* and therefore we must
confesse, *tam pater nemo est in terris*, hee that begot us is not so
much our Father, as the King is.[17]

[15] Ibid., pp. 4–5 and 15.
[16] [Digges], *An Answer*, p. 5. In his *Review*, p. 2, he said, 'God creating
man single, left him not other meanse of multiplying, than only by propagation, and in propagating, he gave the Rule and Soveraignty of the issues
propagated, to the Father of whom they were propagated; and in defailance
of the Father, He gave the Rule of all the younger (and consequently
of their descendants too) unto the first borne.... So that all men in the
beginning were born Subjects, either to him that naturally was their
Father, or to him that by right of primogeniture was representatively the
Father.'
[17] Digges, *Unlawfulnesse*, pp. 61–2. Cf. the passage from pp. 14–15 quoted
above and the interpretations of J. H. M. Salmon, *The French Religious
Wars in English Political Thought* (Oxford, 1959), p. 91, and John Neville
Figgis, *The Divine Right of Kings*, 2nd ed., paperbound reprint (New
York, 1965), p. 345.

When Parker finally replied to his critics more than two years after the publication of the *Observations*, his arguments were far more philosophic than the controversy demanded. He was no longer just defending Parlimentary sovereignty, for his answer, *Jus Populi*, was an attempt to provide a full theory of political obligation. Parker was much more precise than Digges in separating paternal from political power and could therefore trace government back to its familial beginnings without making any concessions to the moral patriarchal doctrine. Were it not for some very conspicuous contradictions, Parker's position would be an almost perfect example of neutral anthropological patriarchalism. Despite these slips, his argument was very close to Locke's critique of Filmer.

True liberty, Parker insisted, is an essential requisite for political life; transfering the principles of household government to political rule is inappropriate. It is not enough for a ruler to look after his subjects in the process of protecting his personal interests as a master does with a servant. 'This kind of Authority is not to be endured in a State', Parker wrote, 'because it is incompetent with liberty, provided onely for slaves, and such as have no true interest in the State.'[18] Although he did not identify these nonpolitical, slave-like individuals, Parker's context suggests everyone in a condition of subservience to a patriarchal superior, that is, wives, children, and servants. The liberty of the remaining people was presumably analogous to what other writers often called natural equality, and Parker asserted that it was not incompatible with political authority. The state was originally ordained by God to provide the order required after the Fall from Grace. Thus, even the voluntary establishment of government by man was in accord with the divine scheme, if not with God's very commands.

Nevertheless, Adam had no political authority. This was evident in his failure to punish Cain for the murder of Abel, which he certainly would have done had the power been his. 'But we do not find that *Adam* did claim any such power, or sin, in not claiming it; We find rather that the whole stock of Mankinde then living, were the Judges that Cain feared.' And even if Adam had been granted political power as part of his role as a father, his paternal right 'might better qualifie him to rule, whilst he

18 [Parker], *Jus Populi*, p. 28.

lived only amongst his own descendants, than any other pretence could any particular person amongst his descendants: but it did only qualify, not actually constitute: and since *Adams* death, none but *Noah* could pretend to the same qualification'. But such discussions were only academic, for Parker would not admit that patriarchal authority was ever so great as 'to equal [political] Jurisdiction, or at least absolute Jurisdiction'.[19]

Despite these criticisms of the alleged relation of familial to political dominion, Parker did not deny the anthropological or historical claims of patriarchalism. In fact, he agreed that the first government had been exercised over a family, saying:

Whilst the Universe was but one intire House, and united under one common Father, in whom all tyrannous thoughts were contrary to the worst suggestions of Nature; whilst the neare relation of blood was fresh, and unobliterated; whilst the spacious surface of the Earth (not yet thronged with plantations) afforded few baites of avarice, or objects of ambition, or grounds of difference betwixt brother and brother; whilst so many umpires of equal distance in blood, were at hand to interpose, in case any difference did unhappily arise; The raines of Government might hang more loose and easie upon the necks of Men.

Eventually, familial government became insufficient; as the population of the world increased, the conditions that had been favorable to patriarchal rule disappeared. Then 'Families did incorporate, and grow up into Cities, and Cities into States'. But how long this process took and when it started could never be known. Parker would only say that between the Flood and usurpation of Nimrod men were under the government *'of single Commanders, who nevertheless did not govern as Kings,* but as Fathers'. This meant merely that 'Governours in those days, having small Territories, did claim but moderate Prerogatives, though they were solely supreme in the State, as Fathers are in Families.'[20] In these few sentences Parker virtually retracted his earlier statements against patriarchal right, especially the insistence that it had never been great enough 'to equal Juridisdiction'.

[19] Ibid., pp. 3, 33 and 34.
[20] Ibid., pp. 43, 46, and 45. Cf. W. K. Jordan, *Men of Substance: A Study of the Political Thought of Two English Revolutionaries, Henry Parker and Henry Robinson* (Chicago, 1942), p. 143.

Also, it is clear that the individuals intended by the *Observations* —those persons whose collective consent established government —were the same as the heads of the 'Families [that] did incorporate, and grow up into Cities' in *Jus Populi*. Only patriarchal rulers would have had sufficient authority to establish the incorporated governments.

2

While Digges and Spelman were answering Parker, Henry Ferne, in a tract entitled *The Resolving of Conscience* (1642), was attacking another version of the populist theory. If the doctrine of the original power of the people 'must be a Fundamentall,' Ferne charged, 'it is such a one as upon it this Government cannot be built, but confusion and anarchy may readily be raised'. He substituted unembellished divine right for this faulty popular sovereignty. There was nothing at all patriarchal in Ferne's position, but in his preface he linked divine right with the Fifth Commandment, saying, 'If it be agreed upon as a thing known in this State, that the King is *the higher Power* according to St. Paul, *the Supreme* according to St. Peter, *the Father of the Commonwealth* according to the fifth Commandment, surely it belongs to the Divine to urge obedience, honour, and subjection according to those places [in the Bible], and reprove resistence forbidden there.'[21]

Ferne attracted critics at once, and when he defended his original tract, he added patriarchalism to his divine-right notions and provided a detailed account of the development of fatherly power. This further elaboration of Ferne's arguments illustrates how close to the surface the familial doctrine remained even when it was not actually articulated. After repeating that 'the Governing power was from God', Ferne revealed the nature of that source more clearly:

Well then, this Governing power was not *a populo effluxa,* as he [Charles Herle[22]] above said, but flowed from that providence at

---

[21] Henry Ferne, *The Resolving of Conscience* (Cambridge, 1642), p. 14 and Preface, sigs. 1ᵛ–2.

[22] [Charles Herle], *A Fuller Answer to a Treatise Written by Doctor Ferne* (London, 1642). The title of this work is due to its having been the second or third reply to Ferne's *Resolving the Conscience.*

first through the veines of nature in a paternal or Fatherly rule,
and by that as a Kingly Rule or Government, upon the encrease of
people and Nations; for when the Reins of Paternall Government
could not reach them for their extent, or hold them in for their
unruliness, & injustice, it inlarged it self into a Kingly power, which
bore and used the Sword; for that is given them to use streight
after the Flood. *Gen.* 9: 6.

Noah, his sons, and their descendants all exercised the rights of
paternal monarchs over their families, some of them as the vice-
roys of the universal father. When the patriarchal state became
crowded, Ferne wrote, colonies were 'thrust forth (like swarmes
of Bees) under their Rulers, who were the chiefe Fathers of those
new Progenies, and had the Government, both Regall and Sacre-
dotall by Primogeniture, unless the chiefe Patriarch, from whom
they all issued, saw cause to order it otherwise'.[23]

In replying to Ferne's defense, Charles Herle asserted that the
Bible did not provide sufficient evidence for claiming that the
first government in the world was a universal monarchy. Quite
the contrary, Herle asserted, for men were originally governed
aristocratically by the 'heads or chiefes in their *severall Families
in their Countreyes and Nations* (as the words are[24]) and there it
is that *Nimrod* was singled out among all the rest, as a *mighty
Hunter or Usurper*,[25] in first beginning a Kingdome'. Despite the
important concession to the patriarchal theory inherent in his
notion of paternal aristocracy, Herle said that the symbolic use
of fathers and husbands to represent kings does not mean that
monarchs are patriarchs. Herle's specific denial of the identity of
familial and political authority and his awareness of the role and
limitations of symbols in political discourse are particularly noteworthy:

*Allegoryes* are no good *arguments*, they onely illustrate as farre as
the likenesse holds. Because a *King* may in some respects be call'd
the *Father*, the *Head*, the *Husband* of his *Kingdome* (as the Doctor
insists) doth it therefore follow that because he should governe with

[23] Henry Ferne, *Conscience Satisfied: That There Is No Warrant for the
Armes Now Taken up by Subjects* (Oxford, 1643), pp. 7–8.
[24] See Gen. 10: 5, 20, 31, and 32.
[25] Gen. 10: 9.

the *providence* of a Father, he may therefore governe with the *Arbitrarinesse* of a Father without the Consent of his people, to the laws or rules of his government, as Father doth without that of his children; or because he should governe with the *wisdome* of a *head*, that therefore he may governe not only without the *consent* but without the *Counsell* of the rest of the *Members* as the head doth; or because with the *love* of a *husband*, therefore an absolute power of disposall of whatever the Subject hath, as the husband hath towards the wife?[26]

### 3

The differences between fatherly and political power were extremely important to populist writers. As part of his attack on the patriarchal theory of kingship, Samuel Rutherford, a Scottish Presbyterian, distinguished between liberty and property. 'Fathers may indeed dispose of the inheritance of their children,' he wrote, 'because that inheritance belongeth to the father as well as to the Sonne.' However, the liberty of the son is born with him, 'all men being borne free from all Civill subjection'; the father, therefore, 'hath no more power to resigne the libertie of his children, then their lives'. Rutherford's notion of 'libertie' was extremely limited, for he also said that merely by committing his posterity to the government of a specific ruler, a father did not necessarily deprive them of their natural liberty. 'To be tyd to a lawfull King is no making away of liberty,' he claimed, 'but a resigning of power to be justly governed, protected and awed from active and passive violence.' All that a people who remove themselves from a state of nature surrender is 'their power of doing violence to those other fellows in that same Communitie', not their rights and liberties.[27]

Rutherford was attacking a patriarchal defense of the divine right of kings by John Maxwell, a favorite of Charles I's and a Scotsman and loyal follower whom the King rewarded with the Bishopric of Tuam, Ireland. Maxwell had criticized the idea of popular sovereignty, saying that its origins could be seen in the

[26] [Charles Herle], *An Answer to Doctor Fernes Reply, Entitled Conscience Satisfied* (London, 1643), pp. 16–17.
[27] Samuel Rutherford, *Lex, Rex: The Law and the Prince* (London, 1644), pp. 86–7 and 44.

Conciliar doctrine of papal accountability. Attributing this position to Gerson, John of Paris, and William of Occam, Maxwell said, 'All these were prior to *Luther* or *Calvin*. Our Rabbies then have drawn Doctrines out of their polluted cisternes.'[28] Power had never been in the community, he continued, and therefore the people could not claim an authority above the king. If God had originally given political power to the people, absolute monarchy was contrary to divine law, and this, of course, was not the case!

It was possible to understand the source of governmental authority, Maxwell reasoned, only by looking into the first establishment of political dominion. Strictly speaking, however, government was never 'established' but had always existed. Man simply could not live without it. 'Can we then dreame to ourselves', he asked, 'that God did leave man without this means of subsistence,' and that man had the capacity 'to appoint and specify either no government at all, or what kind and specie of government he pleased?' The answer was clearly in the negative, for everyone is born subject to his father and therefore lacks the right of freedom that populism presupposes. This condition had existed since the creation of man; Adam was an absolute monarch even in the state of innocence. And if such authority was needed before the Fall, it was even more necessary after it, Maxwell said:

I humbly intreat those who are contrary minded [and who doubt that all government was originally established by God] to consider seriously, how Almighty God in the creation of man before the woman was made *of him, and for him*, and before he had any child or subject to governe, fixed authority and power for government in the person of *Adam*. This is to averre, that government was fixed in a governour before hee had [anyone] over whom he was to beare rule, is no paradox in Philosophie (if I pleased to insist philosophically to cleare it) nor a more strange theory to consider, then when a *Posthumus*, one borne after the death of his father, by right inheriteth his fathers honour and revenues. Is it not considerable that

28 [John Maxwell], *Sacro-Santa Regum Majestas: or, The Sacred and Royal Prerogative of Christian Kings* (Oxford, 1644) p. 16. Maxwell was probably correct in his claim to have found the historical sources of populist doctrines. See Zofia Rueger, 'Gerson, The Conciliar Movement and the Right of Resistance (1642–1644)', *Journal of the History of Ideas*, XXV (1964), 467–86.

God did not make *Evah* out of the earth, as he did *Adam*, but made her *of the man*; and declareth too, made her *for man*? It is far more probable then, [that] God in his wisedome did not thinke it fit (that he was able to doe it I hope none dare to deny) to make *two indepen-dents*, and liked best of all governments of mankind, *The Soveraignty of one*, and that with that extent, that both wife and posterity should submit and subject themselves to him. If *Adam* had not fallen, Divines doubt not but [that] government had beene. Govern-ment without subordination is not conceivable, nor subordination without the reall relations of superiority and inferiority. It is not to be controverted, if *Adam* had never fallen, Aristocracie, or Demo-cracie, or mixed Government, had never been existent or apparent in the world.[29]

Maxwell believed that Adam's fatherly authority continued and was passed on to his descendants. Therefore, a people who had all 'sprung up from one root' would obey their common father (or his lineal heir) as a political ruler so long as that person were alive and known. But the states of seventeenth-century Europe lacked this common ancestry and therefore had to choose their rulers. Nonetheless, Maxwell argued, when such nations selected governors, they were merely designating substitutes for their miss-ing common fathers. They gave them no power but just chose someone to exercise the authority bestowed by God.

Consider yet a little more; the King elected to be a Soveraigne to such a headlesse, a discorded multitude, as we presuppose, is sur-rogated in the place of a common father to the whole Communitie over which he is to beare rule. . . . [A]s the naturall Father (suppose that *Adam* were living, had he not just title to the Monarchies of the world?) receiveth not any *paternall right, power, or authority*, from his posterity, or those [who] are come of his loynes; but hath this from God and the ordinance of nature, which is *jus divinum* (as we have said) no more can the *father surrogated* in the place and power of the naturall father be said to receive his Right, his Power, his Soveraignty from the Community. . . . For my part a King designed in such a case, ought, should enjoy his paternall right, no less than *Malchisedeck*, or *Abraham*.[30]

---

[29] [Maxwell], *Sacro-Sancta*, pp. 89 and 84. On the power of Adam before the Fall, see Filmer, *Anarchy*, p. 289.
[30] [Maxwell], *Sacro-Sancta*, pp. 85–7. On the status of Adam were he still alive, see Filmer, *Patriarcha*, p. 61.

Criticizing Parker's denial of the relevance of the patriarchal image to political obligation in the *Observations*,[31] Maxwell said that it was foolish to exalt fathers over their sons and to forget that kings were entitled to even more obedience. 'The obligation to *pater patriae*, to the father of the kingdom, is stronger, is straighter, than to *pater familiae*, to our naturall father,' he insisted. This notion was one of his cardinal tenets, for he had previously stated that 'The tye betwixt King and People, Prince and Subject is greater, is stricter than any betwixt man and wife, father and sonne,'[32] and in his interpretation of the Fifth Commandment he wrote that 'by father is *principally* (according to the Commentaries of ancient and moderne Divines) meant the king'.[33] He left 'mother' out of his text altogether, letting '&c.' take its place. Interestingly enough, Maxwell made no attempt to relate this reading of the Fifth Commandment to his notion of the familial origins of the state; nor did he use it to justify the powers of fathers in general.

Another of the King's favorites, James Ussher, Archbishop of Armagh, who computed the chronology that is still in the margins of the King James Bible, also employed patriarchal arguments in his defense of the monarchy. The 'main aim and scope' of Ussher's treatise was 'no other but to confirm all good Subjects in their dutiful obedience unto their Prince, and to prevent Sedition and Rebellion' among those honest, well-minded, but mistaken subjects who 'might perhaps for want of better information be drawn out of the way, and misguided to their destruction'.[34] The King of England, while no less obliged than his subjects to keep divine law, is answerable only to God.[35] This independence from the people could be traced to the original institution of government by God. By subjecting Eve to the authority of Adam, He 'established an Headship in every single Family'.

---

[31] The passage is quoted in full above, at n. 2. In particular Maxwell objected to the statement that the inferiority of the son to his father had nothing to do with the relation of subjects to the king.

[32] [Maxwell], *Sacro-Sancta*, pp. 169 and 99–100.

[33] Ibid., p. 161; emphasis added. Cf. pp. 7 and 188.

[34] James Ussher, *The Power Communicated by God to the Prince, and the Obedience Required of the Subject* (written *c.* 1644, first published in 1661), 2nd ed. (London, 1683), p. 244.

[35] Ibid., pp. 80–1.

So after the posterity of *Eve* began to be distinguished into Families, the same God, by using the same speech to *Cain* concerning his brother *Abel, Unto thee shall be his desire and thou shalt rule over him,* may seem to have constituted a principality in one man over divers Families, and thereby laid the foundation of Political Government; the Kingdom (as it appeareth by the ordinary practice of the succeeding times) together with the excellency of dignity, and the excellency of Power, the two peculiar characters thereof, being an honour that descended upon the first-born, and not upon the younger Brother.[36]

Large-scale political society probably began when '*the very light of Nature* ... enforced men to conjoin many Families into one Body of a civil Society, and to submit themselves to the Government of some Superiour: For, otherwise a dissolution of mankind would quickly ensue, and all come to ruine'.[37] This doctrine was part of the Archbishop's derivation of governmental authority from the patriarchal (and husbandly) power of Adam. Because of these familial beginnings and the general resemblance of the state to the household, Ussher held that all Biblical statements about the governance of families were equally applicable to kingdoms:

...*A Household is a kind of little Common-wealth, and a Common-wealth a great Household.* ... And therefore what in the one a Husband, a Father, and a Master may expect from those who have such relations to him: the like, by due proportion, is to have place in the other. For *that which the Apostle speaketh of the Master and the Servant, is to be understood likewise of Powers, and Kings, and of all the high Estates of this World,* saith *S. Augustine.*[38]

There is little in Ussher's limited patriarchalism to suggest the form that the theory was going to take in Filmer's writings; in this

[36] Ibid., p. 14; citing for the reference to Adam and Eve Gen. 3: 16, to Cain and Abel Gen. 4: 7, and for the parenthetical statement Gen. 49: 3 and II Chron. 21: 3.

[37] Ussher, *Power*, pp. 14–15.

[38] Ibid., p. 134, citing Augustine's commentary on Psalm 125. On p. 143 Ussher used this doctrine to justify the application of the following Biblical discussions of household governance to political obligation: Ephes. 5: 24 (coupled with I Tim. 2: 11), Colos. 3: 20 and 22 (with Tit. 2: 9), and Josh. 1: 16 and 17.

respect, the Archbishop is certainly not to be compared with Digges or Maxwell. However, his book was not published until 1661 despite its having been written for Charles I sometime during the First Civil War. When the work was issued, it was with the assistance of Robert Sanderson, the Bishop of Lincoln, and James Tyrell, Ussher's grandson, who was to write an attack on Filmer in 1681. Sanderson contributed a lengthy introduction on the origin of government and the problems raised by the contract theory. As I shall indicate in chapter ten, this introduction utilized a great many of the anti-contractual arguments that seem to have been first employed by Filmer, and it may be that Sanderson was directly influenced by Sir Robert.

# VII

## Sir Robert Filmer:
## (1) The Attack on Populism

### I

It 'may be inferred to be the plain mind of Aristotle,' Sir Robert Filmer announced in 1652, '1. That there is no form of government, but monarchy only, [and] 2. That there is no monarchy, but paternal.' These statements are more the quintessence of Filmer's own political theories than they are conclusions objectively drawn from Aristotle; they were followed by four other assertions, also said to have been unambiguously based upon Aristotle: '3. That there is no paternal monarchy, but absolute, or arbitrary. 4. That there is no such form of government as an aristocracy or democracy. 5. That there is no such form of government as a tyranny. 6. That the people are not born free by nature.'[1] In order to substantiate these claims, it was necessary for Filmer to demonstrate not only that patriarchal monarchy was the sole form of government in the world but also that alternative explanations of the nature of political obedience were incorrect. As was shown in chapter one, twentieth-century commentators tend to agree that Sir Robert was far more successful in the critical task than in setting forth his own theory of politics. And a number of authors have suggested that Filmer's attack on the emerging liberal theory was unanswerable while simultaneously proclaiming the uniqueness and absurdity of his patriarchal doctrine.

[1] Sir Robert Filmer, *Observations upon Aristotles Politiques Touching Forms of Government* (1652), *Political Works*, p. 229. Hereafter cited as *Forms*.

The comments on Aristotle were almost the last words that Sir Robert wrote on the general subject of political obligation, a topic that had occupied much of his attention for the preceding decade. Sometime in the early 1640s he wrote *Patriarcha*, the tract on which his reputation has rested for nearly three hundred years. *Patriarcha* was originally composed for Filmer's friends and neighbors, and manuscript copies circulated among the manor houses of Kent, no doubt earning for their author considerable reknown as an enemy of populism. But the work was apparently never intended for a larger audience, and Filmer would not agree to requests that he publish his essay.[2] Thus, *Patriarcha* was withheld from the press during its author's life. It had been written in terms of the controversies that led to the Puritan Revolution but was finally published in 1680, some twenty-seven years after Sir Robert's death, as an attack on the Exclusionists. The arguments of *Patriarcha* are fragmentary, and most of the ideas were more fully developed by Filmer in his later writings, which may partially explain his reluctance to publish the original essay. But it was in the first half of *Patriarcha* that Filmer most clearly and forcefully worked out his patriarchal theory and its Biblical underpinnings.

The *Patriarcha* manuscript also contained a long discussion of the English constitution, and when Filmer decided to offer his political thoughts to the public beyond the County of Kent, his first published work—*The Freeholders Grand Inquest* (offered for sale in January, 1647/8)[3]—was an elaboration of the legal argument. The thesis of the *Freeholder* was that the king was the supreme power in England and did not share any of his authority with the two houses of Parliament. Filmer insisted that Parliament owed its existence to royal grace alone. Parliaments were

[2] For Filmer's life see the following works by Peter Laslett: 'Sir Robert Filmer: The Man versus the Whig Myth', *William and Mary Quarterly*, 3rd ser., V (1948), 523–46; Introduction to Filmer, *Political Works*, esp. pp. 1–10; and 'The Gentry of Kent in 1640', *Cambridge Historical Journal*, IX (1947–49), 148–64. Sir Robert's unwillingness to publish *Patriarcha* is reported by his close friend Peter Heylyn, in *Certamen Epistolare: or, The Letter-Combate* (London, 1659), p. 208 (misnumbered 387).

[3] The months in which Filmer's tracts were available are given by Laslett in his editorial note preceding each work. His information is generally taken from the Thomason Collection in the British Museum.

called to advise the monarch, not to share in his legislative supremacy. Even this power of giving counsel was not a right but was enjoyed only through royal sufferance, for what the crown had granted it could legitimately take away. There is not much in the *Freeholder* to interest students of *political* philosophy, but the structure of its argument reveals Sir Robert's reliance upon genetic methods and the ease with which one could move from the origins of all political organization to the beginnings of a specific institution in a particular nation.

The *Freeholder* demonstrates as well Filmer's rejection of a developmental view of the English constitution, which placed him in direct opposition to the growing common law and traditionalist notions. Sir Robert's point, in brief, was that the first Parliament was not summoned until 1215. Therefore, kings must originally have ruled alone, and Parliament could claim no rights that were imbedded in the English constitution, only privileges that had been granted by the royal sovereign and which were periodically renewed. Filmer was absolutely unwilling to acknowledge that a practice of long standing could become converted to a right; thus, it was essential to see how Parliament began in order to understand its nature.

Filmer's next publication, *The Anarchy of a Limited or Mixed Monarchy* (April, 1648), was an attack on Philip Hunton's *Treatise of Monarchy* (1643).[4] The *Anarchy*, like the *Freeholder*, used much material from *Patriarcha*; it was Sir Robert's first public discussion of political obligation, and its case against Hunton was presented in concise patriarchal terms and without the extensive Biblical history that characterizes the first half of *Patriarcha*. A number of arguments that were not fully developed

---

[4] Hunton capably argued that England was governed by a mixed and thereafter limited monarchy, a doctrine that Corinne C. Weston says was 'the prevailing constitutional theory during the English Civil War'. ('The Theory of Mixed Monarchy under Charles I and After', *English Historical Review*, LXXV [1960], 426–43.)

Hunton's *Treatise of Monarchy* was reprinted in 1680 as an Exclusion tract and twice more in 1689 in defense of the Revolution. For a full analysis see Charles H. McIlwain, *Constitutionalism and the Changing World* (Cambridge, 1939), pp. 186–230. On the first page of the *Treatise* Hunton distinguished between authority in a 'Family, which is called Oeconomicall' and that in 'a publicke society, which is called Politicall. . . '.

E

in the original tract were spelled out more precisely in the *Anarchy*. A few months later, in August, 1648, George Thomason was selling *The Necessity of the Absolute Power of All Kings*, a collection of extracts that Filmer had made from Bodin's *République*. The *Necessity* was a discourse on sovereignty rather than a treatise on political obligation. Again, materials from *Patriarcha* were used, and some of the ideas from the *Anarchy* were repeated as well, showing their origins in Bodin, a thinker who had a most pronounced influence on Sir Robert.[5] For the next three and a half years Filmer published nothing. He was undoubtedly busy writing, for a number of his manuscripts from this period are preserved in the Bodleian Library,[6] and between February and May, 1652, three more of his political tracts were published. The first, *Observations Concerning the Originall of Government*, was a critical examination of Hobbes's *Leviathan*, Milton's *Defensio pro Populo Anglicani*, and Grotius's *De Jure Belli ac Pacis*. Filmer's criticisms attempted to demonstrate that the patriarchal theory solved a number of problems that were present in all three works. Several pages of the Grotius portion were taken verbatim from the *Patriarcha* manuscript, and when *Patriarcha* was finally published in 1680, this entire passage was omitted.[7] While it does not add very much to the doctrines Filmer had already advanced in *Patriarcha* and the *Anarchy*, the *Originall* is of more than routine interest; it shows Sir Robert's defense of the patriarchal case against three very different doctrines. The criticism of the *Leviathan* is particularly interesting, for Filmer confessed his agreement with Hobbes's absolutism but still dissented from the state of nature and contractual parts of the

[5] For Filmer's textual reliance upon Bodin, see Constance I. Smith, 'Filmer and the Knolles Translation of Bodin', *Philosophical Quarterly*, XIII (1963), 248–52. A manuscript in Filmer's hand of the first few pages of the *Necessity* is in the British Museum, MS. Harleian 6867, fols. 253–254ᵛ. See my 'Sir Robert Filmer: Some New Bibliographic Discoveries', *The Library*, XXVI (1971), 135–60, for a discussion of this and other Filmer manuscripts mentioned in this and the next chapter.

[6] Bodleian Library, MS. Tanner 233, fols. 135–47 and 172–82. The manuscripts, written and corrected in Filmer's own hand, deal with such topics as the Engagement Oath controversy and the extent to which a usurping government is entitled to obedience.

[7] A manuscript of *Patriarcha* in Filmer's hand and now owned by the University of Chicago also omits this passage. University of Chicago Library, catalogue number JC381.F5.

theory, offering patriarchalism as a more consistent route to the same conclusion.

The *Originall* was followed by *Observations on Aristotle's Politiques Touching Forms of Government*, to which the six propositions quoted at the beginning of this chapter were the conclusion. This too was partly an elaboration of some arguments that can be found in *Patriarcha*, but the *Forms* also adds a great deal to Filmer's theory. Especially noteworthy is an analysis of republicanism that is not present in any of the other tracts. The last of Sir Robert's political writings was entitled *Directions for Obedience to Governors in Dangerous or Doubtful Times*. It was published with the *Forms* but is actually a separate work; as its title suggests, it is a casuist essay on the extent to which a royalist should consider himself bound to obey the government of Cromwell, which was a central political question after the Regicide. In several respects, the *Directions* is Filmer's most interesting publication, for it was his only sustained attempt to apply his larger theoretical principles—which included prescriptive legitimation and non-resistance as well as patriarchalism—to a situation that should have been the very antithesis of his divine right royalism. In the end, Filmer was able to preserve both his loyalty to Charles II in exile and his duty to obey the government of England as effectively established. The price he paid for this reconciliation was his patriarchal theory.

These works were all published anonymously during Filmer's life, and they attracted conspicuously little attention. Had nothing more ever come of them, Filmer would doubtless be no better known today than Dudley Digges, Sir Henry Spelman, and a host of other minor and justifiably obscure royalists. But in 1679, a number of people recognized that the issues behind the debates in the Exclusion controversy were similar to the conflicts of the 1640s, and a great many tracts and pamphlets from the earlier crisis were reprinted. Among them was the corpus of Filmer's published works, issued for the first time in a single volume entitled *The Freeholders Grand Inquest* and bearing their author's name. By 1684 this collection had been reprinted or reissued five more times.[8] In 1680 *Patriarcha* was finally published. Since that

[8] The extracts from Bodin were omitted from the collection and were published separately in 1680 as *The Power of Kings: And in Particular of the King of England*. This work was added to the collected edition of

year Filmer has been assured of an historical reputation; even if he was to be regarded as an astoundingly naïve and irrational simpleton, he would at least be known.

It is well to keep in mind that in the late seventeenth century Filmer's theories generally escaped the ridicule they meet today. And when they did not—notably in the cases of Locke and Sidney—the scorn served a rhetorical purpose. The patriarchalism was taken quite seriously, for it was the main theoretical opposition encountered by populist writers during the latter part of the Stuart period. Filmer's books became the backbone of the Tory ideology when they were republished in the 1680s, and many men held them and their author in far higher esteem than the caricature by Locke suggests would have been possible. To cite only one instance here of the importance of Sir Robert during that decade, Anthony Wood, the famed antiquary and historian of Oxford, recorded that on 6 September 1683, James Parkinson was expelled from a Fellowship at Lincoln College 'for holding, maintaining and defending some unwarrantable [*sic*] and seditious principles'. One of the charges brought against Parkinson was 'that he commended to some of his pupils Milton as an excellent book and an antidote against Sir Robert Filmer, whom he calls "too high a Tory"'.[9]

2

Filmer did not fully distinguish his critical notions from his patriarchal theories, but his attack on populism provided a basis for those positive aspects of his theory for which he is chiefly remembered and often disparaged today.[10] His criticisms of the fundamental notions and presuppositions of popular sovereignty —including the state of nature, the contractual origins of govern-

---

1684, which was also the first collected edition to contain *Patriarcha*. The republication of Filmer's work in 1679 and after is discussed in part III of my bibliographic essay, 'Sir Robert Filmer'.

[9] Anthony Wood, *The Life and Times of Anthony Wood, Antiquary, of Oxford, 1632–1695, Described by Himself*, ed. Andrew Clark, 5 vols., Oxford Historical Society Publications (Oxford, 1891–1900), III, 69 and 70.

[10] This chapter is devoted to his critical doctrines. His patriarchalism will be examined in Ch. VIII.

ment, and the source and character of private property—were themselves substantial and interesting arguments. They were, moreover, a concise statement of the traditional political beliefs that had to be overcome before constitutional liberalism could become a dominant ideology. It was the fullness of Filmer's attack that forced Locke to depart from traditional modes of thought when he wrote about property, the state of nature, the origins of governance, and political obligation in his *Two Treatises*.

Sir Robert met the genetic thinking of the social compact with a similar origins-determined account of political authority. Attacking what he saw as the logical flaws and historical misrepresentations that abounded in populism, Filmer insisted against the state of nature thesis:

There never was any such thing as an independent multitude, who at first had a natural right to a community: this is but a fiction, or fancy of too many in these days, who please themselves in running after the opinions of philosophers and poets, to find out such an original of government, as might promise them such title of liberty.

If the theory of the natural and orginal freedom and right of sovereignty of all mankind could be refuted, Filmer alleged, it would not be possible to claim legitimacy for any form of government other than monarchy. This matter did not present him with a serious difficulty, for he found that no one had attempted to *prove* the 'supposed natural freedom of mankind'. Its advocates 'only beg it to be granted'.[11] The proposition rested upon the erroneous belief that a 'multitude of men had first sprung out, and were engendered of the earth' at the creation, whereas in fact only one man, Adam, had been created.[12] Filmer's argument against Hobbes was similar:

I cannot understand how this right of nature can be conceived without imagining a company of men at the very first to have been all created together without dependency one of another, or as mushrooms (*fungorum more*) they all on a sudden were sprung out

[11] Filmer, *Forms*, Preface, pp. 188 and 189.
[12] Ibid., p. 204.

of the earth without any obligation on to another, as Mr. Hobbes's words are in his book *De Cive*, chapter 8, section 3; the scripture teacheth us otherwise, that all men came by succession, and generation from one man: we must not deny the truth of the history of the creation.[13]

Filmer's major source for the early history of mankind was the Bible, and his conception of that history was similar to the view defended in Overall's *Convocation Book*. It should not be assumed, however, that Sir Robert's position was untenable or indemonstrable, for the historical authenticity of Holy Writ was one of the most uniformly accepted bases of seventeenth-century thought. Even Locke did not dispute the literal truth of scriptural history in his attack on political patriarchalism. What was at issue, though, was the interpretation to be extracted from certain passages where the meaning was not clear. Locke's analysis was to be rational; his adversary's had been literal.

Filmer's criticism of populism was not derived exclusively from the Bible. Beyond the insistence upon the creation of only one man, in fact, it owed very little to revelation. This was not true of his positive theories, which, at crucial points, were inseparably wedded to Old Testament history. But in the present context his arguments were not primarily historical; his chief point was the moral and logical impossibility of deriving government, private property, and the hierarchical arrangements that exist in society from the conditions of original natural freedom and equality predicated by contractual thinkers. All state-of-nature theories presuppose some binding requirement that legitimate contracts and promises be kept; otherwise, it would be impossible to explain how men who agreed to a compact that created government could be bound to obey the newly instituted sovereign. This moral presupposition—usually thought of as the natural law of *pacta sunt servanda*—was attacked by Sir Robert on the ground that, in the condition of natural equality and common ownership, there could never even *be* pacts, let alone an obligation to keep them. Confounding the economic goods *about* which some agreements can be made with the moral implications and consequences of the very institution of keeping agreements, Filmer asked, 'If

[13] Filmer, *Originall*, p. 241.

all things are common by nature, how could there be any bargains?'[14]

The main thrust of Sir Robert's argument was the demonstration of the logical gulf between natural freedom and government. 'If it be imagined that the people were ever but once free from subjection by nature, it will prove a mere impossibility ever lawfully to introduce any kind of government whatsoever, without apparent wrong to a multitude of people.'[15] The point was, of course, that with the institution of government, natural equality and freedom gave way to status and restraint—and without justification. This attitude was more fully elaborated in Filmer's criticism of Grotius's theory of private property.

Grotius, Filmer held, argued that natural law was so changeless and immutable that even God was powerless to alter it. Nevertheless, *De Jure Belli* placed at least one human institution on an equal footing with the law of nature. Although original equality and primitive communism were dictates of nature, Grotius defended private property as a necessary consequence of man's condition and endowed it with the protection of natural law itself. Thus Sir Robert mockingly concluded:

[Grotius] gives a double ability to man; first to make that no law of nature, which God made to be the law of nature: and next to make that a law of nature which God made not; for now that dominion is brought in, he maintains, it is against the law of nature to take that which is in another man's dominion.[16]

The state-of-nature thesis was so far from providing the basis for government, Filmer asserted, that it actually led to anarchy, for

[14] Filmer, *Originall*, p. 265. Filmer was talking about contracts of exchange, and he failed to see the difference between the duty to keep a specific promise and the justification of promise-keeping in general. For an excellent discussion of this distinction, see John Rawls, 'Two Concepts of Rules', *Philosophical Review*, LXIV (1955), 3–32.

[15] Filmer, *Anarchy*, p. 287. See also *Patriarcha*, p. 81.

[16] Filmer, *Originall*, p. 266. Filmer's objections seem to be warranted. Contrast Grotius's statements in *De Jure Belli*, I, i, 10 (the law of nature) with those in II, ii, 2–4 (original communism and private ownership). See also *Patriarcha*, pp. 63–6, where a similar argument was developed and Filmer called attention to the apparent inconsistency in Selden's having embraced both original communism and the universal dominion of Adam.

every man had an equal right to become a king unto himself. In
order to avoid a universal monarchy, 'we shall run into the
liberty of having as many Kings as there be men in the world'.
Thus, there would be 'no King at all', and all men would be left
with 'their natural liberty, which is the mischief the pleaders for
natural liberty do pretend they would most avoid'.[17]

Leaving aside these matters, Filmer called attention to a number of fundamental questions about consent that proponents of
that doctrine failed to consider, such as 'the manner of the
peoples passing their consent', the determination of 'which of
them is sufficient, and which not to make the right or title;
whether it must be antecedent to possession, or may be consequent: express, or tacite: collective, or representative: absolute,
or conditionated: free, or enforced: revocable, or irrevocable'.
Sir Robert implied that these problems were intentionally ignored
by contractual theorists because of the great difficulties they
would have faced had they attempted to deal with them; 'otherwise surely . . . [these issues] would not have been neglected, con-
sidering how necessary it is to resolve the conscience, touching the
manner of the peoples passing their consent; and what is sufficient, and what not, to make, or derive a right, or title from the
people'.[18] He claimed that Philip Hunton had not specified whom
he meant by 'the people, even though he had rested the power
to determine the form of the government upon their consent:

Literally, and in the largest sense, the word people signifies the
whole multitude of mankind; but figuratively and synecdochically,
its notes many time the major part of a multitude, or sometimes the
better, or the richer, or the wiser, or some other part; and often-
times a very small part of the people, if there be no other apparent
opposite party, hath the name of the people by presumption.

In a rare instance of literary eloquence, Sir Robert observed that
'the people' was in a state of constant flux. 'Mankind is like the
sea, ever ebbing or flowing, every minute one is born another dies;

---

[17] Filmer, *Anarchy*, p. 286.
[18] Filmer, *Forms*, p. 226. Filmer's complaint was, on the whole, justified;
with the partial exception of Hobbes, most thinkers had ignored these
matters. Interestingly enough, Locke addressed himself to every one of
them, albeit only indirectly in some cases.

those that are the people this minute, are not the people the next minute, in every instant and point of time there is a variation.'[19] But if the term were used expansively and included children and servants, Filmer continued, it would mean that their numerical superiority would enable them 'to vote and appoint what government or governors their fathers and masters shall be subject unto, [which] is most unnatural, and in effect [is] to give the children the government over their parents'.[20]

Filmer resolved some of these matters for himself, and if his conclusions contradicted those of the populist writers, it was not because he had treated their premises illogically. The theoretical assumption of original human equality demanded that government and private property be instituted only by the unanimous act of all of the people.[21] Any departure from the principle of unanimity was a violation of someone's rights, for what belongs to someone by nature, Filmer reasoned, can be taken away only by his own consent, not by the agreement of others. But it is physically impossible, Sir Robert further charged, to obtain the agreement of everyone; it could not be done even 'in the smallest kingdom, though all men should spend their whole lives in nothing else but running up and down to covenant'.[22] Against Grotius he wrote:

> Certainly it was a rare felicity, that all men in the world at one instant of time should agree together in one mind to change the natural community of all things into private dominion: for without such a unanimous consent it was not possible for community to be altered: for if but one man in the world had dissented, the alteration had been unjust, because that man by the law of nature had a right to the common use of all things in the world; so that to have given a propriety of any one thing to any other, had been to have robbed him of his right to the common use of all things.[23]

[19] Filmer, *Anarchy*, pp. 285 and 287. In the *Forms* (p. 211) he said, 'The whole people is a thing so uncertain and changeable that it alters every moment, so that it is necessary to ask of every infant so soon as it is born its consent to government, if you will ever have the consent of the whole people.' See also *Forms*, pp. 225–6.

[20] Filmer, *Anarchy*, p. 287.

[21] Filmer, *Forms*, p. 225; *Anarchy*, p. 285.

[22] Filmer, *Originall*, p. 244. Cf. Overall, *Convocation Book*, Canon II, p. 3 (above, p. 93) for a verbal parallel.

[23] Filmer, *Originall*, p. 273.

Similarly, Sir Robert perceived one of the great logical flaws in the state-of-nature/contract theory and observed that agreement to a compact of government presupposed the existence of some social machinery. At the same time, he provided a further demonstration of the impossibility of obtaining unanimous consent:

For except by some secret miraculous instinct they should all meet at one time, and place, what one man, or company of men less than the whole people hath power to appoint either time or place of elections, where all be alike free by nature? and without a lawful summons, it is most unjust to bind those that be absent. The whole people cannot summon itself; one man is sick, another is lame, a third is aged, and a fourth is under age of discretion: all these at some time or other, or at some place or other, might be able to meet, if they might choose their own time and place, as men naturally free should.[24]

This problem is in part identified today as the doctrine of 'two contracts'. As Sir Ernest Barker observed, 'The theory of a contract of government really postulates, as a prior condition, the theory of a contract of society. There must already be something in the nature of an organized community . . . before there can be any contract between ruler and subjects.'[25]

Even a careful spelling out of two distinct contracts would not have satisfied Filmer, for this explanation still leaves unanswered the question of how men were able to agree on an initial *societal* contract. In fact, as Sir Robert himself recognized, there is no reason why there had to be a 'contract of society'. So long as men are legitimately associated, their duly authorized representative may make political decisions for them, and these decisions and the establishment of specific governments may very well be contractual in origin. What is important is to define the political constituency and to show how its members achieved their status. For Filmer, as for Stuart society in general, the politically significant part of the population was limited to fathers (or potential heads of households) who themselves were once sovereign within their own

---

[24] Filmer, *Anarchy*, pp. 286–7.
[25] Sir Ernest Barker, 'The Theory of the Social Contract in Locke, Rousseau, and Hume', reprinted in his *Essays on Government*, 2nd ed. (Oxford, 1951), pp. 90–1. See also Gough, *Social Contract*, p. 128 *et passim*.

families and had derived their powers from nature. At some stage, however, a number of these fathers had combined their separate domains into larger units and transferred the political part of their authority to a single ruler.

In Filmer's own words, 'All such prime heads and Fathers have power to consent in the uniting or conferring of their fatherly right of sovereign authority on whom they please.'[26] This contractual government was built upon a naturalistic and not a voluntary society. Sir Robert was able to avoid the two contracts question because he saw no difference between state and society. In 'conferring . . . their fatherly right' these patriarchs were not *creating* politics as a new kind of authority, as most contract theories seem to suggest. Filmer's handling of this matter is probably the only way in which his own criticisms of the contract thesis can be avoided, but this does not mean that societal naturalism necessarily leads to political absolutism or that a political order cannot be *created* by men who are naturally social.

As we shall see, Locke raised these same issues when he agreed with Filmer that men were social by nature but went on to argue that politics was something new that men had created when they needed it. On this question, however, the difference between Locke and Filmer was very much a matter of their implicit definitions of 'politics'. The many relationships that according to Locke existed in the state of nature and were therefore pre-political would certainly have been understood by Sir Robert as political in nature.

Filmer objected to the principle of contractual association as well as to the method by which people could agree to establish a political order. Tacit acceptance was altogether inadequate because 'If the silent acceptation of a governor by a part of the people be an argument of their concurring in the election of him, by the same reason the tacit consent of the whole community may be maintained.' Thus, Filmer observed that the same principles that were used in support of alleged popular assent could also justify conquest and usurpation.[27] Moreover, tacit consent was contrary to original equality, for it allowed the decision of those who did agree 'to bind the whole people, [which] is both unreasonable and unnatural'. Proxy votes were rejected as a valid

[26] Filmer, *Patriarcha*, p. 61.
[27] Ibid., p. 82.

means of instituting a government by consent for the same reasons.[28]

Criticizing a specific version of the contract theory, Sir Robert pointed out several problems inherent in notions of Hobbes, all of which commend themselves to the attention of some of Hobbes's twentieth-century critics. The essence of Hobbes's contract should be non-resistance, Filmer observed:

> To authorize and give up . . . [one's] right of governing himself, to confer all his power and strength, and to submit his will to another, is to lay down his right of resisting: for if right of nature be a liberty to use power for preservation of life, laying down of that power must be a relinquishing of power to preserve or defend life, otherwise a man relinquisheth nothing.[29]

But this was not the case at all, for Hobbes had placed important —even crucial—limitations on political obligation. Once an individual had become a member of a state, he could not legitimately be compelled to place his own life in jeopardy or to take the lives of others. What was more, the extent of a subject's duty to obey depended upon the intention or purpose of the compact rather than upon the principle of submission to sovereign authority. Hobbes's precise words were:

> No one is bound by the words [of the compact] themselves, either to kill himselfe, or any other man; And consequently, that the Obligation a man may sometimes have, upon the Command of the Sovereign to execute any dangerous, or dishonourable Office, dependeth not on the Words of our Submission; but on the Intention; which is to be understood by the End thereof. When therefore our refusall to obey, frustrates the End for which the Sovereignty was ordained; then there is no Liberty to refuse: otherwise there is.[30]

One of the difficulties in this position, Filmer complained, was that the sovereign might be deprived of his right and power to

[28] Filmer, *Forms*, p. 225, and *Patriarcha*, p. 82.
[29] Filmer, *Originall*, p. 244. Cf. Thomas Hobbes, *Leviathan, or the Matter, Forme & Power of a Common-wealth Ecclesiasticall and Civill* (1651), ed. W. G. Pogson Smith (Oxford, 1909), ch. xvii, esp. the passage preceding the oath, pp. 131–2.
[30] Hobbes, *Leviathan*, ch. xxi, p. 167. For other limitations, see ch. xiv, pp. 99ff.

wage war and defend his subjects. In addition, allowing the intention behind a command 'to execute any dangerous, or dishonourable Office' to determine whether or not a person was bound to obey gave the subject the right of interpretation, which effectively placed him above the sovereign in this respect.[31] 'These last doctrines are destructive to all government whatsoever,' Filmer lamented, 'and even to the *Leviathan* itself.' So detrimental to societal stability are the rights preserved by the subject, he continued, that 'we are at least in as miserable a condition of war as Mr. Hobbes at first by nature found us'.[32]

Another vital element in Filmer's critique of populism was his realization that free submission to government logically entailed the right of withdrawal through the same voluntary actions. 'If it were a thing so voluntary, and at the pleasure of men when they were free to put themselves under subjection,' he asked, 'why may they not as voluntarily leave subjection when they please, and be free again?'[33] Closely related was Sir Robert's attempt to undermine the derivation of a contemporary obligation from an ancestral contract. His major arguments here rested upon the seeming contradiction of having later generations bound by the decisions of their predecessors while asserting that men were endowed with a natural, God-given equality. 'How the consent of mankind could bind posterity when all things were common, is a point not so evident,' Filmer wrote. 'Where children take nothing by gift or by direct descent from their parents, but have an equal and common interest with them, there is no reason in such cases, that the acts of the fathers should bind the sons.'[34]

In other words, natural equality meant that no generation

[31] To Filmer's important criticisms may be added the further objection that auto-interpretation of one's own rights and the intentions of his fellows was one of the dangerous conditions of nature that the creation of a state was designed to overcome.

[32] Filmer, *Originall*, pp. 246–8; quotation from p. 248.

[33] Ibid., p. 273. Filmer also attacked Milton's insistence upon the entitlement of people to reassert any fundamental rights that might have been surrendered in the original voluntary institution of government, saying, 'This doctrine well practised, layeth all open to constant anarchy.' (Ibid., p. 260.) But it must be stressed that he did not deny the validity of inferring this right from the presumption of original equality and *logically* would have been required to accept an intentional and consistent anarchist doctrine.

[34] Filmer, *Patriarcha*, p. 65.

could have less freedom than any that had come before. Therefore, each man had the natural right to conclude his own agreement with the government under which he was born, for men
always had the moral authority to reassert their original rights to
the community of all things.[35] 'If it be allowed, that the acts of
parents can bind the children, then farewell the doctrine of the
natural freedom of mankind; where subjection of children to
parents is natural, there can be no natural freedom.'[36] Either each
generation has the right to make large changes in the political
order it inherits, or the appeal to man's natural freedom and
equality is altogether irrelevant to subsequent political debate.
To hold that men owe something to past generations is to bind
them to the acts of their fathers, and this binding relationship,
said Sir Robert, is the essence of the patriarchal claim.

Another of Filmer's favorite targets was the principle of
majority rule, which, he contended, was not operative unless it
had previously been unanimously agreed to; otherwise, dissenters
were not bound by the will of the majority:

the major part never binds, but where men at first either agree to be
so bound, or where a higher power than nature so commands: now
there being no higher power than nature, but God himself; where
neither God nor nature appoints the major part to bind, their consent is not binding to any themselves who consent.[37]

In an established state, government by the majority would pre-
clude the existence of a constant body of rulers, for the majority
would be composed of different persons on each issue; consequently, every action undertaken by the majority would be the
product of a different government. Furthermore, 'It is false and
improper speech to say that a whole multitude ... doth govern
where the major part only rules, because many of the multitude
that are so assembled, are so far from having any part in the
government, that they themselves are governed against and contrary to their wills ...'[38]

---

[35] Filmer, *Originall*, p. 274.
[36] Filmer, *Anarchy*, p. 287. This point will be taken up in detail in Ch.
VIII.
[37] Ibid., p. 286. The same point was made in *Patriarcha*, p. 82, and *Forms*,
p. 225.
[38] Filmer, *Forms*, pp. 211 and 205. See also *Originall*, pp. 243–4.

3

As a part of his criticism of the theories of natural rights and human equality, Filmer also attacked republicanism and legislatures in general. Representative bodies, he said, were often regarded as alternatives to true popular governments, for it was impossible to have the powers and functions of government exercised by the people. Representatives are collectively 'surmised to be the people', Sir Robert indicated, and exercise for the people the powers they cannot exercise themselves. Filmer made several replies to these assumptions of republicanism. First, since no representatives are chosen at large, none of them truly represents all of the people; instead, each is assumed to stand for only the political subdivision from which he was selected. But even this supposition is unfounded, for the absence of uniform and universal suffrage means that not even a majority of people in each constituency elect their delegates.

Next, Filmer alleged that legislatures do not act as single representative bodies. The frequency and number of absences mean that the body truly representing all the people is rarely if ever assembled. Size is a further hindrance to the genuine operation of the representative principle. Because republican bodies are so large and unwieldy, much important work is delegated to committees. 'Thus those that are chosen to represent the people, are necessitated to choose others, to represent the representatives themselves; . . . [and] nothing can be more destructive, or contrary to the nature of public assemblies' than this transferral of public debates from the general assembly of the kingdom to 'a particular or private assembly'. Third, Sir Robert charged that delegates do not represent the interests of their own areas or constituents on all issues but actually tend to vote as blocs and trade votes according to the designs of their leaders. The system begins to degenerate into anarchy at this stage, as the groups 'epitomize and sub-epitomize themselves so long, till at last they crumble away into the atoms of monarchy, which is the next degree to anarchy, where every man is his own monarch or governor'. Finally, Filmer said that the electors were not prepared to choose the best-qualified representatives because they do not know enough about politics.[39]

[39] Filmer, *Forms*, pp. 223–4. Filmer's questions about the relation of legis-

Concerning the execution of laws, Filmer observed that once legislation had passed, those who voted for it—the majority—and were therefore the composite sovereign who instituted it, became 'incorporated into the whole assembly, and are buried as it were in that lump, and not otherwise considered'. To have the lawmaker bound by his own laws was contrary to the nature of sovereignty, Filmer complained, for the sovereign power must be above the law in order to give it strength. Moreover, 'every law must always have some present known person in being, whose will it must be to make it a law for the present; this cannot be said of the major part of any assembly, because that major part instantly ceaseth, as soon as ever it hath voted'.[40]

Filmer assumed with Hobbes and Bodin that every society had to have a sovereign authority in order to exist. And this authority —whether a legislature or a monarch—was, by definition, arbitrary and above the positive law. 'There never was, nor ever can be any people governed without a power of making laws,' Filmer wrote, 'and every power of making laws must be arbitrary: for to make a law according to law, is *contradictio in adjecto*.'[41] Thus, Filmer saw that legislative power was just as independent as that of kings, and that was potentially no less despotic. Therefore, in answer to Milton's republican claim that parliamentary supremacy would be a safeguard against authoritarian abuses, Filmer identified the possibility of legislative tyranny and wrote:

if all sorts of popular government that can be invented, cannot be one minute, without an arbitrary power freed from all humane laws: what reason can be given why a royal government should not have the like freedom? If it be tyranny for one man to govern arbitrarily, why should it not be greater tyranny for a multitude of men to govern without being accountable or bound by laws?[42]

---

lators to their constituents still plague political theorists. See, for instance, A. Phillips Griffiths and Richard Wollheim, 'How Can One Person Represent Another?' (Symposium), *Proceedings of the Aristotelian Society*, Supp. Vol. XXXIV (1960), 187–224; R. S. Downie, *Government Action and Morality* (London, 1964), pp. 115–20; and especially Hanna F. Pitkin, *The Concept of Representation* (Berkely, Calif., 1967), chs. iv–vii.

[40] Filmer, *Forms*, pp. 227 and 228, citing Hobbes, *Leviathan*, ch. xxvi, p. 210 of the Pogson Smith edition.
[41] Filmer, *Anarchy*, Preface, p. 277. See also *Patriarcha*, pp. 102–3 and 121.
[42] Filmer, *Originall*, p. 254.

What Sir Robert did not acknowledge was that the accountability of Parliament to the voters through elections might limit the excessive use of political power, a function that has frequently been offered in behalf of the principle of elections.[43] But restraints of this kind depend for their effectiveness upon the 'good will' of elected public officials or their 'fear' of reprisals at the next election. A legislator who lacks this concern for the commonweal and does not plan to seek re-election could be just as indifferent to the rights and wishes of his constituents as the most despotical of kings. Thus, Filmer was certainly correct in denying the existence of a necessary connection between republicanism and governmental responsibility.

Pushing his criticism beyond the institutions of popular government, Filmer attacked democracy itself. His most strongly worded criticism occurred in a manuscript that he did not publish. And when the work was published in 1680—twenty-seven years after Filmer's death—from a different version, this passage was omitted:

So as all popular States are but bastard slips, no plants of Gods setting; but the gro[w]th and production of our sins, and the curse of God upon them. For the iniquity of a nation, many are the Princes (or Governours) thereof, Saith Solomon. Yet even then in popular States (so naturall a thing is Monarchy) in what hands soever you place the power, [just] as one Finger will still be Found longer [than] the rest, . . . [one person will] become a Kingly Tyrant, by his over-swaying interest.[44]

[43] See Gerald Pomper, 'The Concept of Elections in Political Theory', *Review of Politics*, XXIX (1967), 478–91.

[44] Sir Robert Filmer, 'Two Treatises Against Rebellion', holograph manuscript, Bodleian Library, MS. Tanner 233, fol. 127. Punctuation and capitals supplied for clarity. Title from Bodleian Library catalogue. The published version of the manuscript was entitled *A Discourse Concerning Supreme Power and Common Right* (London, 1680); this passage should have been printed following p. 94, but fols. 127–9, which comprise the conclusion to the second part of the manuscript, were not published.

The *Discourse* is universally attributed to Sir John Monson (1600–1683) of Lincolnshire, the second baronet of his line and an important figure in the draining of the Lincoln fens. My reasons for challenging this attribution and for ascribing the work to Sir Robert are set forth in detail in Part I of my article 'Sir Robert Filmer: Some New Bibliographic Discoveries'.

His comments in *Patriarcha* were moderate in comparison: 'And I do verily believe never any democratical state showed itself first fairly to the world by any elective entrance, but they all secretly crept in by the back door of sedition and faction.' Democracy is characterized by the dominance of evil and corrupt forces in the government, Filmer continued, because 'the greatest part of the people' are 'wicked and vicious'. The rule of the virtuous members could be brought about only by taking the state away from 'the people'.[45] Another fault of democratic governments is that they lack the unity essential to governance that is always found in monarchies. Therefore, Filmer reasoned that if popular states are to flourish, they need standing armies and warfare, which will provide the missing unity:

if unity in government, which is only found in monarchy, be once broken, there is no stay or bound, until it come to a constant standing army, for the people or multitude, as Aristotle teacheth us, can excel in no virtue but miltary, and that is natural to them, and therefore in a popular estate, the sovereign power is in the sword, and those that are possessed of the arms. So that any nation or kingdom that is not charged with the keeping of a King, must perpetually be at the charge of paying and keeping of an army.[46]

Perhaps Filmer's most damaging complaint about purportedly popular governments was the observation that the Commonwealth of England was not true to its own proclaimed principles of consent and representation. This too was said in an essay that was intended for a limited audience, a casuist manuscript in which Sir Robert attempted to explain how one might take the Engagement oath and still remain loyal to the House of Stuart.

And the present change amongst us, is so far from being advanced or first made by an universall consent; as of individual persons, I am perswaded there is not one in twenty that have concurred in it; And for the Parliament we know it had no such delegation of power from the people when it was a full representative, but so long as it preserved its owne just dignity and freedome the major part opposed our great Innovations; so as the subversions and alterations we suffer under are but the efforts of an unjust and usurped power.[47]

[45] Filmer, *Patriarcha*, pp. 88 and 89.
[46] Filmer, *Forms*, p. 199. See also *Patriarcha*, p. 90.
[47] Sir Robert Filmer, 'Discourse Concerning the Taking of the Engage-

On a more theoretical level, Filmer argued against the adequacy of the logical or hypothetical use of the state of nature and social compact theories because of their implicit denial of the validity of the thesis that they were supporting. When a writer admits that the consent basis of the first government cannot be demonstrated and so must be *assumed*, Filmer asserted, he is accepting that fact that this government was actually established on some other ground. 'If there were at first a government without being beholden to the people for their consent,' he concluded, '. . . I find no reason but that there be so still, without asking leave of the multitude.'[48] As much as anything else that he wrote, this argument illustrates Sir Robert's reliance upon a genetic conception of political obligation and the denial of the possibility of fundamental change that is a necessary part of that doctrine.

If Filmer's criticisms of populism appear irrelevant today, it is because the whole controversy no longer has the meaning it did in the seventeenth century. We have abandoned strict genetic thinking about political duty and agree, on the whole, with J. D. Mabbott's pithy observation that 'My obligation to my country cannot be decided one way or the other by the putative activities of a number of missing links huddled around the altars of Stonehenge.'[49] What Filmer could not realize, of course, was that the very factor he was criticizing in the contract theory when he attacked its claim to logical and rational rather than historical and legal validity was the harbinger of a new conception of political obligation. The emerging rational political philosophy would not have to rely upon either the 'putative activities' of the first citizens or the structure of society originally established by God in order to justify obedience in the modern world.

---

ment: That It May Be Lawfully Taken', holograph manuscript, Bodleian Library, MS. Tanner 233, fol. 139. Title From Bodleian catalogue, which does not attribute this work to Filmer; his authorship can be demonstrated on the basis of the handwriting and the use of certain unique arguments.
[48] Filmer, *Forms*, p. 225.
[49] J. D. Mabbott, *The State and the Citizen: An Introduction to Political Philosophy*, 2nd ed. (London, 1952), p. 13.

# VIII

## Sir Robert Filmer: (2) Patriarchalism and the Descent of Adam's Power

I

Against the state-of-nature and social contract doctrines of populism, Filmer insisted that the state was an extension of the natural hierarchy of the family and that political obligation was the same as the duty to obey fathers. The relation between Sir Robert's critical and positive positions can readily be seen in his analysis of Hobbes, of whom he said:

> With no small content I read Mr. Hobbes's book *De Cive*, and his *Leviathan*, about the rights of sovereignty, which no man, that I know, hath so amply and judiciously handled: I consent with him about the rights of exercising government, but I cannot agree to his means of acquiring it. It may seem strange I should praise his building, and yet mislike his foundation; but so it is, his *Jus Naturae*, and his *Regnum Institutivum*, will not down with me: they appear full of contradiction and impossibilities; a few short notes about them, I here offer, wishing he would consider whether his building would not stand firmer upon the principles of *Regnum Patrimoniale* (as he calls it) both according to scripture and reason.[1]

Sir Robert was in limited company in recognizing Hobbes's use of patriarchal theories. On the contrary, Hobbes was often criticized for his apparent failure to account for the existence of the family in his discussion of the origin of the state.[2]

[1] Filmer, *Originall*, Preface, p. 239.
[2] See Ch. X, sect. 1. Because Hobbes's use of patriarchal doctrines will be examined in detail in Ch. XII, the validity of Filmer's comments will not be discussed here.

Filmer's main argument was that Hobbes had embraced mutually exclusive doctrines, natural liberty and the original authority of the father. Filmer wrote:

I wonder how the right of nature can be imagined by Mr. Hobbes, which he saith, [*Leviathan*] page 64, is a liberty for each man to use his own power as he will himself for preservation of his own life; a condition of war of everyone against everyone; a right of every man to everything, even to one another's body, especially since he himself affirms, page 178, that originally the Father of every man was also his Sovereign Lord with power over him of life and death.[3]

If children were subjugated to their fathers, Sir Robert reasoned, 'there would have been little liberty in the subjects of the family to consent to [the] institution of government'.[4] It was, of course, upon this original and natural power of the father that Filmer built his own theory of politics. The chief historical source for his opinions was the Bible, which 'teacheth us . . . that all men come by succession, and generation from one man'. Filmer thus objected to Hobbes's account of the state of nature because the existence of an independent multitude with the power to conclude a compact of government was contrary to scripture.[5]

The Bible was Sir Robert's most important and frequently used reference. Another favorite authority was Aristotle; I have already quoted the set of political principles Filmer claimed to have deduced from the *Politics*. He also cited the *Politics* against Philip Hunton's claims that monarchies could be limited and mixed.[6] As might be expected, Aristotle was employed only when his teachings could be made to support Filmer's own position. Sir Robert explained that the 'uncertainty and contrariety in him [Aristotle] about the sorts of government' was due to his unfamiliarity with the Bible; this ignorance had prevented his knowing

---

[3] Filmer, *Originall*, p. 241. The citations from *Leviathan* refer to the original (1651) edition and correspond to pp. 99 and 263 of the Pogson Smith edition.

[4] Filmer, *Originall*, Preface, p. 239. See also, Sir Robert Filmer, *Directions for Obedience to Government in Dangerous or Doubtful Times* (1652), *Political Works*, p. 231. Hereafter cited as *Directions*.

[5] Filmer, *Originall*, p. 241.

[6] See Filmer, *Anarchy*, p. 303, citing Aristotle, *Politics*, III, xvi, 1–2 (p. 145 of the Barker edition).

about the power that God had bestowed upon Adam at the Creation. 'It is not probable that any sure direction of the beginning of government can be found in either Plato, Aristotle, Cicero, Polybius, or in any other of the heathen authors, who were ignorant of the manner of the creation of the world', Filmer said. Accordingly, 'we must not neglect the scriptures, and search in philosophers for ... the main principles of government and justice'.[7] 'Because the Scripture is not favourable to the liberty of the people, therefore many fly to natural reason and to the authority of Aristotle', Sir Robert wrote in *Patriarcha*. But when he found Plato and Aristotle favourable to patriachalism, Filmer justified his own use of their doctrines with the curious statement that they were somehow conversant with the Old Testament: 'No doubt but Moses' history of the creation guided these two philosophers in finding out of this lineal subjection deduced from the loins of the first parents ....'[8]

The final test was always scriptural history and not the ancient philosophers. Filmer summarized his attitudes when he wrote:

It is a shame and a scandal for us Christians to seek the original of government from the inventions or fictions of poets, orators, philosophers and heathen historians, who all lived thousands of years after the creation, and were (in a manner) ignorant of it: and to neglect the scriptures, which have with more authority most particularly given us the true grounds and principles of government.[9]

He criticized Hunton for failing to produce a single scriptural example to justify his concept of limited and mixed monarchy[10] and said that the theory that the people elected their kings was without Biblical support and did not deserve serious consideration.[11] The doctrine of original freedom is atheistic, Sir Robert concluded, 'since a natural freedom of mankind cannot be supposed without the denial of the creation of Adam'.[12] The only kind

[7] Filmer, *Forms*, p. 203 and Preface, p. 187. See also, *Patriarcha*, p. 73.
[8] Filmer, *Patriarcha*, pp. 78 and 80.
[9] Filmer, *Anarchy*, Preface, p. 278.
[10] Ibid., p. 280.
[11] Filmer, *Patriarcha*, pp. 83–4.
[12] Filmer, *Forms*, Preface, p. 189.

of government that could be justified through an appeal to the Bible was patriarchal monarchy.

Filmer's interpretations of the Bible were not significantly different from views that have already been considered; his treatment was close to that of the *Convocation Book.* Sir Robert began with the divine enthronement of Adam at the Creation, traced the development of monarchy to the institution of kings among the Hebrews (in fact, if not always in name), and concluded that because no other form of government was mentioned in the Old Testament, only monarchical rule had the sanction of God.

2

In two significant details, however, Sir Robert's discussion differed from previous ones. First, Filmer inextricably united his argument for divine right of kings with patriarchal authority. In doing so, he went far beyond the superficially anthropological arguments that had characterized the patriarchalism of Digges or even Spelman; Filmer's entire case for royal absolutism depended upon his patriarchal theory. The argument from fatherhood was not just one of several supports for monarchy; it was the bed-rock itself. Filmer's other addition to English divine-right theory was the direct derivation of all political authority from the power of Adam, which, according to Sir Robert, had been a fatherly power. In both respects, Filmer changed the character of patriarchal political thought and generally set the tone for its development and use until the end of the Stuart period. Limited, anthropological patriarchalism certainly did not disappear with the publication of Filmer's works; in fact, it was an important element in the political thought of Sir William Temple and provided an essential argument for the *Whig* and *anti*-Jacobite theorists of 1688 and after. Sir Robert's reformulation of patriarchalism, however, influenced the doctrines of Tory and Jacobite writers. After Filmer, patriarchal apologists for absolute monarchy relied much more heavily upon the fatherly power of Adam, Noah, and the Hebrew patriarchs than they had in the past. Appeals such as Ussher's and Digges's to a vague and unrecapturable past in which separate families expanded into larger associations and eventually united into a complex political order were replaced

by more specific accounts of man's early political life that could
be taken from the Bible. And in almost all cases, the arguments
were of a distinctively Filmerian character.[13]

The authority of Adam was manifested in his having been 'the
Father, King and Lord over his family: [to him] a son, a subject
and a servant or slave, were one and the same thing at first'
Filmer wrote.[14] In the published version of one of his Civil War
manuscripts he said:

[God centered] all Power (of Families, Societies, Kingdoms) in one
Supreme and Paternall Head, both for perfection and permanence:
So as all other Forms argue not only weakness in, but tend to the
perversion, nay subversion of the Fabrick, (the several Policies of
Men would seem to raise) because not agreeing to the Model,
which God first erected in *Adam*. For even there he established
Regal and Paternal Power, that differ only in proportion, not
similitude; (it being the same, as a Child is a Man in little).[15]

Apparently following the Thomistic doctrine that governance had
existed in Paradise, Filmer wrote that as soon as he was created,
Adam 'was monarch of the world, though he had no subjects;
for though there could not be actual government until there were
subjects, yet by the right of nature it was to Adam to be governor
of his posterity: though not in act, yet at least in habit'. Before
the Fall, Adam's power did not extend to 'those things which
were necessarily and morally to be done; yet things indifferent,
that depended merely on ... free will, might be directed by the

---

[13] Cf. R. W. K. Hinton, 'Husbands, Fathers and Conquerors', *Political
Studies*, XV (1967), 291–300, esp. 297–9, who contends that Filmer 'stood
outside the English [patriarchal] tradition' that stretched from Sir Thomas
Smith to John Locke. 'The normal tradition of patriarchalism,' Hinton
concludes, 'found its ablest exposition in Filmer's contemporary, Hobbes'
(p. 300). Hinton reached this conclusion by ignoring the score of minor
writers whose positions were very much like Filmer's and who, with Sir
Robert, comprise a most formidable 'tradition'. Hinton has concentrated,
instead, on a number of highly articulate authors; the second part of his
article is devoted almost exclusively to Hobbes and Locke (*Political
Studies*, XVI [1968], 55–67). For a sharp and compelling methodological
confutation of Hinton's approach, see Quentin Skinner, 'The Limits of
Historical Explanation', *Philosophy*, XLI (1966), 199–215, esp. 213.
[14] Filmer, *Forms*, Preface, p. 188.
[15] [Filmer], *Discourse*, pp. 6–7.

power of Adam's command'.[16] After the expulsion from Eden, God said to Eve, 'I will greatly multiply thy sorrow and thy conception; in sorrow thou shalt bring forth children; and thy desire *shall be* to thy husband, and he shall rule over thee,' which, according to Filmer, was 'the original grant of government, and that fountain of all power'. 'Neither Eve nor her children could either limit Adam's power, or join others with him in the government.'[17] Adam was the absolute 'monarch of the whole world; none of his posterity had any right to possess anything, but by his grant or permission, or by succession from him'.[18]

The power that God had conferred upon Adam 'was given in his person to his posterity', to whom it passed at his death according to the rule of primogenitive succession. In this manner, 'paternal power continued monarchical to the Flood',[19] after which Noah divided the world among his three sons, each of whom ruled his portion as his ancestors had governed the whole. These microcosms of the universal monarchy of Adam did not last long, Filmer continued, for at the confusion of tongues at Babel 'there were seventy-two distinct nations erected'. These nations 'were not confused multitudes, without heads or governors, and at liberty to choose what governors or government they pleased, but they were distinct families, which had Fathers for rulers over them'. Thus, Filmer concluded, 'God was careful to preserve the fatherly authority by distributing the diversity of languages according to the diversity of families.'[20]

According to Sir Robert, Nimrod—described in Genesis as the 'mighty hunter before the LORD'—was among the patriarchal rulers whose sovereignty began at Babel. Many writers believed that monarchy was first established with the rule of Nimrod.

---

[16] Filmer, *Anarchy*, pp. 289 and 290.
[17] Ibid., p. 283. The Biblical passage is Gen. 3: 16.
[18] Filmer, *Forms*, Preface, pp. 187–8.
[19] Filmer, *Anarchy*, p. 283.
[20] Filmer, *Patriarcha*, p. 58–9, quotation from p. 58. This argument was repeated in *Anarchy*, p. 290, and in the manuscript 'Taking the Engagement', Bodleian Library, MS. Tanner 233, fol. 138. Filmer seems to have been the first writer who advanced this interpretation of Babel in print, and the appearance of this doctrine in 'Taking the Engagement' is one of my reasons for attributing that work to him. This view was anticipated in the *Convocation Book*, ch. vi, but that work was not published until 1690.

Filmer rejected this interpretation but used it, nonetheless, as a further argument against the consent theory. Nimrod, he asserted, enlarged his empire by 'seizing violently on the rights of other lords of families, and in this sense he may be said to be the author and first founder of monarchy'. Moreover, all those who attribute to Nimrod 'the original of regal power do hold he got it by tyranny or usurpation, not by any due election of the people or multitude, nor by any paction with them'.[21] Carried to a logical conclusion, this view was at one with the statement that hypothetical rather than historical use of the contract theory denied the voluntarist account of the origin of the state.[22]

Sir Robert's interpretation of Old Testament history held that after Nimrod and his descendants 'this patriarchal power continued in Abraham, Isaac and Jacob, and even until the Egyptian bondage' and equally so 'amongst the sons of Ishmael and Esau'. Indicating specific instances in which the Hebrew patriarchs had exercised sovereign power over the members of their families, he wrote:

For power of life and death we find that Judah, the Father, pronounced sentence of death against Thamar, his daughter-in-law, for playing the harlot.... Touching war, we see that Abraham commanded an army of 318 soldiers of his own family. And Esau met his brother Jacob with 400 men at arms. For matters of peace, Abraham made a league with Abimelech, and ratified the articles with an oath. *These acts of judging in capital crimes, of making war, and concluding peace, are the chiefest works of sovereignty that are found in any monarch.* Not only until the Flood, but after it, this patriarchal power did continue, as the very name of Patriarch doth in part prove.[23]

'By manifest footsteps we may trace this paternal government unto the Israelites coming into Egypt, where the exercise of [supreme] patriarchal jurisdiction was intermitted, because they were in subjection to a stronger Prince.' But at the Exodus, God 'chose Moses and Joshua successively to govern as Prince in the place and stead of the supreme Fathers'. The regal power that Moses held through divine commission was the same as that

---

[21] Filmer, *Patriarcha*, p. 59. The description of Nimrod is from Gen. 10: 9.
[22] See Filmer, *Forms*, p. 225. Quoted above, p. 135.
[23] Filmer, *Patriarcha*, pp. 59 and 58. Emphasis added. The Biblical examples are drawn from Gen. 38: 24; 14: 14; 33: 1, and 21: 23-4.

'which before was Natural and Paternal in Adam'. The Judges similarly governed the Children of Israel as substitutes for natural patriarchs and were individually commissioned by divine appointment. 'But when God gave the Israelites Kings, He re-established the ancient and prime right of lineal succession to paternal government.'[24]

## 3

It was at this point that genuine patriarchal government vanished from history (and temporarily from Filmer's analysis), and men began to rule as the 'reputed' heirs to the power of Adam, Noah, and one of the seventy-two father-kings who were raised up at Babel. Sir Robert explained and attempted to justify this transition:

> It may seem absurd to maintain that Kings now are the fathers of their people, since experience shows the contrary. It is true, all Kings be not the natural parents of their subjects, yet they all either are, or are to be reputed, as the next heirs of those progenitors who were at first the natural parents of the whole people, and in their right succeed to the exercise of supreme jurisdiction. . . .
>
> As long as the first Fathers of families lived, the name of Patri-archs did aptly belong unto them. But after a few descents, when the true fatherhood itself was extinct, and only the right of the Father descended to the true heir, then the title of Prince or King was more significant to express the power of him who succeeds only to the right of that fatherhood which his ancestors did *naturally* enjoy. By this means it comes to pass, that many a child, by succeeding a King, hath the right of a Father over many a grey-headed multitude, [and hath the title of Pater Patriae].[25]

Filmer's notion of prescriptive legitimacy—the position into which sucession by reputation necessarily resolves itself—will be ex-amined at greater length below when his theory of usurpation is discussed. It will suffice here to consider the more immediate problem that this passage raises: the relevance of Adam, Noah, and the rest to political obligation once it is admitted that kings are no longer fathers.

[24] Ibid., p. 60 (bracket in Laslett's text), and *Discourse*, p. 38.
[25] Filmer, *Patriarcha*, pp. 60–1; bracket in Laslett's text.

It must be remembered that Filmer's patriarchalism is an extreme example of the preoccupation of seventeenth-century English political philosophy with origins. This attitude dictated that political obligation could be found in, and had to be consistent with, the beginnings of government. As used by Filmer and many other writers, origins referred to the beginnings of political authority *per se* rather than the establishment of a specific state. The first form of rule that was instituted in the world was, for Filmer, patriarchal monarchy; I have already quoted his statements—supposedly extracted from Aristotle—that no other form of government was legitimate. What had been created by God Himself or flowed from the very order of nature could not be altered by man. (The same reasoning lay behind his insistence that if men were originally equal and free, it was morally impossible for them to be changed—except perhaps by their own voluntary actions, but even that possibility was not clear.)

Sir Robert was not so blinded by his discovery of the origins of all authority in the familial power of Adam as to insist that only the literal first or prime fathers of nations had valid titles to crowns. Royal houses died out; monarchs were driven from their thrones by revolutions and wars; kingdoms were consolidated and divided—Filmer was aware of all these factors and realized that knowledge of true lineal heirs could have been lost or even that such claimants were not always able to obtain or hold their thrones. What was more, God may have decided to transfer a kingdom to a new family. Thus, the external *form* of patriarchal rule had undoubtedly disappeared in every nation in the world. The *substance*, however, was still there; the *proper* manner of conducting government had not altered since the universal kingship of Adam and would never change unless God directly intervened again. Therefore, if men were to understand the character of government as God had intended it and were to comprehend their respective roles in society, they had to know what had transpired before humans were so brazen as to depart from *jus divinum.*

There was also a polemic reason for employing the government of Hebrew patriarchs as a basis for the powers of a seventeenth-century sovereign: to demonstrate by repeated examples that God *had* actually sanctioned patriarchal monarchy. In addition, Filmer had to prove against the critics of patriarchalism that there were no distinctions between political and familial authority during the Biblical period.[26] His case could have been considerably strengthened had he been able to show that the powers exercised by Abraham and Judah belonged to them initially because they were prime fathers. By the same token, powers of nonpolitical fathers under the rulers of the Old Testament were important to Sir Robert's explanation of the nature of monarchy; his discussion is riddled with references to fatherly authority that cannot be ignored or abstracted out if the sense of his doctrines is to be preserved.[27]

Monarchy is natural to the world, Filmer said, because 'God is a God of order' and has established 'a kind of Hierarchy and Regiment amongst all the several Societies of the Creatures, even from the lowest to the highest Story of created Beings, (so that levelling is contrary to his Design) . . .'. This order can be seen on all levels of existence—from the enthronement of the sun and moon in heaven 'to govern over their several Spheres', through 'the Unreasonable Creatures' such as 'Bees, which of all others maintain a most perfect Polity of monarchical Government', to the hierarchy of offices in the church and state and the orders of angels.[28] So considered, monarchy was the first and for a time the only government in the world. It was not 'until wantonness, ambition or faction made . . . [the people eager to] attempt new kinds of regiment' that democracy and other forms of rule were substituted for monarchy. But these actions did not change the

[26] See Filmer, *Patriarcha*, pp. 75–6, where he argued—contrary to the views of Aristotle and Suarez—that these powers were identical.

[27] Hinton contends that there is 'surprisingly little on fathers as a whole' in Filmer's writings; he then uses this apparent absence to support his claim that Locke's 'Second Treatise'—in which fatherly authority was discussed extensively—was not directed against Sir Robert but was probably aimed at Hobbes. ('Husbands, Fathers and Conquerors', *Political Studies*, XV [1967], 299, and XVI [1968], 61.) I think he is simply incorrect about Filmer, but even if Sir Robert had written very little about fatherhood *per se*, he continually insisted that political authority was familial. Therefore, it could easily be argued that Locke's analysis of paternal power was indeed part of his critique of Filmer. What Locke argued in the relevant sections of the 'Second Treatise' was that fatherly authority was not absolute, that it was a trust from God, and that it was to be exercised for the good of the child. It followed, then, that even an acceptance of the patriarchal theory did not lead to divine right absolutism. See Ch. XIII.

[28] [Filmer], *Discourse*, pp. 4–6.

character and value of kingship; it was still true that 'The best order, the greatest strength, the most stability and easiest government are to be found in monarchy, and in no other form of government.'[29] Similarly, 'It was impiety, to think, that God who was careful to appoint judicial laws for his chosen people, would not furnish them with the best form of government.' Therefore, it is foolish to attempt to improve on monarchy.[30] What was more, Filmer said, no other type of rule was legitimate in the sight of God, 'For when he [God] saith, *By me Kings Reign*, he implies all others Forms of Government to derive their Pedigree only from men, not Divine Institution. They have his permission, but Kings only his Commission.'[31] Against Hunton he wrote:

If those who live under a monarchy can justify the form they live under to be of God's ordinance, they are not bound to forbear their own justification, because others cannot do the like for the form they live under; let others look to the defence of their own government: if it cannot be proved or shown that any other form of government had ever any lawful beginning, but was brought in or erected by rebellion, must therefore the lawful and just obedience to monarchy be denied to be the ordinance of God?[32]

## 4

The various part of Filmer's theory were held together by his conception of the relationship of regal and paternal authority; it is most important to realize that he saw them as *identical*, not merely *similar* or in some way analogous. This distinction between identification and comparison is most important for understanding various modes of political argument. An identification requires a *total* transference of meaning from one entity to the institution for which it is being used as a symbol. A comparison or simile, on the other hand, leaves open the questions of the ways in which the two entities or institutions are alike and different. It allows, and even invites, debate about how well and how much a particular symbolic explanation fits. Argument by analogy was

---

29 Filmer, *Patriarcha*, p. 86.
30 Filmer, *Anarchy*, Preface, p. 278.
31 [Filmer], *Discourse*, p. 3, citing Prov. 8: 15
32 Filmer, *Anarchy*, pp. 284-5.

quite frequent in the seventeenth century, and Filmer himself at times appeared to be talking analogically. However, Sir Robert carefully avoided the possibility of a debate about the relevance of his familial symbol to politics. The authority 'of Parents, Patriarchs, and Kings, being but the same Power, under several Dresses and Appellations,' Filmer wrote, 'the same Beams of Majesty, though reflecting several Lusters, and challenging alike Obedience from all that are subjected to them, [comes] from one and the same Divine Right'.[33] This identification of familial and political authority was the denial of the distinction between state and society that, as I observed earlier, had to be refuted by Locke in his answer to Filmer.

It will be remembered that Aristotle had criticized Plato for insisting in the *Statesman* that 'political science' was identical to the 'science of household management'. In a most explicit rejection of this position, Sir Robert wrote that Aristotle's argument showed

> only this, that conjugal and despotical communities do differ. But it is no consequence that therefore economical and political societies do the like. For, though it prove a family to consist of two distinct communities, yet it follows not that a family and a commonwealth are distinct, because, as well in the commonweal as in the family, both these communities are found.

Aristotle's thesis was premised upon the teleological differentiation of things according to their ends or purposes, and since the end of the household—generation—was different from the purpose of the state—preservation—it followed that familial and political rule were different in essence. But Filmer said that even though generation and preservation 'differ about the *individuum*,' they 'agree in the *general*' and both serve 'the conservation of mankind'. By the same token, he continued, servants differ 'in particular ends or offices, one to brew and another to bake, yet they agree in the general preservation of the family'.[34]

The difference between the 'natural duties' of a father and those of a king is only a matter of degree, Filmer wrote in *Patriarcha*, and here his argument paralleled the metaphorical use of

---

[33] [Filmer], *Discourse*, p. 8. In the *Forms*, he referred to the 'supreme power' as 'an indivisible beam of majesty'. (Preface, p. 189.)
[34] Filmer, *Patriarcha*, p. 76.

power by James I: 'As the Father over one family, so the King, as Father over many families, extends his care to preserve, feed, clothe, instruct and defend the whole commonwealth ... so that all the duties of a King are summed up in an universal fatherly care of his people.'[35] But the metaphor gave way once again to a strict identification. In his last tract, the discussion of the loyal subject's obligation to obey Cromwell, Filmer said, 'All power on earth is either derived or usurped from the fatherly power, there being no other original to be found of any power whatsoever.'[36] Thus, since every nation began as a 'fatherly empire', each of which was '*alienable* by the parent, and *seizable* by a usurper as other goods are: ... every King that now is hath a paternal empire, either by inheritance, or by translation or usurpation, so a Father and a King may be all one'.[37] This statement, incidentally, should settle the question raised above about the relevance of the patriarchal kingship of Adam and Noah to the government of seventeenth century England.

Filmer rejected the notion that paternal rule had existed in the early days of the world and was eventually replaced by government based on contract. In answer to this version of the anthropological patriarchal thesis and in anticipation of complaints that were to be made against his own theory, Filmer asserted that Adam's power had not been lost upon his death, for 'the paternal power cannot be lost; it may either be transferred or usurped; but never lost, or ceaseth. God, who is the giver of power, may transfer it from the Father to some other.' Similarly, the fact that 'God hath ... given to the Father a right or liberty to alien his power over his children to any other'[38] answered in advance the charge that Noah had violated the primogenitive rights of Shem by dividing the world among all three sons, a complaint that, oddly enough, is still being made.[39] While this defense is weak, it deserves to be taken into account by those who criticize the legitimacy of Noah's voluntary partitioning of the world.

Unless it was lost or surrendered, the power of the father over

---

[35] Ibid., p. 63. Cf. James I, *Trew Law, Political Works*, ed. McIlwain, pp. 55–6.

[36] Filmer, *Directions*, p. 233.

[37] Filmer, *Originall*, p. 256.

[38] Filmer, *Directions*, p. 231. See also, *Forms*, Preface, p. 188.

[39] Plamenatz, *Man and Society*, I, 182.

his offspring was life-long, according to Filmer.[40] Grotius, on the contrary, had maintained that children remained under the control of their parents only so long as they lived with them and lacked powers of judgment.[41] Sir Robert's answer to Grotius is one of his most forlorn and desperate attempts to uphold the supremacy of paternal power. It is not by the decree of nature, Filmer insisted, that children become free of the powers of their Fathers, but by the positive laws of individual nations. And these positive laws 'are made by the supreme fatherly power of princes, who regulate, limit, or assume the authority of inferior Fathers for public benefit of the commonwealth'. Thus, it is only through 'the transcendent fatherly power of the supreme prince, [that] children may be dispensed with, or privileged in some cases, from obedience to subordinate parents'.[42] Since these emancipated children would owe their freedom to the prince, they would still be subject to patriarchal authority. This was obviously not a suitable reply, for it presumed the validity of the very argument that Sir Robert was trying to prove against Grotius, the identity of kingly and familial right. Once again, it was Filmer's inability and unwillingness to distinguish between political and social associations that was at the root of his difference with another thinker.

The pre-discretionary phase in the life of the child referred to by Grotius was known as the period of 'nonage', and it was a very useful—if not altogether satisfactory—means of avoiding one of Filmer's most damaging criticisms of voluntarism. Sir Robert had maintained that the subordination of children to the rule of their parents was incompatible with natural equality and freedom and meant that no one had ever possessed enough liberty to agree to a contract of government.[43] Locke and Tyrrell used the doctrine of nonage to great advantage in criticizing political patriarchalism. However, neither thinker directly answered Filmer's allegation that 'in nature there is no *nonage*; if a man be not born free, she doth not assign him any other time when he shall attain his freedom'.[44]

[40] Filmer, *Patriarcha*, pp. 72–3.
[41] Grotius, *De Jure Belli*, II, v, 2–6.
[42] Filmer, *Originall*, pp. 268–9.
[43] See especially Filmer's criticism of Hobbes, *Originall*, pp. 239–50, and the passages quoted on pp. 129–30 above.
[44] Filmer, *Anarchy*, p. 287.

F

5

By pursuing this reasoning, Sir Robert unwittingly led himself into a series of compromises, and the resultant doctrine was similar to the moderate patriarchalism of Dudley Digges. Filmer said that even the consent theory—if it has any validity at all—presupposes that fatherly authority was the source of the original agreement to form a government:

all those who affirm that power is conveyed to persons by public consent, are forced to confess that it is the fatherly power that first enables a people to make such conveyance; so that admitting (as they hold) that our ancestors did at first convey power, yet the reason why we now living do submit to such power [even though we have not given our consent to it], is, for that our forefathers every one for himself, his family, and posterity, had a power of resigning up themselves and us to a supreme power.[45]

In *Patriarcha* he had written,'By the uniting of great families or petty Princedoms, we find the greater monarchies were at first erected, and into such again, as into their first matter, many times they return' when there is no heir apparent to the throne and selection of a new ruler falls to the heads of constituent families. 'All such prime heads and Fathers have power to consent in the uniting or conferring of their fatherly right of sovereign authority on whom they please.'[46] Short of engaging in an intolerable kind of extrapolation and supplying the missing history of the seventy-two patriarchal nations formed at Babel, there is no way of reconciling the notions that were behind these statements with the rigorous disavowal of consent that is otherwise so prevalent in Filmer's writing. Moreover, Filmer was so imprecise and careless in general that logical analysis would be of limited value if not impossible.

But before these passages are dismissed as aberrations, it should be pointed out that the ones from *Patriarcha* were a part of a larger discussion of 'what becomes of the right of fatherhood in case the Crown does escheat for want of an heir, [and of] whether

[45] Filmer, *Anarchy*, p. 284. See also, p. 289, and *Patriarcha*, p. 71.
[46] Filmer, *Patriarcha*, pp. 61–2.

it doth not then devolve to the people'. The second question, of course, was answered negatively, for 'the Kingly power escheats in such cases to the prime and independent heads of families'. A ruler selected by this patriarchal aristocracy, Filmer said, 'claims not his power as a donative from the people, but as being substituted properly by God, from whom he receives his royal charter of an universal Father, though testified by the ministry of the heads of the people'.[47]

All this notwithstanding, it is beyond doubt that the authority was still regarded by Filmer as fatherly, if for no other reason than that it was a collective 'fatherly right of sovereign authority', which is why a comparison with Digges was suggested. Beyond this level of inference, there is Filmer's own statement in the passage just quoted and his further remark that no matter how one comes to a crown—by usurpation, election, or succession—and no matter 'whether some few or a multitude govern', the power of ruling 'is the only right and natural authority of a supreme Father. There is, and always shall be continued to the end of the world, a natural right of a supreme Father over every multitude, although, by the secret will of God, many at first do most unjustly obtain the exercise of it.' Concluding this argument, Sir Robert said that the 'natural right of regal power' was confirmed in the Decalogue, where 'the law which enjoins obedience to Kings is delivered in the terms of "Honour thy Father", as if all power were originally in the Father'.[48]

It has already been suggested that Filmer's attitude toward the question of legitimacy was, in the final analysis, a prescriptive theory of monarchical power. This is certainly the only interpretation that can be placed upon such assertions as kings either are 'or are to be reputed, as the next heirs of those progenitors who were at first the natural parents of the whole people'. Sir Robert

[47] Ibid. pp. 61–2.
[48] Filmer, *Patriarcha*, p. 62. See also *Directions*, p. 233, *Anarchy*, pp. 283 and 289, and *Discourse*, p. 8, for similar references to the Fifth Commandment. The omission of 'mother' occasioned comments by Filmer's critics during the 1680s, but whether it was intentional is far from clear. It would have been in keeping with the rest of Filmer's doctrine and his general attitude concerning innate female inferiority—based on Gen. 3: 16—to have ignored it, but the sentence immediately following the one just quoted begins with the words 'If obedience to parents...', which casts some doubt on the entire matter.

preceded this statement with the more emphatic observation that 'Kings are either Fathers of their People, or Heirs of such Fathers, or the Usurpers of the Rights of such Fathers'.[49] An important implication of this reasoning was that the means by which sovereign power was acquired had no bearing on its nature and proper exercise:

That which giveth the very being to a King is the power to give laws, without this power he is but an equivocal King. It skills not which way Kings come by their power, whether by election, donation, succession or by any other means, for it is still the manner of the government by supreme power that makes them properly Kings, and not the means of obtaining their crowns.[50]

The point was that all authority came from God, and the obligation of men to obey their political superiors was part of their duty to obey God, whose commands were to be accepted without question. As Filmer wrote in one of his manuscripts, 'When God commandeth or condemneth an act, though he declareth not the cause whereof, we must submit our judgment to him.'[51] This principle applied to politics where God often used 'the minestry of the wickedest men for the removing and setting up of Kings'. When this happens, 'the subjects' obedience to the fatherly power must go along and wait upon God's providence, who only hath right to give and take away kingdoms, and thereby to adopt subjects into the obedience of another fatherly power'.[52] But Sir Robert also insisted that 'the ministry of men who execute God's judgments without commission is sinful and damnable'.[53]

Filmer failed to explain how subjects could distinguish between usurpers who acted without God's commission and those who succeeded because of divine endorsement. Moreover, he did not indicate that different kinds or degrees of obedience were due to the types of usurpers. In fact, in the tracts written before the

---

[49] Filmer, *Patriarcha*, pp. 61 and 60. The same doctrine was repeated in *Anarchy*, p. 288.
[50] Filmer, *Patriarcha*, pp. 105–6.
[51] British Museum, MS. Harleian 4685, fol. 60. Fair copy in Filmer's hand, titled 'A judgment as it were of the 72 elders touching 72 acts in the Scripture set down in nine rules'.
[52] Filmer, *Anarchy*, p. 289.
[53] Filmer, *Patriarcha*, p. 62.

Regicide—that is, *Patriarcha* and the *Anarchy*, the essays from which the preceding quotations have been taken—Filmer did not even suggest that there was a difference between the obedience to which kings and usurpers were entitled. He said only that subjects (and servants) owed their rulers (and masters) absolute non-resistance. They could not question their orders, even if their silence meant working on the Sabbath instead of going to church or fighting in an apparently unjust war. If they were required to act against God's law, the sin would fall on the one who issued the command rather than upon the one who obeyed.[54]

## 6

In 1652, with usurpation an actuality for the first time since the crown passed from a bush at Bosworth field to the head of Henry Tudor, Filmer's tone was decidedly different on all these matters. Non-resistance became passive obedience, and Sir Robert wrote that 'if men command things evil, obedience is due only by tolerating what they inflict: not by performing what they require'.[55] In the anonymous *Discourse* he stated that while magistrates are not to be resisted under any circumstances, they are 'not [to be] obeyed in contrary [sic] to Divine, and sometimes Humane National Laws'.[56] Neither of these statements was explicitly limited to obligation to a usurper, but the limitations that Filmer placed upon his theory of usurpation in the *Directions* and *Discourse* suggest that these works were reactions to Puritan rule. These arguments are paralleled by comments in his manuscript essay on the Engagement Oath.

In the *Directions* Sir Robert specifically defined the extent to which usurpers were to be obeyed and apologetically explained the need for continued obedience: 'Every man is to preserve his own life for the service of God, and of his King or Father, and is so far to obey a usurper as may tend not only to the preservation of his King and Father, but sometimes even to the preservation of the usurper himself, when probably he may thereby be reserved to the correction, or mercy of [God] his true superior.' However,

[54] Ibid., p. 105.
[55] Filmer, *Directions*, p. 235.
[56] [Filmer], *Discourse*, p. 48.

a usurper's commands are not to be obeyed in 'anything tending to the destruction of the person of the [true] governor; whose being in the first place is to be looked after'. Quite similar was Filmer's justification for fighting on the side of the usurper against the attack of a foreign nation: 'Where a man hath been born under the protection of a long and peaceable government, he owes an assistance for the preservation of that government that hath protected him . . .'.[57] Thus, when one's home land is attacked 'I ought only to join with any force to defend my self and the Kingdom against any such Invasion, so as I neither fight for the Usurper's Interest and Establishment, nor against those of my lawful Soveraign.'[58] But in *Patriarcha* Filmer had written without qualification that when ordered by the king to serve in a war, a subject 'may not examine whether the war be just or unjust, but must obey, since he hath no commission to judge of the titles of kingdoms or causes of war. . . .'[59]

Because God has allowed him to come to a throne, Filmer said, 'the title of a usurper is before, and better than the title of any other than of him that had a former right'. This 'qualified right is found at first in all usurpers,' he continued, 'as is in thieves who have stolen goods, and during the time they are possessed of them, have a title in law against all others but the true owners, and such usurpers to divers intents and purposes may be obeyed'.[60] In the manuscript Sir Robert introduced an explicit distinction between legitimate rulers and usurpers and indicated that they did not deserve the same kind of obedience. The 'lawful magistrate' was supported by 'divine sanction', but the usurper had 'only . . . prudence and election' on his side:

Human laws bind conscience only in relation to divine sanction and so oblige me to obey my lawful magistrate in lawful things. But where an usurped power imposes anything, my submission to it is only [a] matter of prudence and election and obliges me no farther than my own promise ties me; or [obliges me no farther than] the literal sense of my engagement would do in any civil contract

---

[57] Filmer, *Directions*, pp. 232 and 234. These arguments were repeated in the manuscript 'Taking the Engagement', Bodleian Library, MS. Tanner 233, fols. 138 and 144.
[58] [Filmer], *Discourse*, p. 161.
[59] Filmer, *Patriarcha*, p. 105.
[60] Filmer, *Directions*, pp. 232 and 234.

between party and party—where the instrument signed ought to be the measure of my performance and not the intention of him I capitulate with.[61]

This distinction, as we shall see, contradicts the insistence in *Patriarcha* that the source of political authority—'election, donation, succession or by any other means', as Filmer put it—is irrelevant to its nature.

The same contradiction also appeared in the *Directions*. Sir Robert said that when a usurper has reigned so long that the people no longer remember who is the heir to the true sovereign, the 'usurper in possession is to be taken and reputed by such subjects for the true heir, and is to be obeyed by them as their Father'. Nevertheless, the usurper would not have a divine right to his title, for 'though by humane laws, a long prescription may take away right, yet divine right never dies, nor can be lost, or taken away'.[62] This doctrine had been suggested in *Patriarcha* where Sir Robert asserted, 'If Adam himself were still living, and now ready to die, it is certain that there is one man, and but one in the world, who is next heir, although the knowledge who should be that one man be quite lost.'[63] The *implication*, then, was that even the established thrones in the world did not actually enjoy the protection of *jus divinum*, for Filmer had already admitted that ruling monarchs were no longer lineally descended from the legitimate heirs to Adam's powers.

Once again Filmer's reasoning will not survive the rigid analysis to which he subjected the state-of-nature and social contract doctrines. This time, however, more of an explanation is possible. It is undoubtedly incorrect to conclude that Filmer intended to deny to Charles I the divine sanction of his title. But it is equally inaccurate to say that he believed that Charles was a lineal descendant of one of the seventy-two patriarchal kings who came into being after the confusion of tongues at Babel.[64]

---

[61] Filmer, 'Taking the Engagement', Bodleian Library, MS. Tanner 233, fol. 146.

[62] Filmer, *Directions*, p. 232.

[63] Filmer, *Patriarcha*, p. 61. See also *Anarchy*, pp. 288–9.

[64] That he endeavoured to prove this—or at least that he actually believed it—is one of the charges most frequently hurled at Filmer. See Laslett, Introduction to Filmer, *Political Works*, p. 15; Herbert H. Rowen, 'A Second Thought on Locke's "First Treatise"', *Journal of the History of*

Nothing in Filmer's writings supports such a view. However, some men did believe it, for there are a number of sixteenth and seventeenth century manuscript genealogies that purport to trace the lineal descent of English sovereigns from Adam and Noah.[65] Filmer's theory of usurpation saved him from taking so extreme a stand, for he certainly believed—before 1649—that a title derived from a long-standing prescription conveyed a moral as well as a legal right. His difficulty was that he attempted to employ his own interpretation and use of scriptural arguments whenever possible to prove the validity of his thesis.

Sir Robert should have avoided further references to the power of Adam after his discussion of the unsuccessful attempt to build a tower to heaven. There is a mitigating factor, however. Filmer had criticized Grotius for allowing human actions to eliminate the community of property that was ordained by natural law. In effect, Grotius had elevated prescription above nature.[66] Filmer would have been guilty of the same inconsistency had he failed to differentiate between usurpation and lineal descent from Adam and Noah. At first, he blurred the distinction in such statements as 'It skills not which way Kings come by their power'; kings are the natural fathers of their people, the heirs of such fathers, 'or the usurpers of the right of such Fathers'; and all kings 'either are, or are to be reputed' as the legitimate heirs to natural fathers.[67] It may have been, then, self-defense that caused Sir Robert to reassert the right of Adam's litc... heirs in the middle of the seventeenth century. If so, it was an unfortunate move, even though it anticipated the separation of divine institution from prescriptive rights that Filmer was to make after the Regicide.

---

*Ideas*, XVII (1956), 130; and R. W. K. Hinton, 'Husbands, Fathers and Conquerors', *Political Studies*, XV (1967), 299. Cf. Greenleaf, *Order, Empiricism and Politics*, pp. 82–4.

[65] I have examined three such documents: British Museum, MS. Harleian 53 (Adam to Henry VI); Trinity College, Cambridge, MS 0.5.54 (Adam to Henry VIII); and one displayed in the library of Hatfield House (Adam to Elizabeth I). For a discussion of other similar manuscripts and of the prominence of the belief in regal descent from Adam in Stuart England, see W. H. Greenleaf, 'Filmer's Patriarchal History', *Historical Journal*, IX (1966), 157–71, esp. 163–6.

[66] Filmer, *Patriarcha*, p. 64, and *Originall*, p. 274.

[67] Filmer, *Patriarcha*, p. 106, *Anarchy*, p. 288, and *Patriarcha*, p. 61.

The conflict between these two bases of sovereignty had previously been smoothed over by Filmer. He had suggested that successful usurpation established a title because it had God's approval—otherwise it would have failed—not because it had succeeded. Prescription itself was not the source of legitimacy but was a sign of divine sanction, and it was God's will alone that justified political authority. A prescriptive basis for political standards and for judging political conduct is generally part of an historicist or developmental view of society. Such a theory would hold, with Burke, for instance, that the historical conditioning of institutions and their endurance over time are the essence of social and political vitality. Change must be gradual and consistent with established and evolving practices. But this was the very conception Filmer was at pains to deny. He had no theory of change and social growth, and the genetic presuppositions of his patriarchalism ultimately prevented him from developing his doctrines of usurpation and prescriptive sovereignty into such a theory. Even his understanding of English law was antagonistic to traditionalism and the notion of organic growth over time. The law was simply the command of the monarch, whom Filmer saw as the 'author, interpreter and corrector of the common law' as well as of the positive or written law.[68] Continuity of the common law from one reign to the next came from the free and personal determination of successive kings to retain the practices of their predecessors and not from any inherent or self-preserving feature of the common law itself. If a king were to be bound by the laws promulgated before he came to his throne, his monarchical power would be limited, which was contrary to the nature of monarchy.[69] Filmer did not specifically say so, but the fact that succeeding monarchs had accepted and upheld the growing volume of law and custom was due only to circumstance and fortunate contingency, not to the irrepressible nature of the common law.

All this is a far cry from historical conditioning, but it does accord with the conception of usurpation as a reflection of God's will that Sir Robert held to in his earlier writings. Unfortunately, this doctrine could have justified the rule of Cromwell—and anyone else who succeeded in overthrowing an established ruler.

[68] Filmer, *Patriarcha*, p. 106, chapter title.
[69] Ibid., pp. 103–6.

# IX

## Patriarchalism and Its Critics During the Interregnum

I

The execution of Charles I did not, by any means, end the pamphlet war on the nature of the English commonwealth. Many of the same questions—especially the dispute between patriarchalists and contractualists—were still at issue, and examples can be found of all the forms of patriarchalism that have previously been identified. Shortly after the Regicide, the patriarchal justification of kingship was attacked by Francis Rous, who said that this doctrine proved nothing unless the ruler was the literal father of his people. If patriarchalism is to be at all useful in settling the present controversies, Rous asserted, there must be no question 'That the former Magistrate was our naturall parent and that we all derive from him, as from a *Genarcha*.' However, the entire claim is 'evidently false' and 'ill supposed. For in this confusion of Families in the world, in which the originall Families are lost; we owe no naturall duty to any but to those from whose blood we derive.'[1]

Rous contended, against the claims of the royalists, that the republican government was entitled to the subjects' obedience because it was the legitimate supreme authority. Accordingly, he was forced to accept successful usurpation and conquest as valid sources for titles. He said in another tract that the way in which a government came to power was of no consequence to political

[1] [Francis Rous], *The Bounds and Bonds of Publique Obedience* (London, 1649), p. 17.

obligation, for all rulers achieved their positions only through the permission of God.[2] These arguments were not at all representative of the defenses of the Commonwealth. Most authors delved more deeply into the moral and theoretical issues and attempted to justify obedience to the new government in terms either of individual conscience or of the requirements of nature. But even when legitimacy was reduced to possession and effectiveness, the argument was seldom allowed to rest upon unembellished divine right.

An anonymous work of 1650, *The Engagement Vindicated*, held that despite the familial and monarchical beginnings of government, a republic was the most desirable and revered political form because it satisfied the demands of nature and the needs of men better than any type of rule:

The first Governments came in neither by Election nor Conquest, but by the right of Primogeniture. Heires of families were heires of Kingdomes, and had the power of life and death; and so long then were the lives of men continued to them, that they might see a competent Kingdome rising out of their families; their childrens children, and servants children, all members of the family, and subject to the first-borne.

No other government is individually a constitution of the law of nature; for if it were, they must needs offer force to nature, that are not moulded under such a government. . . . Nature hath not punctually obliged men to any individual or particular Form of Government, but only generally impress'd the notion of Government upon men, yea, and beasts too, at least a resemblance of it.

A Republique comes nearest to the law of nature, since the disbanding of men from that family-government, which was the necessary consequent of their abridg'd lives. . . .

Monarchs are meerly Creatures of the Peoples choice, and dependent upon the continuation of their pleasure.

As usual, there were no clear statements of how non-familial government came into being and of the consequences of changing fatherhood into a new form of authority. The most important of these results seems to have been that the people could lawfully

[2] [Francis Rous], *The Lawfulness of Obeying the Present Government* (London, 1649), p. 7. Cf. Filmer, *Patriarcha*, pp. 60–1, 62, and 106; *Forms*, p. 232; and *Anarchy*, p. 288.

resist the improper action of political rulers,[3] a right they presumably did not have under the government of patriarchs.

2

A more specific use of the anthropological patriarchal thesis can be found in Gerrard Winstanley's radical 'digger' work, *The Law of Freedom* (1652). Winstanley traced the origins of government back to Adam and regarded the head of the household as the basic official in a 'free commonwealth', but he also argued against arbitrary government and insisted that 'the Law of Righteousness and Peace' was the source of magisterial authority. 'The Original Root of Magistracy,' Winstanley wrote, 'is *common Preservation*, and it rose up first in a private Family.' The first family was Adam's; it consisted of a great many people over whom Adam reigned as 'the first Governor or Officer in the Earth, because as he was the first Father, so he was the most wise in contriving, and the most strong for labor, and so the fittest to be the chief *Governor*'. Adam himself was ruled by the 'Law of Necessity, that the Earth should be planted for the common preservation and peace of his household'. Because this law was 'clearly written in the hearts of his people, they all Consented quietly to any counsel he gave them'. Thus, from the very beginning, mankind was ruled simultaneously by the will of Adam, 'the Will of his People', and the 'Law of common Preservation, Peace and Freedom'. In this manner, Winstanley not only founded governance upon the weakness and inexperience of children and the consequent authority of fathers but also argued that the 'Law of common Preservation is the Rule and Foundation of true Magistracy' and a protection against the abuse of political power.[4]

Adding a doctrine of tacit consent, Winstanley used the familial origins of political authority to demonstrate that all political officials were to be chosen by their subjects instead of

---

[3] T. B., *The Engagement Vindicated* (London, 1650), pp. 6–7, quotation from p. 6.

[4] Gerrard Winstanley, *The Law of Freedom in a Platform: or, True Magistracy Restored* (London, 1652), reprinted in *The Works*, ed. George H. Sabine (Ithaca, New York, 1941), pp. 536–7.

succeeding to or acquiring their positions:

> In the first Family, which is the Foundation from whence all Families sprang, there was the Father, he is the first link of the chain of Magistracy. The necessity of the children that sprang from him doth say,
>
> Father, do thou teach us how to plant the Earth, that we may live, and we will obey. By this choyce, they make him not onely a Father, but a Master and Ruler. And out of this root springs up all Magistrates and Officers, To see the Law executed, and to preserve Peace in the Earth, by seeing that right Government is observed.
>
> For here take notice, That though the children might not speak, yet their weakness and simplicity did speak, and chose their Father to be their Overseer. . . .
>
> . . . a true Commonwealths Officer is to be a chosen one, by them who are in necessity, and who judg him fit for that work.
>
> And thus a Father in a family is a Commonwealths Officer, because the Necessity of the young children choose him by a joynt consent, and not otherwise.[5]

Fatherhood for Winstanley had not been altered since the time of Adam; the responsibilities of the office continued to outweigh its powers by far. The commonwealth was basically an association of households,[6] and the father was the most fundamental political official. The father's role, acording to Winstanley, is to 'cherish his children till they grow strong and wise', to instruct them in reading and language or to teach them a trade or find one for them, and to teach them to live together in mutual respect and moderation: 'That so children may not quarrel like beasts, but live in Peace, like rational men, experienced in yielding obedience to the Laws and Officers of the Commonwealth, every one doing to another as he would have another do to him.'[7]

## 3

Winstanley certainly did not derive his arguments from Filmer. Rather, his theories exemplify the genetic preoccupations of Stuart political thinkers and demonstrate the presence of patriarchal pre-

---

[5] Ibid., p. 539.          [6] Ibid., pp. 538–9.          [7] Ibid., p. 545.

sumptions in populist doctrines. John Hall's *Of Government and Obedience* (1654), on the contrary, appears to have been influenced by Filmer and to have combined moral patriarchalism with arguments drawn from Hobbes, though neither of these sources was mentioned. Instead, Hall claimed that he reached his conclusions without depending on the writings of others, asserting, 'I am neither Thief nor prisoner to the Text or Tenet of any man.'[8] Very little is known about Hall (who identified himself as 'John Hall of Richmond'), and his writings have not received much attention in the past.[9] Hall was a bitter critic of popular sovereignty. He wrote *Of Government and Obedience* because he feared that utter chaos would result from the 'disrespect and contempt of the present Soveraign power'. His attitude was due in part to those theorists who defended the Commonwealth by insisting upon the 'derivation of power from the people', a view that led straight to 'Princes by Paction'. These notions convince people that they are capable of judging when the power entrusted to rulers has been abused. Consequently, subjects feel that political authority may be withdrawn as easily as it was conferred and come to regard themselves as 'the Supreme power and above Kings'.[10]

Attacking populism on historical grounds, Hall asserted that it was obviously a false theory because it erroneously presupposed

[8] John Hall, *Of Government and Obedience as They Stand Directed and Determined by Scripture and Reason* (London, 1654), Preface, sig. a1.
[9] Hall wrote one other tract, *The True Cavalier Examined in His Principles* (London, 1654). He is not in the *D.N.B.* and should not be confused with the poet of the same name who is. Hall is mentioned several times in the Duppa–Isham correspondence. See Sir Giles Isham, ed., *The Correspondence of Bishop Brian Duppa and Sir Justinian Isham, 1650–1660*, Publications of the Northamptonshire Record Society, XVII (1955), 91, 92, and 117. (I owe this reference to Mr. Keith Thomas.)
There have been only two previous analyses of Hall's political thought: J. A. W. Gunn, *Politics and the Public Interest in the Seventeenth Century* (London, 1969), pp. 97–104, and Zagorin, *History of Political Thought*, pp. 91–3. Gunn's discussion is quite full and recognizes the closeness of Hall to Hobbes. Neither author comments on the similarity to Filmer. For an enlightening analysis of the historical and theoretical relationships between patriarchalism and the Hobbesian doctrine, see Quentin Skinner, 'The Ideological Context of Hobbes's Political Thought', *Historical Journal*, IX (1966), 286–317, esp. 300–2.
[10] Hall, *Of Government*, Preface, sigs. a2–a3.

that the people had once been free and were the original possess-
ors of power. Moreover, the consequences of the populist doctrine
were untenable. Hall examined the development of government
from its patriarchal beginnings in the Garden of Eden. Discussing
what could pass for the Hobbesian state of nature, he observed
that men are naturally covetous and desire power over each
other and therefore could never have been free. Unrestrained
men would be at one another's throats, and those who were
sympathetic and cared for the weak would soon be overpowered
by the less considerate. 'To this end, God placeth man at first in
a state of subjection to one head: so that (no doubt) had *Adam*
lived', Hall continued, 'he had been (as natural Father, so) King
of all mankinde.' But Adam died, and in order to avoid endless
strife among his descendants, 'this power of one man's command
over another was the established due of birthright'. Like Filmer,
Hall asserted that Adam did not need subjects in order to possess
his authority, for '*Adam* (before he had family) was by God made
Monarch of all Creatures below; and of *Eve* also'.[11]

Carrying this argument further, Hall wrote that even if the
members of his household 'dye or depart the family', the
master retains his authority, even though he is no longer a
husband or father. 'For although his power be not so extensive
over few, yet it is as absolute.' Similarly, 'A master of a family of
a hundred servants is but equal to him that hath but three.'[12]
Applied to more narrowly political matters, this doctrine meant
that that the king was logically and temporally prior to his subjects and even created their status, for 'the Monarch and
Governor, is so far from receiving his essential honor and power
from the subjects and governed, as he may . . . be accounted
constitutive of them; even in that very relation'. It followed that
monarchy was man's natural condition. From the beginning of
time men lived under the universal patriarchal monarchy of
Adam and his heirs, and so long as peace prevailed, the world was
united under the rule of one supreme father who took the name
king when his domain became sufficiently large. Eventually,
'Ambition, Covetousness, Revenge, and the like' began to play
a role in human affairs, and they introduced revolt and dis-

[11] Ibid., Preface, sig. a2$^v$ and p. 30. Cf. Filmer, *Patriarcha*, p. 61, and
*Anarchy*, p. 289.
[12] Hall, *Of Government*, pp. 35 and 110.

obedience. From these civil wars came separate kingdoms, 'which had their first rise from popular discontent and insurrection', not the virtue and justice that king-flatterers would claim.[13] The relation of the family to governance was extremely important to Hall; he said that any attempt to set monarchy on its 'true foundations' had to begin with the 'Father of the Family; who, in his less Territory is a little Prince, as the other is a Master of a greater Family'.[14]

Hall departed from the traditional patriarchal doctrine in his discussion of the source of paternal authority. He was probably influenced by the Hobbesian notion that power derived from generation belonged to the mother. Like Hobbes, Hall concluded that the father's title to the obedience of his children came, in the first instance, from his control over their mother (and his wife). Humans marry because their children grow so slowly that the mother cannot take care of them alone; whereas among the animals, by the time that a second litter is born, the first one is no longer in need of the mother's attention. Authority arising from procreation belongs more to the mother than to the father, according to Hall, because she 'hath part of her own substance imployed in nourishment of the young whilst it is within her (and passeth her time in bearing, not in pleasure, but mostly in affliction). . .'.[15]

His criticisms of the contractual explanation of governmental authority demonstrate Hall's probable reliance upon Filmer. He said that it was a denial of natural freedom to bind children and all later generations to an authority established by the consent of their ancestors, unless all people are presumed to have retained the right to cast off the government they inherited. Also, it is illogical to justify the prevailing political arrangements in which women, children, and servants are disenfranchised while simultaneously claiming that man is free by nature. 'And so further,' Hall asked, 'by this maxime, how can conquest or succession have

---

[13] Ibid., pp. 23, 79, and Preface, sig. a2ᵛ. The patriarchal monarchy of Adam and Noah is discussed on p. 52.

[14] Ibid., p. 29.

[15] Ibid., pp. 32–3. Cf. Hobbes, *Leviathan*, ch. xx, ed. Pogson Smith, pp. 154–5, where the same arguments and examples were used. The implications of these problems for an understanding of Hobbes will be dealt with in Ch. XII.

any right? which it hath, by confession of all.' Finally, he questioned the right of the government to take life if its powers were derived from the consent of its original subjects. An individual does not have a title to his own life, Hall argued, for that belongs to God. Since no one can surrender a power that is not his, the exercise of capital punishment by governments indicates that all authority must have come from God.[16] This last point has been a popular argument against the consent theory. It still poses problems unless it is remembered that what was conferred upon the contractually constituted sovereign was the individual's authority to interpret and apply the law of nature for himself; this authority included the right to kill other men when circumstances so warranted. Only in this indirect manner were governments given the power of capital punishment.[17]

## 4

After Thomas Hobbes, the most important and best-known political writer of the interregnum period was undoubtedly James Harrington. Harrington showed little interest in political obligation and the origins of governance, the two problems that were fundamental to patriarchal theorizing in seventeenth-century England. Nevertheless, he examined the patriarchal doctrine and its implications several times, criticizing it in some respects and modifying and then adopting it in others.

Rejecting the entire analogy between kings and fathers, Harrington wrote:

Now if they [the claimants to monarchical authority] say, they are Fathers of the People, and for that reason they call themselves the Heads, inferring the People to be no more than a Trunk, it's only metaphorical, and proves nothing: for they must remember, that since *Father* has a relation upon which it depends, and upon whose removal it vanishes, they themselves cannot bring any such; for by physical procreation they will not offer it; and for metaphorical Dependence, it will come to nothing, we seeing People languish when their Princes are fullest, and, like Leeches, rather willing to burst than to fall off; and on the contrary, the People on the removal of a

16 Hall, *Of Government*, pp. 42–3. Cf. Filmer, *Anarchy*, p. 287.
17 See, for instance, Hugo Bedau, 'The Right to Life', *The Monist*, LII (1968), 550–72, esp. 567–8.

Prince, chearful [*sic*] and reliev'd. Now if there were so strict a Union between these two, such a Contrariety and Antipathy could never appear; for certainly when any two Persons endeavour to gain Ground one upon another, there is an Enmity, whatever is pretended. Besides, if these men would be Fathers, it were then their duty to do like Fathers, which is to provide for and cherish; whereas on the contrary, it is they themselves that eat the Bread out of the Mouths of their Children, and through the Groans of the Poor.[18]

Moreover, Harrington asserted in *The Art of Law Giving*, 'Family Government may be as necessarily Popular in some cases, as Monarchial in others.' To prove this claim, he fell back upon his fundamental principle that political power was identical to economic control. As an example of a monarchical patriarchy, he posited a man with an annual income of 1,000 pounds whose wife, children, and servants were all dependent 'upon him (at his good will) in the distribution of his Estate for their livelihood'. If that estate should be lost or spent, Harrington asked, 'where is the Monarchy of this family? But if the Master was no otherwise Monarchical than by virtue of his Estate, the foundation or balance of his Empire consisted in that thousand pounds a year.' Having established to his own satisfaction that estate rather than fatherhood was the source and justification of patriarchal authority, he insisted that the same principle could give rise to a popularly ruled family. If six or ten persons, each with an income of five hundred pounds annually, 'shall agree to dwell together as Family', no one of them could 'pretend to be Lord and Master of the same' and claim the right 'to dispose of the Estates of all the rest'. Would not these men 'agree together upon such Orders, to which they consent equally to submit?' If this were the case, 'then certainly must the Government of this Family be a Government of Laws or Orders, and not the Government of one, or of some three or four of these men'. Emphasizing the specifically political meaning of his remarks, Harrington asked princes and parliaments to consider:

whether, without violence or removing of Property, they can make a

---

[18] James Harrington, *The Grounds and Reasons of Monarchy Considered* (n.d.) printed in *The Oceana of James Harrington, Esq; and His Other Works*, ed. John Toland (Dublin, 1737), p. 12. All references to Harrington will be to the names of the individual works as published in this edition.

Popular Family of the Monarchical, or a Monarchical Family of the
Popular? Or, whether that be practicable or possible in a Nation,
upon the like balance or foundation in Property, which is not in a
Family? A Family being but a smaller Society or Nation, and a
Nation but a greater Society or Family.[19]

Against the attempt to derive kingship from the power of
Adam, Harrington wrote in *The Grounds and Reasons of
Monarchy Consider'd*, 'As for the Antiquity from ADAM, it is
true before his Fall his dominion was large and wide, but it was
over the Beasts that after his Fall learn'd to rebel against him;
and economically, not despotically, over his Wife and Children.
But what is this to Civil Government?'[20] But in *The Prerogative
of Popular Government*, he took the claim far more seriously
and agreed that 'If ADAM has liv'd till now, he could have seen
no other than his own Children; and so that he must have been
King by the right of Nature, [which] was his peculiar Prerogative.' But Adam was not alive, and his power had not passed intact
to his primogenitive successors; 'because it was early when
ABRAHAM and LOT, dividing Territories, became several Kings;
and not long after when the Sons of JACOB being all Patriarchs,
by the appointment of God, whose Right sure was not inferior
to that of ADAM'. After Adam, therefore, the appeal to the rights
of fatherhood proved nothing about the nature of government,
for:

Fathers of Families are of three sorts, either a sole Landlord, as
ADAM, and then he is an absolute Monarch; or a few Landlords, as
LOT and ABRAHAM, with the Patriarchs of those days; who if
they join'd not together, were so many Princes; or if they join'd,
made a mix'd Monarchy: or, as GROTIUS believes, a kind of
Common-wealth administer'd in the Land of *Canaan*, by
MELCHISIDEC, to whom as King and Priest ABRAHAM paid Tythes
of all that he had. Such a Magistracy was that also of JETHRO,
King and Priest in the Common-wealth of *Median*. Fathers of
Families for the third sort, as when the Multitudes are Landlords
(which happen'd in the division of the Land of *Canaan*) make a
Common-wealth.[21]

[19] James Harrington, *The Art of Law Giving* (1659), pp. 385–6.
[20] Harrington, *Grounds and Reasons*, p. 8.
[21] James Harrington, *The Prerogative of Popular Government: Being a
Political Discourse in Two Books* (1657), pp. 248–9.

Despite this ambiguity in the nature of familial power, the image of fatherhood and its authority were most important to Harrington; he used them in *Oceana* to justify the principles of a natural aristocracy as well as the rule of the community by its elders. In a group of twenty men who come together at random, Harrington wrote, approximately six will be wiser and superior to the rest and will become the leaders. 'Wherefore in matters of common concernment, difficulty, or danger, they [the remaining fourteen] hang upon their [the leaders'] lips as Children upon their Fathers; and the influence thus acquir'd by the six, the eminence of whose parts is found to be a stay and comfort to the fourteen, is the *Authority of Fathers*.' This leadership, he added, was that same 'natural aristocracy discuss'd by God throughout the whole Body of Mankind to no end and purpose, but a positive Obligation to make use of their Guides'. Somewhat later in the book, Harrington acknowledged, 'It is with all Politicians past dispute, that paternal Power is in the right of Nature; and there is no other than the derivation of Power from Fathers of Families, as the natural root of a Common-wealth.' In Israel, he said, sovereignty 'came clearly from this natural Root, the Elders of the whole People'. In both cases, however, Harrington insisted that the authority was not hereditary but was based strictly upon merit.[22] Even when the hereditary principle appeared to be at work, as among the ancient Hebrews, patriarchal succession to power was not a necessary consequence of fatherly right but was a contingency that could be explained on other grounds:

The [Hebrew] Patriarchs, or Princes of Families, according as they declar'd their Pedigrees, had the like right as to their Families; but neither in these nor the former, was there any hereditary right to the *Sanhedrim*: though there be little question but the wise men, and understanding, and known among their Tribes, which the People took or elected into those or other Magistracies, and whom MOSES made Rulers over them, must have been of these; seeing they could not choose being the most known among the Tribes, and were likeliest by the advantages of Education to be the most wise and understanding.[23]

[22] James Harrington, *The Common-wealth of Oceana* (1656), pp. 47 and 87.
[23] Ibid., pp. 135–6.

The people of Oceana were to be divided into 'Freemen or Citizens, and Servants, while such; for if they attain to Liberty, that is to live of themselves, they are Freemen or Citizens'.[24] This statement is an important indication of the patriarchal structuring of society that Harrington incorporated into his political views. Although it initially appears that servitude itself disqualified people from citizenship,[25] Harrington's later amplifications of his position suggest that he was at least equally interested in the positive notion that those who are able 'to live of themselves' are to be citizens. The independence that living of oneself presupposed was widely regarded as a characteristic of fatherhood in Stuart England. It was generally agreed that the ability to head one's own household was a primary qualification for full membership in society. Harrington does not appear to have questioned this conception of citizenship, for he wrote in *Oceana* that each man was to be given enough income 'to maintain himself, his Wife, and Children'.[26] In *The Prerogative of Popular Government*—the first part of which was subtitled, 'A full Answer to all Such Objections as have hitherto been made against OCEANA' —he was much more explicit and said, 'The Land of *Oceana* . . . [is] levell'd or divided equally among the Fathers of Families.'[27] And finally, in *A System of Politics*, Harrington clearly tied the possession of property to the capacity to have dependants and to governmental authority. 'If a Man has some Estate,' he wrote, 'he may have some Servants or a Family, and consequently some Government, or something to govern: if he has no Estate, he can have no Government.'[28] Thus, Harrington demonstrated his acceptance of the traditional Christian and Aristotelian doctrines that the family was the most basic unit in society and that through the exercise of fatherly authority one prepared for participation in the political order itself.

---

[24] Ibid., p. 83.
[25] See C. B. Macpherson, *The Political Theory of Possessive Individualism: Hobbes to Locke* (Oxford, 1962), pp. 181–2.
[26] Harrington, *Oceana*, p. 166.
[27] Harrington, *Prerogative*, p. 265.
[28] James Harrington, *A System of Politics Delineated in Short and Easy Aphorisms* (written *c.* 1661), p. 497. On Harrington's acceptance of the traditional view of society as a community of patriarchs, see also J. G. A. Pocock, *Politics, Language and Time* (New York, 1971), pp. 112–13.

5

Passing criticisms—such as Harrington's—of some aspects of the patriarchal defense of monarchy were common by the mid-seventeenth century; the patriarchal theory was so firmly established that it was virtually impossible to justify republican and populist doctrines without making at least a few comments on familial authority. However, it was not until the publication in 1658 of Edward Gee's *Divine Right and Original of the Civill Magistrate* that patriarchalism was thoroughly and systematically attacked. Gee, a Presbyterian minister from Lancashire, focused his attempted refutation on Filmer's *Anarchy*, which he specifically cited several times.[29] Gee's critique was very much to the point; as Locke was to do, he clearly recognized that a fusion of political and familial authority was behind Sir Robert's doctrine. Unlike Locke, however, Gee was not able to avoid incorporating patriarchal principles into his own reasoning, and in the end he had conceded far more to Filmer than he realized.[30]

'The Question here is not,' according to Gee, 'Whether the Father, and First-born have some preeminency' over their children and younger brothers, 'But whether the preeminency be the same with Civill Magistracy: Or whether the political power in a Common-wealth be not one thing, and that [i.e., familial] superiority another, and those two be not really and essentially different?' While not questioning the father's claim to absolute obedience on familial matters, Gee held that since the 'publique state or Common-wealth' was established 'as a distinct

[29] Gee is only the second Englishman known to have *mentioned* any of Filmer's works in print. The first was William Prynne, the Parliamentary historian, who cited *The Freeholders Grand Inquest* in his *Plea for the Lords and House of Peers* (London, 1648; 2nd ed., 1658). Prynne was interested only in Filmer's constitutional theories, which have not been dealt with here. However, see William M. Lamont, *Marginal Prynne, 1600–1669* (London, 1963), p. 187, and Pocock, *Ancient Constitution*, p. 157.

[30] Both Allen and Laslett have commented on the similarity of Gee's arguments against Filmer to those of Locke. See Allen, 'Sir Robert Filmer', *Augustan Age*, ed. Hearnshaw, p. 45, and Laslett, Introduction to Filmer, *Political Works*, p. 38. There is a brief analysis of Gee in Zagorin, *History of Political Theory*, pp. 75–7, but only Laslett refers to Gee's acceptance of patriarchalism.

society from that of a household, . . . the paternal power hath been (and that duly, and necessarily) taken to be another, or a distinct authority from that of the Civil Magistrate, and inferior, or subordinate to it.'[31] This sharp differentiation between magistrates and fathers was the basis of Gee's position. Even if the fatherly and primogenitive rights had once been political, Gee reasoned, that was now irrelevant, for no ruler claimed or held his throne 'by a right of Fatherhood, or of Primogeniture derived from the First Father, or the first eldest son'. Filmer himself had recognized this much, according to Gee, when he said that 'all Kings that now are, or ever were, are, or were either the Fathers of their people, or the heirs of such Fathers, or usurpers of the right of such Fathers'. In this statement, Sir Robert confessed that patriarchalism is 'now out of use, and . . . [that it is] an impossible thing, to build any soveraign power that now is, or can be expected to be, or for most the ages of mankinde past, hath been in the world, upon it'.[32]

In his most acute criticism of Filmer, Gee saw that Sir Robert's use of sovereignty and his emphasis upon prescription and providence[33] destroyed all moral right to title and nullified whatever distinction there might have been between legitimate rulers and usurpers.

Hereby the Fatherly right and power are made a meer *Equivocum* [Gee wrote], or to signify power entitled, or coming any way whatsoever, though it do not only derive from the right of Fatherhood, but be privately opposed to, or destructive of it: and thus he [Filmer] confounds, and makes to meet together in one name, and title, the thing he had argued against, with the thing he had asserted. And the saying that *Providence in dispossessing of a Crown, him that is the true heir (and so hath the right) and disposing it to the hands of an unjust invader, doth put a fatherly power in*

[31] Edward Gee, *The Divine Right and Original of the Civill Magistrate from God* (London, 1658), pp. 144–5.
[32] Ibid., pp. 153 and 155. The Filmer passage is from *Anarchy*, p. 288.
[33] Filmer, *Anarchy*, p. 289: 'many times by the act either of a usurper himself, or of those that set him up, the true heir of a crown is dispossessed, God using the ministry of the wickedest men for the removing and setting up of Kings: in such cases the subjects' obedience to the fatherly power must go along and wait upon God's providence, who only hath right to give and take away kingdoms, and thereby to adopt subjects into the obedience of another fatherly power.'

*that invader, and adopt the subjects to an obligation to it;* is to deny the right both of paternity and of birth-right, and of the consent of the people, and of every other special way of conveying a title to Government, and to make the right thereof only to follow, come by, and consist in possession, and to die forthwith in the Father, and heir upon dispossession. And to what purpose then is all his plea for Fatherhood, and primogeniture, or any other means for any other title? what a void distinction is that of his when he distinguisheth of a natural, and an usurped right? According to him now there is no Power, but Fatherhood, no Fatherhood, but possession.[34]

Gee's alternative to patriarchalism was at least superficially a form of populism, and he attempted to show that universal consent to the original institution of government was not necessary. Filmer had emphasized the impossibility of getting everyone in a pre-political condition to attend a meeting let alone to agree on a specific form of government.[35] Some do not participate, Gee replied, because they are unable to give their consent, such as those who either lack the use of reason (presumably children and idiots) or 'are involved (as to these) in their Husbands, Parents, Masters, or Guardians'. The lame and ill are never a very significant number; furthermore, their infirmities temporarily remove their interest in the community. Those who are voluntarily absent do not prevent the others from acting, 'but rather by their default they put off the right as to the present act, and invest it in the rest. We account (and justly) that a countrey-meeting,' Gee continued, 'at which we choose our Parliament men, to which the people therein are called, though the twentieth part of them that are called do not appear.'[36]

An important aspect of Gee's own position was revealed in his admission that some people so lack political significance that they 'are involved' in their 'Husbands, Parents, Masters, or

---

[34] Gee, *Divine Right*, pp. 159–60. The final passage may have been a paraphrase of Filmer's closing remarks in the *Forms*, p. 229, quoted above, p. 115. The italicized sentence is Gee's rendering of Filmer's words quoted in the previous note.

[35] See Filmer, *Anarchy*, p. 287, discussed above, p. 126.

[36] Gee, *Divine Right*, pp. 180–1, citing Grotius, *De Jure Belli*, II, v, 20: 'If any members cannot avail themselves of their right by reason of absence or some other hindrance, their right in the meantime accrues to those present.' (Kelsey translation, p. 252.)

Guardians', in short, in their patriarchal superiors. Gee actually agreed with much of Filmer's position despite his perceptive criticisms. Not only did he regard patriarchal headship as one of the basic requisites for political participation, but—as was befitting a member of the clergy—he saw the Fifth Commandment as the divine basis of all social relations. However, Gee did not look to divine right as the justification of political obligation but regarded conscience as 'the surest, and firmest groundwork' for government. Conscience, he said, 'is both the strongest, and most lasting obligation to any relative duty'.[37] But given Gee's implicit patriarchalism, the only consciences that could have been politically significant were those of the heads of households. For instance, after asserting that patriarchalism and primogeniture would have destroyed the continuity of Adam's power, Gee suggested that individual governments were instituted at Babel and elsewhere by the consent of fathers who spoke for their families as well as for themselves:

Suppose we *Adam* to have ruled as sole Monarch during his life; afterward some one of his sons in succession to him, or all his sons each over their own progeny as distinct societies; after by the confusion of languages they being forced to sever; or when those distinct races of *Adam* became so numerous, and dispersive over many countries that they were too vast to be continued in one society, they may be supposed each of them voluntarily to withdraw, or part themselves into several Commonwealths, and the Fathers of families in every [one] of these new erected Commonwealths having in them the interest of power each in relation to his children, and family, and agreeing together for themselves, and theirs to some one as their publique civil-head, or King; and thus cometh in Magistracy to be voluntarily constituted in that way wherein the right of Fatherhood is preserved, and continued in subordination to any civil publique power ... [but] in relation to those only who were natural children to it. ... And with this the *Assertors of the sole right of Fatherhood are driven in a sort to comply*.[38]

Similarly, Gee agreed with the patriarchal insistence that men are not naturally and originally free. Instead, 'the Master of the Family, having rule thereof, representeth all the persons of his house'. Thus, freedom is not a universal human right but belongs

---

[37] Ibid., Preface, sigs. (a7) and (a7ᵛ)–(a8).
[38] Ibid., pp. 158–9, citing Filmer, *Anarchy*, pp. 287–8.

only to those 'who are not by the act either of themselves, or of their progenitors, or others representers compacted into society with others'. The 'whole people to this effect', Gee wrote, consists of them 'that are the Masters of families with them who are Masters of themselves', or, differently stated, everyone who is 'without [a] Domesticall head' and is himself 'capable of heading a family'.[39]

The power of fathers to enter into agreements that bound the members of their households was the source of social continuity for Gee. 'They that think it irrational that the Father should represent and involve the family' had to explain how the religious and civil agreements of the Israelites 'did comprehend, and bind as well as the absent as the present, and their posterity born, and yet unborn; and also how the lawes, and contracts continually passed by some do take in others not personally consenting'.[40] However, if the acts of fathers could impose political commitments upon children and servants, patriarchal authority had to be partially political. Gee did not appreciate this implication of his own conclusions and therefore did not explain how these claims could be reconciled with his attacks on Filmer. It is possible that Gee was not conscious of any major inconsistencies in his argument. He might have believed that he was writing against the excesses of the anonymous author of *The Anarchy of a Limited or Mixed Monarchy* rather than against the patriarchal theory in general. The more likely explanation, however, is that Edward Gee was no less confused than he was verbose.

## 6

Filmer's doctrines provided a direct and acknowledged source for Peter Heylyn, the High Church prelate and a friend of Sir Robert's. Because Filmer had refused to publish *Patriarcha*, Heylyn admitted in 1659, 'I have adventured on that work, which the Consciousness of my own inability might deter me from, if the desire of satisfying such a modest and ingenious Adversary [*i.e.*, James Harrington] had not over-ruled me.' This statement appears in a letter that Heylyn wrote to Filmer's son comforting

---

[39] Ibid., pp. 172 and 186.    [40] Ibid., p. 172. Cf. Filmer, *Anarchy*, p. 287.

him on the death of his father. Praising Sir Robert and the manuscript of *Patriarcha*, Heylyn said that publication of the work
'would have given such satisfaction to all our great Masters in
the Schools of *Politie*, that all other Tractates of that kind, had
been found unnecessary'. He also identified Sir Robert as the
author of the *Forms, Originall,* and *Anarchy*.[41] Part of the letter
was reprinted in the editions of *Patriarcha* published in 1680 and
1685, but Heylyn's statements about having used Sir Robert's
ideas in his own writings were omitted. The influence of Filmer's
patriarchal ideas upon him can be seen by comparing some of
Heylyn's earlier political writings with his 1659 tract.

In 1637 he asserted that monarchy sprang from natural beginnings and that kings were therefore absolute and could be limited
only by their own actions:

So that in case the kings in some particulars had not prescribed
limits unto themselves, and bound their owne hands, as it were to en-
large the peoples: neither the people, nor any lawes by them enacted
could have done it. Besides the law, *Monarchie* is founded on the
Laws of *nature*, not on *positive lawes:* and *positive lawes* I trow
are of no such efficacie, as to annihilate anything, which hath its
being and originall, in the *law* of *nature*. Hence it is, that all sover-
eaigne Princes in themselves are above the lawes, as Princes are
considered in *abstracto,* and extent of power; and how farre that
extent will reach, you may see in the first of *Sam.* and 8 *chap.*
though in *concreto* a just Prince will not breake those lawes which
he hath promised to observe. Princes are debtors to their subjects, as
God to man.[42]

This passage is important simply because Heylyn said nothing
more specific about the origins of monarchy than that it began
in nature. While a genetic conception of obligation apparently
was significant to Heylyn in 1637, patriarchalism clearly was
not. Origins were prominent again in 1658, and once more
patriarchal thinking was not included. In this instance, however,
the Norman Conquest and the beginnings of the English mon-

---

[41] Heylyn, *Certamen Epistolare: or, The Letter-Combate* (London, 1659), p.
208 (incorrectly numbered 387).
[42] Peter Heylyn, *A Briefe and Moderate Answer, to the Seditious and
Scandalous Challenges of Henry Burton* (London, 1637), pp. 32–3.

archy were discussed rather than the establishment of monarchical authority in general.[43]

The next year, in *Certamen Epistolare*, Heylyn did employ patriarchal arguments to show that monarchs could not be forced to share their powers with parliaments. God's establishment of a fatherly political authority was evident in the government of Hebrews, Heylyn said; it continued during their enslavement in Egypt when the Hebrews were ruled by 'the Heads or Chiefes of their several Families, who by a paternal right derived on them from their first Father *Adam*, challenged and enjoy'd a Fatherly authority over all those who descended of them'. It was these governors whom Moses addressed when he spoke to the 'elders'. Moses had unified this power in himself, and Joshua acquired it from him, both ruling as 'Kings in fact, though not in title',[44] and upon the death of Joshua, 'the Ordinary Government returned again to the Heads of the several Families, as before in Ægypt'.[45] This reversion to the rule of individual fathers suggests Filmer's notion that when a king dies without heir, 'The Kingly power escheats . . . to the prime and independent heads of families.'[46]

The acceptance of monarchy by all nations proves that kingship is a natural form of government, Heylyn continued. This uniformity can be explained by the natural kingship of fathers: 'I believe that none can shew me a better reason' why all nations adopted monarchy than that they were guided 'by the light of natural reason, by which they found that Government to be fittest for them, or that the first Kings of every Nation, were

[43] See P[eter] H[eylyn], *The Stumbling Block of Disobedience and Rebellion . . . Removed* (London, 1658), p. 267. This tract was answered by James Harrington in a work of the same title. Harrington was answered by Heylyn in the third part of *Certamen Epistolare*, which begins with the letter to Filmer's son.

[44] Cf. Filmer, *Patriarcha*, p. 60: 'By manifest footsteps we may trace this paternal government unto the Israelites coming into Egypt, where the exercise of [supreme] patriarchal jurisdiction was intermitted, because they were in subjection to a stronger Prince. After the return of these Israelites out of bondage, God, out of a special care of them, chose Moses and Joshua successively to govern as Princes in the place and stead of the supreme Fathers.' (Bracket in Laslett's text.)

[45] Heylyn, *Certamen Epistolare*, pp. 264 (citing Exod. 3: 16 and 4: 29), 265, and 266.

[46] Filmer, *Patriarcha*, p. 61.

the Heads of Families that retained that paternal right over all such as descended of them, as might entitle their authority to divine institution.' Finally, Heylyn denied that men were naturally free; the hierarchical structure of the family precludes the existence of such freedom for no matter what their ages, children 'are *required* by God to do the *duty of servants*, till either their Fathers free consent, or the Constitution of the Government under which they live, shall release them from it'.[47]

[47] Heylyn, *Certamen Epistolare*, pp. 272–3 and 277–8.

# X

## Patriarchalism and the Contract in the Political Literature of the Restoration

### I

The extensive use of patriarchal reasoning by the critics of Hobbes's *Leviathan* is a striking demonstration of the pervasiveness of patriarchalism and of its role as the major alternative to the contract theory in seventeenth-century English political thought. The political writings of Hobbes, unlike those of his admiring but critical contemporary Sir Robert Filmer, attracted attention almost as soon as they were published.[1]

Stuart thinkers—like their nineteenth- and twentieth-century successors—viewed Hobbes's political doctrine as extremely individualistic in its conception of the relations between man and his government. According to this interpretation, Hobbes's individualism can be found in his accounts of the state of nature and its original equality and in his conception of the beginnings of political organization. It is generally asserted today that the state of nature of the *Leviathan* was not intended as an historical description of man's pre-political life; it was, rather, a logical and reductionist device by which Hobbes attempted to demonstrate the necessity of absolute governmental authority. Hobbes himself suggested that there 'was never generally . . . [a state of

---

[1] There have been two recent studies of seventeenth-century reactions to Hobbes: John Bowle, *Hobbes and His Critics: A Study of Seventeenth-Century Constitutionalism* (London, 1951), and Samuel Mintz, *The Hunting of Leviathan* (Cambridge, 1962). Bowle deals primarily with criticisms of Hobbes's political philosophy, and Mintz is interested in metaphysical and theological evaluations.

nature], over all the world'.[2] The extent to which Hobbes
actually eschewed an historical theory of the state of nature is
not important in the present context, for the seventeenth-century
critics of the *Leviathan* were generally unable to distinguish between logic and history. It was sufficient for their purposes that
Hobbes had at least employed the traditional genetic forms of
argument, forms that implied a derivation of obligation from
origins. Whether he had used these principles in a new manner
was irrelevant.

Alexander Rosse, a prolific Scottish author, misinterpreted
Hobbes's statement that 'Nature hath made men ... equall, in
the facilities of body, and mind',[3] and argued that the existence
of familial status in Paradise demonstrated that inequality was
natural:

Doubtless, in the state of innocency, there should have been naturally
a subordination and subjection, as of children to their parents, of
wives to their husbands, and of inferiours to their superiours; for
there should have been no more equality then among men, on earth,
than there was, and is in heaven among Angels, and in hell among
Devils. . . . To say then that there is no inequality by nature, is to
say, that there is no order in nature which cannot be without subordination. . . .[4]

Rosse's claim, of course, presupposed the identity of familial
and political relationships. Implicitly relying upon the same
presumption, William Lucy, appointed to the Bishopric of St.
David's at the Restoration, held that the natural subordination of
children to their parents meant that men were never equal. Adam
had unquestionably been Eve's superior, and on these same
grounds, he said, 'We will therefore see ... [that] by *nature* he
[man] was made a poor helpless Child, in the greatest dispropor-
tion, both of *Soul and body*, to his Parents, that possibly can be.'
Hobbes, Lucy contended, talks of men 'as if they were *Terrigenae,
born out of the earth*, come up like Seeds, without any relation
one to the other'. Lucy rejected Hobbes's belief that the absence
of a higher authority made the state of nature into a condition of

[2] Hobbes, *Leviathan*, ch. xiii, ed. Pogson Smith, p. 97.

[3] Ibid., ch. xiii, p. 94.

[4] [Alexander Rosse], *Leviathan Drawn out with a Hook* (London, 1653),
pp. 19–20.

war. He asserted that men are generally subordinated to their parents and that parental rule is so gentle that conditions 'in that estate [of nature] are most peaceable and free from warre'.[5]

Hobbes, however, was not unaware of traditional patriarchal arguments; chapter twenty of *Leviathan* was entitled 'Of Dominion PATERNALL, *and* DESPOTICALL, but when Lucy criticized this chapter in a later polemic, he said nothing about the political aspects of patriarchal power. Instead, the Bishop dealt only with familial authority *per se* and with the relationships between husbands and wives and parents and children, apparently unaware of the identification of the family and the state that was implicit in his original criticism.[6]

Like Filmer, George Lawson recognized Hobbes's political patriarchalism, but Lawson criticized the notion that generation is one way to acquire dominion and attempted to separate familial and political authority. 'What have we to do with Family-power in a Common-wealth?' Lawson asked. 'For Families as they make vicinities, and vicinities a Community civil, are but a remote part of Politicks.'[7] Lawson's position was not quite so rigid as his criticisms of Hobbes would suggest, for in a later work he held that the Fifth Commandment applies to political as well as domestic obedience and 'determines the right of persons, who are superiours, inferiours, and equals'. He employed the image of the expansion of families into 'vicinities' that he had used against Hobbes and wrote:

A family is the seminary both of the Church, and civil State: And, as a State, or Church, may be said to be a great family; so a family well ordered may be called a little common-wealth, civill or ecclesiastical. Therefore I proceed, from oeconomical to politick dutyes, which by analogy are reducible to this 5th commandment. A

---

[5] William Lucy, *Observations, Censures and Confutations of Notorious Errours in Mr. Hobbes His Leviathan* (London, 1663), pp. 138–9 and 148. This work was originally published in 1657 with a slightly different title and under the authorship of William Pike, a name that is now recognized as a pseudonym employed by Bishop Lucy. (See Bowle, *Hobbes and His Critics*, p. 24.) The reference to Hobbes is to *Leviathan*, ch. xiii, p. 95.
[6] [William Lucy], *An Answer to Mr. Hobbes His Leviathan* (London, 1673), pp. 63–8.
[7] George Lawson, *An Examination of the Political Part of Mr. Hobbes His Leviathan* (London, 1657), p. 48.

G

family, which seems to be onely a private society, may multiply into severall familyes, and they into Vicinityes, and greater multitudes. And though every family hath an order of superiority, and subjection; yet the several families and Vicinityes, being distinct, have no power one over another, but in that respect are equall. Yet these may associate, and unite themselves into a community, and become one body, not onely by confederation for friendship, and mutuall help, commerce, and defence, but may enter into a stricter bond of Union, and become politick, and establish an order of superiority and subjection, either for matters of this life, or for Religion, or for both.

Lawson attempted to distinguish between political and familial subjection, and his argument is similar to the implicit Aristotelianism of Sir Thomas Smith and Althusius. Political authority, Lawson believed, is 'an higher, and publick power of the supreme Governours of a State, as such' and therefore pertains to the entire community; but paternal power extends no further than the private association of the household.[8]

Another critic who questioned the identification of civil and patriarchal authority was John Shafte, whose tract does not seem to have been known by previous students of anti-Hobbesian literature. Kings are not the same as fathers, according to Shafte, because political rulers should be more concerned about the welfare of their subjects than patriarchs are for the well-being of their families. Pointing to the rise and fall of English noble families since the Conquest, he asked:

If Kings then were as Masters of Families, and governed after the same manner, as freely and arbitrarily disposing of all the Profits and Revenues of the Nation, and the Labours of the people; what man is so blinde, as not to see that Kingdoms would be things of no firmer foundation, nor longer continuance, at least under one and the same form of Government, and Race of Princes, then Families are, or the Estates appertaining to these Families continue under, and in the hands of the same Lineal Masters, whereof one in a hundred doth not continue its felicity a hundred years together; but is

---

[8] George Lawson, *Theo-politca: or, A Body of Divinity, Containing the Rules of the Special Government of God* (London, 1659), pp. 186 and 193–194. See also his *Politica Sacra & Civilis: or, A Modell of Civil and Ecclesiasticall Government* (London, 1660), pp. 12–15.

without any other default or cause then that of the Governour, or *Pater Familia's* thereof, reduced to the greatest extremities, and in some respects annihilated? Where is then this care that each man hath of his own Properties?[9]

Roger Coke, a nephew of the Chief Justice, did not notice the patriarchalism of the *Leviathan*. Instead, he insisted that the alleged natural equality of the Hobbesian state of nature had never existed. Coke used the standard identification of familial and political authority and cited the patriarchal monarchy of Adam and the filial subordination of all subsequent generations in support of his contentions.[10] However, even granting that there may have been a state of nature and contract of government, Coke asked, 'If onely these be *cives* who made this *civitas*, and they onely subject to it? then were Women and Children, who were none of the *cives* that made this *civitas* free and independent from it.'[11]

This criticism is similar to Filmer's arguments against Hunton, but Coke did not have so thorough a command of the patriarchal doctrines as Sir Robert; he obviously did not realize that the premise on which his objections were based also provided a possible answer to his question. Women and children 'were none of the *cives* that made this *civitas*' because they were ineligible to participate. They were dependent upon their husbands and fathers and therefore had no political significance but were still bound to the state by the acts of their superiors. While Coke may not

[9] [John Shafte], *The Great Law of Nature, or Self-Preservation Examined, Asserted, and Vindicated from Mr. Hobbes His Abuses* (London, 1673), pp. 56–7.
[10] Roger Coke, *Justice Vindicated from the False Fucus Put upon It by Thomas White Gent., Mr. Thomas Hobbes, and Hugo Grotius* (London, 1660), p. 26. In another work Coke asserted that the powers given to Adam by God in Gen. 1: 27 and 28 were not fatherly: 'And that this supreme power was given to *Adam*, not as a Father, Husband, or Master of a Family, is manifest; for he was neither Father, Husband, nor Master of a Family; there being no Man or Woman in the world at that time.' (Coke, *Elements of Power & Subjection: or The Causes of all Humane, Christian, & Legal Society* [London, 1660], p. 34.) Nonetheless, Coke admitted on the next page that at least until the enslavement of the Hebrews, monarchical authority was the preserve of the first father to whose son it descended by primogeniture. Cf. Filmer, *Anarchy*, p. 289.
[11] Coke, *Justice Vindicated*, Preface, sig. A3.

have accepted this reasoning, his criticism of Hobbes was invalid at least at this point.

Thomas Tenison, who became Archbishop of Canterbury in 1690 when the non-juring William Sancroft was deprived of his See, also opposed Hobbes's egalitarian state of nature and presented the pre-political family as an alternative. 'Common sense, whereby one apprehends in another's birth, the manner of his own, doth sufficiently instruct us in this truth', according to Tenison, 'that we are born, and grow up under Government; Our Parents being before the Institution of Commonwealth, absolute Soveraigns in their own Families.' Therefore, to talk about 'such a state of nature as supposeth an Independency of one person upon another' is to disregard human experience as well as the history of Moses 'and to put some such cheat upon the World, as Nurses are wont, in sport, to put upon unwarry Children, when they tell them, they started out of the Parsley-bed'.[12]

Edward Hyde, the first Earl of Clarendon, also accepted the patriarchal origin of government but qualified its use in his critique of the *Leviathan*. 'I will gratifie him [Hobbes], by not insisting upon the Paternal Dominion', he wrote, 'otherwise than as it must be confessed to be the original of Monarchy, because we will do the Mother no wrong, who is so meet a help in the generation.' This patriarchal headship was transformed when families became so large and extensive that in order to wield sufficient authority 'they who had the Soveraign Power, exercis'd less of the paternal Affection in their Government, and looked upon those govern'd as mere Subjects, not as their Allies'. Like Filmer, Clarendon suggested that a theory of original and natural equality was incompatible with the continuous transmission of obligation from one generation to the next,[13] though he certainly need not have derived the argument from Sir Robert.

[12] [Thomas Tenison], *The Creed of Mr. Hobbes Examined; in a Feigned Conference between Him and a Student in Divinity* (London, 1670), p. 132. Tenison went even further than Filmer in examining the patriarchal elements in Hobbes's position, and I shall incorporate some of his remarks into my analysis of Hobbes rather than present them here without the texts at which they were directed.

[13] Edward Hyde, *A Brief View and Survey of the Dangerous and Pernicious Errors ... in Mr. Hobbes's Book Entitled Leviathan* (Oxford, 1676), pp. 65, 69, and 51–2.

2

The logical and moral gulf between contemporary political obligation and an earlier original compact was one of the major problems confronted by contract theorists,[14] and Filmer was not the first critic to exploit it. However, he does appear to have been the first English writer who developed this criticism into an elaborate and tenable position. His formulation may well have influenced later thinkers, even though they did not refer to any of his writings. Robert Sanderson, for instance—in his 1661 Preface to Archbishop Ussher's *Power Communicated by God*— used notions that had previously been employed only by Filmer. Who actually agreed to a contract of government? Sanderson asked, and his examples reflect an obvious patriarchal bias and suggest that he relied upon the *Anarchy*:

Of what sort of persons did the People, who are supposed to have made the first Contract in this kind, consist? Were all, without difference of Age, Sex, Condition, or other respect, promiscuously permitted to drive the bargain, or not? Had Women, and Children, and Mad-men, and Fools, the freedom of suffrage, as well as men of Age and Fortunes, and understanding? Or were any of them excluded? If any excluded, who excluded them? by whose order, and by what Authority was it done? and who gave them that Authority? If all were admitted, whether with equal right to every one, or with some inequality? Was the Wifes interest towards making up the bargain equal with that of her Husband? and the Childs with that of his Parents? and the Servants (if there were or could be any such thing as Master or Servant) with that of his Master? If every one had not an equal share and interest in the business, whence did the Inequality arise? who made the difference between them? and what right had any man, and how came he to have that right, to give more or less power to one than to another? If all were equal, who could summon the rest to convene together? or appoint the day and place of meeting? or when they were met, take upon him the Authority and Office of regulating their proceeding, of presiding or moderating in the Assembly, or determining such doubts and differences as might arise while matters were under debate, of calculating the

---

[14] See Gough, *Social Contract*, pp. 18 and 139 *et passim*, and J. F. M. Hunter, 'The Logic of Social Contracts', *Dialogue*, V (1966), 31–46.

voices and drawing up the Articles of Agreement, in case they should agree?'[15]

Sanderson also attacked the notion that a contract of government could bind even those who had not accepted its provisions or were not present when it was ratified. Before a government has been created, he said, there would be no laws that could either establish majority rule or require attendance at a meeting. And, of course, he asked how 'a Contract made by such Persons that were at Liberty before, can debar those that shall succeed them in the next Generation from their use of that Liberty their Ancestors had enjoyed?' There was no contractual basis for government, Sanderson concluded, for Adam, Noah, and Noah's sons had been made absolute patriarchal monarchs by the direct commission of God 'without awaiting the Election or consent of, or entering into any Article or Capitulations with the People that were to be governed by them'. The great noise that 'this supposed Pact or Contract' makes 'in the World, proveth to be but a Squib, Powder without shot, that giveth a Crack, but vanisheth into Air and doth no execution'.[16]

Fourteen years earlier, in 1647, Sanderson had given a course of lectures at Oxford entitled *De Obligatione Conscientiae*, in which his derivation of the state from patriarchal beginnings was much more vivid:

*Political Domination at the Beginning* was only the off-spring of *paternal power:* . . . Nations did not grow up into Kingdoms and Commonwealths by the mutual consent of the people, but . . . all Empire amongst the posterity of *Noah*, did for a while consist within the bounds of paternal Authority.

However, there were no kings at the time of Noah or even in ancient Greece, Sanderson said, distinguishing between political and familial authority. People were ruled by the love and gentleness of fathers and did not need the coercive restraints of magistrates. 'All Domination at that time consisted in the power of Heads of Familys,' and the eldest son of each family, 'without

[15] Robert Sanderson, Preface to Ussher, *The Power Communicated by God*, 2nd ed., sect. xvi (sigs. D6–D7ᵛ). Cf. Filmer, *Anarchy*, p. 287.
[16] Ibid., sects. xvii (sigs. D7ᵛ–D8), and xviii (sigs. E2ᵛ–E3).

any suffrages or election, was by a certain Right privilege of Nature, the Governour of all things both *Holy* and *Civil*'. As these family units grew larger and further apart, the power by which they were governed became more overtly political. Eventually the distinctions between family and state disappeared:

so little is the difference betwixt the Prince of a great Family, and a King of a small Territory, that they seem to differ more in Name, and Bulk, than in Deed, and Power, so that it is not to be doubted (if a true Calculation be made) but that the Domination of a family in the processe of Time, did by degrees, and by an unperceived inlargement, grow up into a Kingly Name, and Power; And the Original of the greatest Empire, is no where else to be exhacted [*sic*], but from this Head. And this far there is nothing more plain, nothing more sure, than that in the conferring Kingly power, the people had no part at all, neither indeed could have.[17]

Sanderson insisted that a people was entitled to select its ruler only when a king died without leaving an heir. But even in this case, the electors were not the authors or source of political power; they merely designated its next holder.[18] Sanderson's argument was clearly genetic, for he moved from the origins of kingship in familial rule to the inability of the people to choose their governors. In the same manner, he used the divine institution of primogenitive succession in the pre-political family to show that monarchy was the most natural form of government. The political order in 'which the first born of the whole Family doth succeed to his Fathers rights, as the next heir, is justly to be preferred before the rest, for many considerable reasons,' he wrote, 'but especially for this, because it best of all answers to that Original, to which it seems that Nature itself in some sort hath

[17] Robert Sanderson, *Several Cases of Conscience Discussed in Ten Lectures*, trans. Robert Codrington (London, 1660), Lect. vii, sect. 16, pp. 254–7. Although they had been delivered in 1647, the lectures were not printed until 1660; Codrington's translation appeared the same year as the original Latin edition. Locke drew much from this work in writing his early *Tracts on Government*, as they are now called. See Philip Abrams, Introduction to John Locke, *Two Tracts on Government*, ed. and trans. Abrams (Cambridge, 1967), pp. 71–4, and Abrams' notes to his translation of the 'Second Tract', pp. 210ff.

[18] Sanderson, *Several Caces*, vii, 20, p. 260. Cf. Filmer, *Patriarcha*, pp. 61–2.

made man'.[19] In general, Sanderson's position was a common-place and sketchy statement of the moral patriarchal thesis. There was nothing in the 1647 lectures to suggest the attack on the un-stated suppositions of the contract theory he was to employ in his Preface to Ussher. In the intervening period, his argument was expanded, and it is not unreasonable to suggest that a reading of Filmer might have contributed to the changes.

## 3

Richard Cumberland, afterward Bishop of Peterborough, writing in 1672, conceived of the origin of *'civil Societies'* in two laws of nature: the inviolability of private property 'as well in Things as in human Labour' and the *'peculiar Benevolence of Parents towards their Children'*. This benevolence led to the voluntary tempering of what was apparently an absolute author-ity. Thus, it was quite likely, according to Cumberland, that when the number and size of families increased, *'some* Heads of Families, either in their own Life time, or by their Testaments at their Death, might divide their Dominion among many Sons, by giving to each an absolute Command over his Family, or over many'. This division would have created numerous monarchies; 'Other Heads of Families might also elsewhere settle *Aristocracies, others, Democracies.*' Cumberland followed traditional patriar-chal reasoning and drew his account of political origins from Mosaic history, which, he said, 'acknowledges no *antienter Authority*, under God, over Things and Persons, than is that of *Fathers of Families* over their Wives and Children, and after them, of their eldest Sons'.[20]

In an obvious rejection of the Hobbesian state of nature,[21] Cumberland maintained that nowhere in the Bible is it stated ' "That *Adam* and *Eve* had such a Right to all things, as made it lawful for them," (if they had through a mistake imagin'd it

---

[19] Sanderson, *Several Cases*, vii, 17, p. 257.
[20] Richard Cumberland, *A Treatise of the Laws of Nature*, trans. John Maxwell (London, 1727), Introduction, sect. 26, pp. 32–3. (This work was originally published in 1672 as *De Legibus Naturae*.)
[21] Much of Cumberland's massive book was a diatribe against Hobbes's moral and political theories.

conducive to their own Preservation,) "to wage War with GOD, and with one another, without the Provokation of an Injury; and so mutually deprive one another of Food and Life."' On the contrary, man's life in the earliest days was virtually without care, and there was no communal ownership that would lead to strife and war because property was already divided. Yet, the Bishop subsequently implied that property as estate was originally held in common and was appropriated by the individual labor of each person, a source of title that was 'ratify'd and ascertain'd by common Consent for the future'.[22]

Cumberland's patriarchalism was anthropological, and he does not appear to have drawn any moral inferences from his reading of Biblical history. However, when the Bishop made his statements about the paternalistic origins of governance and said that a family 'was the *first regular Society*, and the *first Civil State*', John Maxwell, his translator of 1727, vigorously objected in a note, 'Parental Power is wholly upon a different Foundation, see Mr. *Locke* on Government'.[23] Yet Cumberland and Locke were closer on this particular question than Maxwell realized. Although Cumberland rejected the contractual explanation of the origin of government and insisted upon its familial beginnings, he did not derive political obligation from filial obedience but from the natural law requiring every man to promote the 'common good', which was itself justified on utilitarian grounds:

The Endeavour, to the utmost of our power, of promoting the common Good of the whole System of rational agents, conduces, as far as in us lies, to the good of every Part, in which our own Happiness, as that of a Part, is contain'd. But contrary Actions produce contrary Effects, and consequently our own Misery, among that of others.[24]

---

[22] Ibid., pp. 33–4 and Bk. I, sect. 23, pp. 66–7. Cf. I, 30, p. 80 (existence of private property at the time of Adam), VII, 2, p. 314 (consent as the basis of private ownership), and VII, 8, p. 321 (a communal society preceding the private ownership of property).

[23] Ibid., IX, 6, p. 350 and Maxwell's note.

[24] Ibid., Introduction, sect. 12, p. 16. See also IX, 5, p. 348. Cumberland has been described as 'the first English moralist who can properly be termed a Utilitarian'. Ernest Albee, *A History of English Utilitarianism* (1901), paperbound (New York, 1962), p. 30. See pp. 30–62 for an account of Cumberland with an emphasis upon the utilitarian aspects of his doctrines.

While Cumberland was publishing his *De Legibus Naturae*, Sir William Temple was writing his 'Essay on the Original and Nature of Government', in which he developed a theory of limited government based on patriarchal beginnings and without referring to the Bible. Temple's analysis was, on the whole, the fullest and best of the patriarchal accounts of political origins that appeared with increasing frequency after the Restoration. He rejected the warlike state of nature as psychologically and historically untenable and asked, apparently of Hobbes, how men who were naturally like wolves could possibly endure government. The contract theory, Temple said, was more relevant to poetry than to political history, for it was 'some of the old Poets' who raised men 'out of the ground by great numbers at a time, in perfect Stature and Strength'. Those persons who met and agreed to a compact of government, he countered, assembled 'not as so many single heads, but as so many heads of families, whom they represent, in the framing of any Compact or common accord; and consequently, as persons, who have already an Authority over such numbers as their families are composed of'. These fathers would be able to exercise a patriarchal power, Temple held, so long as they protected and adequately cared for their children and thereby retained their respect. Properly trained children will be inclined

to believe what he [their father] teaches, to follow what he advises, and obey what he commands. Thus the Father, by natural Right as well as Authority, becomes a Governour in his little State: and if his life be long, and his generations many (as well as those of his Children) He grows [into] the Governour or King of a Nation, and is indeed a *Pater patriae*, as the best Kings are, as all should be; and as those which are not, are yet content to be called.[25]

'Thus a Family seems to become a little Kingdom, and a Kingdom to be but a great Family', Temple wrote; he then described the practice of according power to elders, succession by primogeniture, and the rise of the household as something more than the nuclear family, all of which strengthened the principle

[25] [William Temple], 'An Essay upon the Original and Nature of Government' (written in 1672), *Miscellanea* (London, 1680), pp. 62–6. On the last quotation, cf. Locke, *Two Treatises*, II, 75 and 76.

and operation of patriarchal government. He admitted that 'Governments founded upon Contract, may have succeeded those founded upon [paternal] Authority' but suggested that the first contract of government 'seems to have been agreed between Princes and Subjects, [rather] than between men of equal Rank and Power'.[26] Temple was here referring to the subjugation that arose out of conquest; in his previously quoted remarks about the consent of fathers, he was apparently thinking of the amalgamation of several familial states.[27]

[26] Ibid., pp. 68–76.
[27] For previous recognitions of the patriarchalism in Temple's 'Essay', see Frank I. Herriot, 'Sir William Temple on the Origin and Nature of Government', *Annals of the American Academy*, III (1892–3), 150–79; Homer E. Woodbridge, *Sir William Temple: The Man and His Work* (New York, 1940), pp. xi and 141; and Isaac Kramnick, *Bolingbroke and His Circle: The Politics of Nostalgia in the Age of Walpole* (Cambridge, Mass., 1968), pp. 108–10. Kramnick, who sees Temple as a possible source for Bolingbroke's attack on the contract, has provided the most balanced account.

# XI

## Exclusion, Expulsion and Jacobite Loyalty: English Patriarchalism from 1679 to 1714

### I

If the quality and temper of the tracts published prior to 1678 are accurate indications, the first eighteen years of Charles II's reign were relatively free of major political controversies. But from October, 1678, when the false depositions of Titus Oates touched off the hysteria of the Popish Plot, until the King's death in 1685, Charles was at the center of disputes about the nature of governmental authority, at least in the writings of his subjects if not always in fact. The growing animosity toward the monarchy increased when the Roman Catholic James II succeeded his brother. These differences were certainly not settled by the 1688 Revolution, for James left behind an exceptionally articulate group of supporters when he departed for France. Their cause was hopeless, but they continued to insist that William and Mary ruled illegally because Parliament had overstepped its authority in summoning them. Behind this Jacobite reasoning lay the venerable doctrine of non-resistance to established powers, which became the ideology of the Tories in the early eighteenth century.

The Exclusion Controversy raised the same issues that Englishmen had been debating since James I championed the theory of absolutism early in the century, the relationship between King and Parliament and the sources and extents of their separate authorities. Three successive Parliaments attempted to disqualify the Duke of York from succeeding to the throne. These Parliaments thereby claimed that the legislature at least shared in the exercise of sovereignty because it was the spokesman for the people and the guardian of their interests. The royalists countered that the powers of government belonged exclusively to the monarch and were the unassailable gift of God.

This doctrine had, of course, been fully expounded by Sir Robert Filmer, whose works were issued in 1679 and 1680 as answers to the Exclusion tracts. They were frequently republished during the next sixteen years, and the Archbishop of Canterbury, William Sancroft, personally provided an authentic text of *Patriarcha* from which Edmund Bohun published the second edition in 1685.[1] The Filmerian position very nearly became the official state ideology. As Algernon Sidney complained just before his execution for treason in 1683, 'The whole matter is reduced to the Papers said to be found in my Closet by the King's Officers.' These papers 'plainly appear to relate unto a large Treatise written long since in Answer to *Filmer's* Book, which by all intelligent Men, is thought to be grounded upon wicked Principles, equally pernicious unto Magistrates and People'.[2] James Tyrrell's *Patriarcha non Monarcha* was also a critique of Filmer as were portions of other Whig tracts. However, the most renowned of Sidney's 'intelligent Men' was John Locke. Peter Laslett suggests that the *Two Treatises* may have been composed at the request of the Earl of Shaftesbury, Locke's patron and the leader of the exclusionists in Parliament.[3]

There would be no point in examining the minute details of the attacks on Filmer by Locke, Tyrrell, and Sidney. Their books were often page-by-page critiques of *Patriarcha* and the other works, and many of their arguments were directed at Sir Robert's

[1] Edmund Bohun, *Diary and Autobiography*, ed. S. Wilton Rix (Beccles, Suffolk, 1853), p. 67. See also Bohun's Preface to Robert Filmer, *Patriarcha . . .*, 2nd ed., ed. Bohun (London, 1685), sig. (a). Cited throughout as Bohun's *Patriarcha*.

The publication of the second edition of *Patriarcha* and the reissue of Filmer's works from 1680 on are discussed in my article, 'Sir Robert Filmer: Some New Bibliographic Discoveries', *The Library*, XXVI (1971), 135–60.

[2] Algernon Sidney, *The Very Copy of a Paper Delivered to the Sheriff* (1683), reprinted in *The Dying Speeches and Behaviour of the Several State Prisoners that Have Been Executed in the Last 300 Years* (London, 1720), p. 434.

[3] Laslett, Introduction to Locke, *Two Treatises*, pp. 58–61

interpretations of Scripture and English constitutional history. Nonetheless, the central questions were always the nature of familial authority and its relations to politics. The critics agreed that Adam's power was irrelevant to political obligation in seventeenth-century England, for Filmer had not shown how that authority had descended to the house of Stuart. Locke's comments in section one of the 'Second Treatise' would undoubtedly have been approved by Sidney and Tyrrell:

> it is impossible that the Rulers now on Earth, should make any benefit, or derive any the least shadow of Authority from that, which is held to be the Fountain of all Power, *Adam's Private Dominion and Paternal Jurisdiction*, so that, he that will not give just occasion, to think that all Government in the World is not the product only of Force and Violence, and that Men live together by no other Rules but that of Beasts, where the strongest carries it, and so lay a Foundation for perpetual Disorder and Mischief, Tumult, Sedition and Rebellion, (things that the followers of that Hypothesis so loudly cry out against) must of necessity find out another rise of Government, another Original of Political Power, and another way of designing and knowing the Persons that have it, then what Sir *Robert F.* hath taught us.[4]

''Tis not enough to make a Man a Subject, to convince him that there is *Regal Power* in the World,' Locke wrote in the 'First Treatise', 'but there must be ways of designing, and knowing the Person to whom this *Regal Power* of Right belongs'. A man cannot be obliged to submit to any authority without first knowing 'who has the Right to Exercise that Power over him'. Therefore, even assuming that Adam had absolute political power, Filmer had to show that Adam's authority was conveyed to someone else at his death and that sovereigns now ruling 'are possessed of this *Power of Adam*, by a right way of conveyance derived to them'. Failing these, either a new source of governance must be found, or all present governments are illegitimate, and subjects are freed from their obligations to them.[5] Filmer had admitted that knowledge of the true heir to Adam's power was lost,[6] and Tyrrell therefore concluded that 'this Right of *Adam*,

---

[4] Locke, *Two Treatises*, II, 1.

[5] Ibid., I, 81, 82, and 83.

[6] Filmer, *Patriarcha*, p. 61.

as Lord and King of the whole World, as the first man, must certainly be extinct, since none but the true Heir could have a Right to that (according to the Author's principles)'.[7] Locke and Sidney reached the same conclusion.[8] Thomas Hunt, a previously unrecognized critic of Filmer's, wrote that since the heir to Adam's power is unknown, 'we can have no rightful King in the World'. The duties and rights that result from familial relations cannot be 'exercised or exacted by and between any persons, but the Relatives themselves', Hunt continued. Thus, this patriarchal power 'of Sir *R. F.* hath no foundation of [*sic*] reason in the nature of things, was in Fact never exercised, and is now utterly fallen to the ground, and all Government with it'.[9]

Locke, Tyrrell, and Sidney examined the entire patriarchal argument and asserted that Adam had never been an absolute monarch. The authority that all men possessed as fathers and husbands was the only power they conceded to Adam.[10] Sidney held that even if Adam had been an absolute patriarchal ruler, later ages would not be required to follow the same pattern. The conditions of life change, and men are no more bound to accept the governmental structure of their ancestors 'than to live upon acorns, or inhabit hollow trees, because their fathers did it, when they had no better dwellings, and found no better nourishment in the uncultivated world'. Sidney explicitly rejected the genetic presuppositions of the patriarchal doctrine and accepted instead a notion of historical change. 'Men are subject to errors', he said, 'and it is the work of the best and wisest to discover and amend such as their ancestors may have committed, or to add perfection to those things which by them have been well invented.'[11] Tyrrell similarly criticized Filmer's use of origins to determine successive obligation, writing that even if Adam's power was monarchical

---

[7] [James Tyrrell], *Patriarcha non Monarcha: or, The Patriarch Unmonarched* (London, 1681), p. 12. Cited throughout as [Tyrrell], *P.N.M.*
[8] Locke, *Two Treatises*, I, 104 and 105; Algernon Sidney, *Discourses Concerning Government* (1698), in *Works*, ed. J. Robertson (London, 1772), i, 12 and 14. Cited throughout as Sidney, *Discourses*; all quotations will be from the Robertson edition.
[9] Thomas Hunt, *Mr. Hunts Postscript for Rectifying Some Mistakes in the Inferiour Clergy* (London, 1682), pp. 59–60.
[10] Locke, *Two Treaties*, I, 40; [Tyrrell], *P.N.M.*, p. 13; and Sidney, *Discourses*, ii, 2, p. 69.
[11] Sidney, *Discourses*, ii, 8, p. 99, and iii, 25, pp. 403–4. See also i, 6.

through 'Gods bare Approbation, [this fact] lays no Obligation for all mankind to practise it now, any more than it is a good Argument to say, that it is now not onely lawful, but necessary for men to marry their Sisters, because God approved of that way of propagation of mankind at first'. Locke simply asserted that 'at best an Argument from what has been, to what should of right be, has no great force'.[12]

Even if Adam had possessed the power of an absolute Monarch, and even if his authority had descended by the right of primogeniture, Tyrrell said, Noah's dividing the world into three parts[13] ended the patriarchal basis of political authority, for that act destroyed the claim of the first-born. If the children of Noah 'could divide themselves into as many distinct Governments as there were Sons', Tyrrell asked, 'Why might not they do so *in infinitum*? And then there could never be any common Prince or Monarch set over them all, but by Force or Conquest, or else by Election; either of which destroys the notion of Natural Right of Eldership'.[14] In other words, as Locke pointed out, if the right of fatherhood 'does give *Royal Authority*, then every one that has *Paternal Power* has *Royal Authority*, and then by our *A's* Patriarchal Government, there will be as many Kings as there are Fathers'.[15] The controversy was not about the power of Adam and Noah but concerned the nature and political significance of patriarchal authority itself. Accordingly, all Filmer's critics examined primogenitive succession and agreed that whether fatherly power was political or merely familial, it could not be inherited or transferred. As Sidney argued, in sentiments that were echoed by Locke, Tyrrell, and Hunt, 'No man can be my father but he that did beget me; and it is as absurd to say I owe that duty to one who is not my father, which I owe to my father, as to say, he did beget me, who did not beget me; for the obligation that arises from benefits can only be to him that conferred them.'[16]

[12] [Tyrrell], *P.N.M.*, p. 94; and Locke, *Two Treatises*, II, 103 (see also I, 58 and 59).

[13] See Filmer, *Patriarcha*, pp. 58–9.

[14] [Tyrrell], *P.N.M.*, p. 38. See also Locke, *Two Treatises*, I, 65 and 139.

[15] Locke, *Two Treatises*, I, 70. See also sect. 68. The same argument was made by Sidney, *Discourses*, i, 9.

[16] Sidney, *Discourses*, i, 17, p. 43; Locke, *Two Treatises*, I, 74; [Tyrrell], *P.N.M.*, p. 48; and Hunt, *Postscript*, p. 72.

In a very important sense, the entire question of the power of Adam and its literal descent to the House of Stuart was academic, for Filmer had not claimed that any reigning monarch was the lineal descendant of Adam or of one of the sons of Noah. On the contrary, he had stated that it was 'the manner of government by supreme power that makes them [i.e., rulers] Kings, and not the means of obtaining their crowns'.[17] The critics were unanimous in their insistence that Filmer's theories of usurpation and prescriptive sovereignty provided no foundation for government but actually detracted from the patriarchal thesis. Locke mockingly rebuked Filmer for being 'the first Politician, who, pretending to settle Government upon its true Basis, and to establish the Thrones of lawful Princes, ever told the World, That he was *properly a King, whose Manner of Government was by Supreme Power, by what Means soever he obtained it*'. Sir Robert's doctrines, he implied, could justify a Cromwell's claim to the throne. Tyrrell concurred, and Sidney believed that the theory would be an invitation to usurpers.[18] In addition, Sidney observed that if the title of a usurper can be passed on to his heirs, monarchy cannot be identified with fatherhood.[19] Hunt wrote:

[Filmer's] hypothesis will not allow at all of Hereditary rightful Succession: For he, establishing the right of the universal Empire of the world in *Adams* right Heir, since this Illuminatio[n] hath enlightened the World, no Successor can, according to his Doctrine, derive any hereditary right from his Predecessor. His title can only be his own possession; for no man can claim by descent the Usurpation of his Father, but he that is not conscious to this wrong, and is bonae fidei possessor, under the presumed right and title of his Father.[20]

According to his critics, Filmer was not even correct in his description of the *familial* powers of the father. Tyrrell, Locke, and Hunt charged that in the first place paternity does not itself constitute the basis of the father's powers, for men often become

---

[17] Filmer, *Patriarcha*, p. 106. See also *Directions*, p. 233, *Originall*, p. 256, and *Anarchy*, p. 288.

[18] Locke, *Two Treatises*, I, 79; [Tyrrell], *P.N.M.*, Preface, sig. A3, and pp. 65 and 69; and Sidney, *Discourses*, i, 19, p. 48.

[19] Sidney, *Discourses*, i, 14, pp. 31–2.

[20] Hunt, *Postscript*, pp. 43–4.

parents involuntarily. As Hunt observed, God planted in man 'powerful and irresistible instincts to procreation' and commanded him to increase and multiply to preserve the human race. When men follow these instincts, they generally are not aware that they are obeying a command of God but instead are usually 'gratifying their own Natures. What from all this can give them a right over their Child?' Parents 'do not give us life,' he continued, 'but hand it over to us from the fountain of being, the Universal Father of all things.'[21] Locke and Tyrrell added that the mother as well as the father would have to be included in any title derived from generation.[22] The actual source of parents' rights to the obedience of their children, Tyrrell wrote, 'is not merely natural, from generation; but acquir'd by their performance of that nobler part of their duty'. Because discipline is essential to education, according to Hunt, parents have the 'duty' to correct their offspring. He was insistent, however, that parental correction 'doth not participate any thing of the Nature of Civil Government. It hath nothing of the Nature of Punishment, examplarity, or vindicative Justice.'[23]

Tyrrell was more specific than Hunt in attempting to prove that subordination to his parents did not deprive an individual of his political freedom. His argument relied in large part upon the doctrine of 'nonage' and children's needs for education and discipline during their minority when they lacked rationality and were not yet responsible for their actions. Filmer had claimed that 'in nature there is no nonage; if a man be not born free, she doth not assign him any other time when he shall attain his freedom'.[24] Tyrrell held in response, 'There really is an Age of Nonage in nature . . . in which though the Child be indeed free, yet (by reason of his own want of strength and discretion) is obliged to submit himself to his Parents judgment in all things conducing to that end.' He supported his claim by referring to an earlier part of *Patriarcha non Monarcha* in which he had written:

In the first Period [of their lives], all the actions of Children are under the absolute dominion of their Parents: for since they have

[21] Ibid., pp. 62–3.
[22] [Tyrrell], *P.N.M.*, pp. 14–16; and Locke, *Two Treatises*, I, 54, and II, 6, 52, and 53.
[23] [Tyrrell], *P.N.M.*, p. 16; and Hunt, *Postscript*, pp. 65–6.
[24] Filmer, *Anarchy*, p. 287.

not the use of Reason, nor are able to judge what is good or bad for themselves, they could not grow up nor be preserved, unless their Parents judged for them what means conduced to this end; yet this power is still to be directed for the principal end, the good and preservation of the Child.

Parental dominion ended when the child developed judgment and had repaid his father's 'charge and trouble in bringing him up', which, Tyrrell suggested, 'may very well be by that time the Child attains to twenty five years of age at farthest'.[25]

These comments about nonage do not adequately answer Filmer, for it had not yet been demonstrated that paternal power was *different in kind* from political authority. Strongly arguing that there was such a distinction, Tyrrell said:

I will not deny that the Heads of separate Families, being out of Commonwealths, have many things analogous to them, though they are not Commonwealths themselves: And the reason why I do not allow them to be so, is, because the ends of a Family and a Commonwealth are divers.[26]

In a later work, *Bibliotheca Politica*, a collection of thirteen dialogues, each of which was published separately from 1691 to 1694, Tyrrell was more precise and explicitly distinguished between 'oeconomical' and civil authority. A father has 'oeconomical' power merely 'for the well ordering and preservation of his Family', but civil authority, he said, is designed to protect subjects and their lives and properties from one another and from foreign enemies and to make laws for those purposes. Even this distinction broke down, however, for Tyrrell subsequently admitted that the two authorities 'do not differ in kind, but in largness or extent'.[27]

---

[25] [Tyrrell], *P.N.M.*, pp. 75, 19, and 32.

[26] Ibid., p. 35. Tyrrell's argument is similar to the Aristotelian notion that Filmer had criticized in *Patriarcha* (p. 76, quoted above, p. 147). Tyrrell neither cited this passage nor showed how his formulation of the distinction escaped Filmer's criticisms. In fact, because the two positions rest upon incompatible assumptions about the nature of social and political relationships, it is probably not possible to defend one in terms that would be acceptable to proponents of the other.

[27] [James Tyrrell], *Bibliotheca Politica: or An Inquiry into the Ancient Constitution of the British Government* (London, 1691–1694), pp. 10 and 64.

Despite their adamant objections to Filmer's patriarchal thesis, all four of these critics recognized the close relationship between familial and political authority at some historical point. Although they generally attempted to maintain a normative distinction between the family and the state, these writers embraced the anthropological theory and agreed that the familial association was the progenitor of the political order. Tyrrell, at least, was consistent enough to maintain that there was never a *necessary* relation between the two forms of authority. Government, he contended, may spring from fatherly authority—not as an expression of the father's right but as a concomitant to it. If he had 'sufficient strength to perform the ends of a Commonwealth', the father of a large family might have become a prince. Nevertheless the tranformation of patriarchal into political power did not make the two kinds of control equivalent. Even if 'the first Kings were Fathers of Families', Tyrrell contended, it is not thereby proven 'that this proceeded from that natural perpetual subjection which Children owe their Parents; or that because they are Parents, they are therefore Lords and Kings over them'. A father's rule becomes political only for the good of the members of his family 'and by their implied consent'.[28] Government, according to Tyrrell, is 'an Authority over the person of a man' that had to be rooted in consent, for 'a man without his own act or consent can never lawfully fall into the power or possession of another'.[29]

Sidney suggested that political society might have originated in the uniting of independent and patriarchally ruled family groups but added that the process was purely voluntary. Like Tyrrell, he so qualified his doctrine as to make it totally distinct from Filmer's:

We have already seen, that the patriarchal power resembles not the regal in principle or practice; that the beginning and continuance of regal power was contrary to, and inconsistent with the patriarchal; that the first fathers of mankind left all their children independent of each other, and in an equal liberty of providing for themselves; that every man continued in this liberty, till the number so increased,

28 [Tyrrell], *P.N.M.*, pp. 47, 60, and 35. On 'implied consent', cf. Locke, *Two Treatises*, II, 74–6. The similarity between the positions of Locke and Tyrrell on this point is striking.
29 [Tyrrell], *P.N.M.*, pp. 63–4.

that they became troublesome and dangerous to each other; and finding no other remedy to the disorders growing, or like to grow among them, joined many families into one civil body, that they might the better provide for the convenience, safety, and defence of themselves and their children.[30]

Hunt merely acknowledged that fathers had exercised political authority over their families before the time of Noah. But this patriarchal rule was too gentle; it resulted in a 'Relaxation of Justice in the World before the Flood', for it sprang from the father's love of his children rather than from the need to discipline them. Because men were not adequately governed, the evil in the world increased. As a direct result, God sent the Deluge, a 'sad consequence of the natural Love in Parents toward their Children, which was intended for the propagation and advancement of Mankind'.[31] On a related issue, Tyrrell accepted Filmer's judgment that the division of the people of the world into distinct nations at Babel followed family lines, but he argued that the confusion of tongues still did not confirm a patriarchal right to governmental authority. God probably established familial nations, Tyrrell conjectured, 'for the better conservation of mutual Love and concord of neer Relations, since men would more readily obey their Ancestor or Common Father, than a meer stranger'.[32] Locke, on the other hand, ridiculed Filmer's position and asserted that there was nothing in the Bible to justify the claim that each language group was a family and therefore a state. The Biblical evidence, however, appears to support Sir Robert.[33]

Tyrrell's discussion of Babel and its aftermath brought him close to Filmer in yet another respect and demonstrated the underlying patriarchalism of his own libertarian doctrines as well as his implicit acceptance of the patriarchal ordering of Stuart society. Filmer, it will be recalled, had objected to the state of nature and contract theories on the ground that servants, children, and women would have outvoted their masters, fathers,

---

[30] Sidney, *Discourses*, ii, 1, pp. 59–60.

[31] Hunt, *Postscript*, p. 69.

[32] [Tyrrell], *P.N.M.*, p. 82. See Filmer, *Patriarcha*, pp. 55–9, and *Anarchy*, p. 290.

[33] Locke, *Two Treatises*, I, 144–5. Gen. 10: 31, for instance, is as follows: 'These are the sons of Shem, after their families, after their tongues, in their lands, after their nations.' See also verses 5 and 20.

and husbands.[34] Tyrrell replied that even a government that had originated in consent 'needed no Compact of all the People of the world, since every Father of a Family being independant [*sic*] upon any man else, had a power to confer his Authority of governing himself and his Family upon whom he pleased'. Women would not have taken part, he reasoned, for they are 'concluded by their Husbands, and [are] commonly unfit for civil business'. Children still living with their fathers would not have participated either, for they were included 'under the notion of Servants, and [were] without any Property in Goods or Land, [and therefore] had no reason to have Votes in the Institution of the Government'.[35] Similarly, Tyrrell prefixed the following 'Advertisement' to the first dialogue of *Bibliotheca Politica*: 'I Desire always to be understood, that when I make use of the word People, I do not mean the vulgar or mixt multitude, but in the state of Nature the whole Body of Free-men and women, *especially the Fathers and Masters of Families*; and in a Civil State, all degrees of men, as well the Nobility and Clergy, as the Common People.'[36]

Of Filmer's supporters in the 1680s, only Edmund Bohun attacked Sidney's scaffold paper in an anonymous defense of Sir Robert,[37] and the next year he published his edition of *Patriarcha* with 'A Preface to the Reader in which this Piece is vindicated from the Cavils and Misconceptions of the Author of a Book stiled *Patriarcha non Monarcha*'.[38] Bohun used all the standard patriarchal arguments, especially Adam's superiority to Eve before the Fall as the origin of kingship and the universal monarchy of Adam and Noah. 'If neither *Adam* nor Noah had a Sovereign Authority,' he claimed, 'then could their Children never have nor create any, for they succeeded to their Fathers Rights and no others.'[39] In only one respect did Bohun add to the moral patriarchal theory, but he does not seem to have appreciated the importance of the point he was making. The familial explanation of political obligation was regularly attacked because it did not

[34] Filmer, *Anarchy*, p. 287.
[35] [Tyrrell], *P.N.M.*, pp. 83–4. See also pp. 73–4 and 91–3.
[36] [Tyrrell], *Bibliotheca Politica*, sig. A3$^\mathrm{v}$.
[37] [Edmund Bohun], *A Defence of Sir Robert Filmer against the Mistakes and Misrepresentations of Algernon Sidney* (London, 1684).
[38] Bohun's *Patriarcha*, title page.
[39] Ibid., Preface, sigs. (a7)$^\mathrm{v}$–(b) and (e2)$^\mathrm{v}$.

account for the difference between the obedience that a child would owe to his father and grandfather. Filmer's explanation made it impossible to reconcile the multiplicity of rulers in the world with the origins of kingship in the universal, patriarchal monarchy of Adam. As Tyrrell complained, there can be no legitimate political power in the world other than what has been passed on to the lineal descendants of Adam.[40] Bohun replied that independent political authorities arose through the permission of the supreme ruler:

Mankind spreading apace, it is very probable that *Adam*, though he had a right, did not actually Govern all his own descendants to the time of his death, but left them to the care and government of their more immediate Parents, with or near whom they lived, who by his permission and appointments had as good Anthority to Govern under him as the *Deputy of Ireland* has by his Majesty's Authority, under him.

And when *Adam* died *Seth* was no ambitious youngling, and therefore it is probable left things in the state he found them, without aspiring to the Title or exercise of an universal Monarchy. And so as Mankind encreased in the World, new Principalities or Patriarchates arose, from the same principles and causes, the People in the mean time having no more hand in Electing their Governours *than* of their Fathers.[41]

So conceived, the government of the Biblical world would have resembled the theoretical structure of the medieval polity in which all power potentially belonged to a sovereign who sat astride a pyramid of delegated authority. Bohun's explanation was orderly, but his quasi-feudal interpretation of patriarchalism went too far, for the prime father was reduced to a meaningless figurehead. 'If *Ruben pledged his two Sons to his Father Jacob* for the *restoring Benjamin to him again*,' he said, 'it is as plain as the Nose on a

[40] [Tyrrell], *P.N.M.*, pp. 11–12.
[41] Bohun's *Patriarcha*, Preface, sigs. (b6)ᵛ–(b7). Cf. sig. (c7)ᵛ, where Bohun attributed the multiplicity of ruling fathers to circumstances rather than to the will of the prime head, saying that after the division of the world among Noah's sons, the different languages and wide dispersion of the population made it impossible for individuals to rule any one of the three parts. 'Therefore the Heads of the several Families took this care upon them, wherein they had the direction of God Almighty who had commanded them to obey their parents.'

Man's Face, that till this was done by *Ruben, Jacob* had no manner of Authority over his Grandchildren.'[42] This position is a
significant departure from Filmer's teaching; carried to its logical
conclusion, it supports the frequent criticism that the patriarchal
scheme would establish as many kings as there were fathers.


2


One of the most interesting but neglected tracts of the Exclusion Controversy was Henry Neville's *Plato Redivivus*, a work in
the tradition of Harrington's *Oceana* in its claim that property
and consent are the foundations of government.[43] Neville generally ignored the patriarchal theory of governmental origins, writing that he 'did not think it worth the taking notice of'. While he
acknowledged the difficulty of disproving patriarchalism directly,
Neville attacked the doctrine on historical grounds and suggested
that 'if we could trace all foundations of polities that now are, or
ever came to our knowledge since the world began; we shall find
none of them to have descended from paternal power'. This
patriarchal 'fancy' was originated 'not by the solid judgement of
any man,' he wrote, 'but to flatter some prince; and to assert,
for want of better arguments, the divine right of monarchy'. The
Biblical supports for the doctrine are also invalid, Neville believed, for he could find no texts that suggested that Adam and
Noah exercised paternal rule over the entire world; Abraham and
Isaac, for instance, were not governors but were merely 'ordinary
fathers and families', who simply 'governed their own household[s] as all others do'.[44]

---

[42] Ibid., Preface, sigs. (c5)–(c5)$^v$. See Gen. 13: 37.
[43] See Caroline Robbins, ed., *Two English Republican Tracts* (Cambridge,
1969), Introduction, pp. 5–20, for an account of Neville and his book.
(This work reprints Neville's *Plato Redivivus* and Walter Moyle's *Essay
upon the Constitution of the Roman Government* [first published in 1726].)
See also Robbins, *The Eighteenth Century Commonwealthman* (Cambridge, Mass., 1959), pp. 32–41. I am indebted to Professor Robbins for
assistance in identifying some of the attacks on Neville discussed in the
next few paragraphs.
[44] [Henry Neville], *Plato Redivivus: or, A Dialogue Concerning Government* (London, 1681), pp. 31–2; corrected according to the 2nd ed. as reprinted in Robbins, ed., *Tracts*, p. 86.

Neville's belief in the popular origins of political authority and his casual dismissal of patriarchalism were answered by at least three authors. John Northleigh, an ardent opponent of republicanism, said that the patriarchal power of Adam proves that God's sanction could not have extended to democracy. He relied upon the thirteenth chapter of Romans and wrote that in its first verse 'we have the Authority for the sole Sovereignty of every *Father of a Family*, from the very first Original of the World'. '*Popular* Supremacie', Northleigh continued, 'never commenced but by some Division in a Tribe or Family, and even they made some Head in that Division, which was no more than what we now call Rebellion and Usurpation.'[45] A critic, who identified himself only by the initials W.W., held that sovereignty could never have resided in the people because of the plenary powers God gave to Adam. This authority was inherited according to the principle of primogeniture, which was established 'by the universal and Eternal Law of God', and men were unable 'to interrupt or disturb it, less God sent his extraordinary commission'. Once the rights of primogeniture had been instituted, this author continued:

the Elders or Fathers of Families had by their Eldership not only Paternal but Regal power; . . . and from these original stock-fathers, Kingdoms and Monarchies, I suppose for the most part, have had their beginning without popular Election in their Commencement; But Violence of War, Vulgar Commotions and otherwise may in most places have interrupted and altered the course of Succession contrary to this divine institution.[46]

Finally, Thomas Goddard viewed paternal authority as the source of political right in the pre-Mosaic world and of the natural inequality of men for all time. Little is known about the period between Adam and Noah, he wrote, but it is evident

[45] John Northleigh, *The Triumph of Our Monarchy, over the Plots and Principles of Our Rebels and Republicans* (London, 1685), pp. 164–5. (Northleigh's book was anonymously republished in 1699 as *Remarks upon the Most Eminent of Our Anti-Monarchical Authors and Their Writings*. The only known copy is in the British Museum, where it is catalogued as an anonymous work; Wing follows the B.M. [Wing no. R-949].)

[46] [W.W.], *Antidotum-Britannicum: or, A Counter-Pest against the Destructive Principles of Plato Redivivus* (London, 1681), pp. 26–8.

that after the Flood the world was 're-peopled and govern'd absolutely by *Fathers of Families*'. If the world was 'peopled, as well before the Flood as since' by procreation, which 'begets Inequality', Goddard reasoned, '*Noah*, as well as *Adam*, being our first Parent, should have been an Universal Monarch,' for 'Inequality necessarily produces Superiority'.[47]

At one point, Northleigh, unlike Filmer, took the patriarchal doctrine literally and attempted to show that the ancient Saxon rulers of Britain claimed their titles by direct descent from a grandson of Noah. The Saxon Heptarchy continued by a 'Paternal Right', he said, which 'is proved by the most learned Pens, and these Saxons are believed to have been the relict of the race of *Cimbrians*, that inhabited that *Chersonese*, so called from its Inhabitants, of whom *Gomer* the son of *Japhet* was the Original *Father* or *Prince*'.[48] On another level, however, Northleigh attacked the literal interpretation of the descent of political authority from Noah. Sidney had asserted that lineal descent from one of Noah's sons was the only legitimate base for monarchy that could be reconciled with patriarchalism.[49] Northleigh charged that this argument is an 'absurdity which is truly their *own*, by supposing it *ours*, when it can't be truly deduced from the Doctrine and defense of a *Divine* right'. Therefore, he wrote —switching from a moral to an anthropological patriarchalism— it is 'one thing to say a paternal Right was once Monarchical; but must it make all Monarchs to Rule by a paternal Right?' There is no reason 'why Monarchy may not still be said to have been first founded in a paternal Right, though the claims to Sovereign power since, in such several Kingdoms, and Nations where it is now Establish'd, are of as several sorts too, as there are Subjects that have submitted to be govern'd by it'.[50] However, Northleigh did not explain why patriarchal origins would even be relevant once it was acknowledged that there were 'several sorts' of presumably valid 'claims to sovereign power'.

[47] Thomas Goddard, *Plato's Demon: or, The State-Physician Unmaskt* (London, 1684), pp. 78 and 15.
[48] Northleigh, *Triumph*, p. 26.
[49] Sidney, *Very Copy*, in *Dying Speeches*, p. 437. This argument, of course, was quite popular among anti-patriarchalists.
[50] Northleigh, *Triumph*, pp. 618 and 628.

3

On 21 July 1683, the Convocation of Oxford University passed its famous *Judgment and Decree* 'Against certain PERNICIOUS BOOKS *and* DAMNABLE DOCTRINES, Destructive to the Sacred Persons of PRINCES, their STATE and GOVERNMENT, and of all HUMANE SOCIETY'.[51] The *Judgment and Decree* was largely an attack on voluntarist and populist principles, but it also censured the presumed individualism and prescriptivist notions of Hobbes. In short, anything detrimental to passive obedience and divine right absolutism was denounced. Among the propositions singled out for condemnation were the following: that 'All Civil Authority is derived originally from the People' and that 'There is a mutual compact, tacit or express, between a Prince and his Subjects; and that if he perform not his duty, they are discharged from theirs.'[52] The Convocation did not identify acceptable alternative principles, but there are grounds for believing that the patriarchal theory of obligation would have met with its approval. It was only a few months after the issuance of the *Judgment and Decree*, in September 1683, that James Parkinson was expelled from Lincoln College, Oxford, for, among other things, urging his students to read Milton as an antidote to Filmer. And it has been shown that throughout the century moral patriarchalism was regularly offered as a divine right answer to contractualism.

The reaction of Richard Baxter to the *Judgment and Decree* further reveals the relationship between the two doctrines. Baxter's *Holy Commonwealth* (1659) was one of the books proscribed by the Convocation for espousing the contractual theory. If the contractual basis of authority is eliminated, Baxter asked in a manuscript defense of his own book, what is left?

Will you lay it upon *paternal right* as natural? I hope you will not put all kings to prove such a right of primogeniture, as continued from Noah, and not founded in contract? Nor expose their title whenever such right of continued primogeniture is disproved? There

[51] *The Judgment and Decree of the University of Oxford Past in their Convocation, July 21, 1683*, title page.
[52] Ibid., p. 2.

being therefore no title within my notice pleadable but 1. by revelation from heaven, 2. or by conquest, 3. or by natural primogeniture, 4. or by consent or contract, if I erred in fixing on this, it was because I knew of no other, and was afraid to dethrone all kings on earth.[53]

A further suggestion of the status of patriarchalism at Oxford can be inferred from the reception accorded George MacKenzie's tract, *Jus Regium*. MacKenzie, who was the Crown's Advocate in Scotland, employed patriarchalism to discredit the state of nature and original equality arguments of the proponents of Exclusion. Since the creation of Adam, he said, all men have been born as natural subjects to their fathers. 'And therefore the Jesuitical and Fanatical Principles, that every Man is born Free, and at Liberty to choose what form of Government he pleaseth, was ever, and is most false', for if these fathers were not subjects of a superior themselves, they 'might judge and punish them [their children] capitally, lead them out to War, and do all other things that a King could do, as we see the Patriarchs did in their own Families'. Thus the people have no say in the selection of their rulers 'as long as it is known who is the Root of the Family, or who represents it'.[54]

MacKenzie implicitly acknowledged that literal patriarchalism was not a valid basis for monarchy in the seventeenth century, but, like Filmer, he appears to have believed that the paternal right was still an adequate description of the nature of kingship. He claimed that 'such as overcome the Heads of Families in Battel, succeed to them in their Paternal Right'. MacKenzie said very little about patriarchal authority itself. He treated political fatherhood and its primogenitive complement as historically necessary rather than morally binding in the present. 'This Power over all the Family was justly given by nature', he wrote, 'to shun divisions, or else every little Family should have erected it self in a distinct Government, and the weakest had still been a Prey.' Therefore, until the patriarchal form of government was super-

---

[53] Richard Baxter, 'A Sheet in Reference to the Decree of the University of Oxford' (1683), in Richard Schlatter, *Richard Baxter and Puritan Politics* (New Brunswick, N.J., 1957), pp. 152–3.
[54] George MacKenzie, *Jus Regium: or, The Just and Solid Foundation of Monarchy* (London, 1684), pp. 23–4.

seded—and MacKenzie did not describe the process—the eldest son of the eldest line ruled and was succeeded by his first-born son who had power over his uncles as well as other members of his family. Succession also adds to the order of a society, 'for if the wisest or strongest were to be chosen, there had still been many Rivals, and so much Faction and Discord; but it is still certain who is the Eldest Son, and this shuts out all Debate, and prevents all Dissention'.[55] MacKenzie dedicated *Jus Regium* to Oxford University, and Wood recorded that on 8 June 1684, a Convocation sent the author a letter of thanks 'for the service he had done his majesty in writing and publishing . . . *Jus Regium*'.[56]

4

The dispute between patriarchalism and the contractual theory was frequently at the center of the controversy in the pamphlet wars of the 1688 Revolution. Opponents of the Revolution concluded that Parliament had illegally declared the throne vacant, for subjects always owed a passive obedience to their sovereign. This was the argument of one of the most fascinating of the anti-Revolution tracts, Abednigo Seller's anonymous *History of Passive Obedience* (1689), a singularly rich compilation of royalist commentary. Seller's *History* is best described in the words of Thomas Bainbridge, one of its severest critics:

Why must so much pains be taken in the perusal of Sermons, popular Discourses and lesser Tracts, to find out, and report to the rest of the World what such and so many Men have said upon this Subject? They have *writ* excellent things, and those many; but all of them it seems are insipid to the palate of this Searcher; save their delicious touches of Passive Obedience.[57]

Among the passages quoted by Seller were many of the patriarchal attacks on populism that have been discussed here, including statements by Ussher, Sanderson, and Maxwell.[58] In the

---

[55] Ibid., pp. 23–5.
[56] Wood, *Life and Times*, III, 96.
[57] [Thomas Bainbridge], *Seasonable Reflections, on a Late Pamphlet, Entituled, A History of Passive Obedience* (London, 1689), p. 2.
[58] [Abednigo Seller], *A History of Passive Obedience* (Amsterdam, 1689), pp. 7, 17, 61, and Appendix, p. 5. This work was anonymously republished

second volume of his work, Seller reproduced with approval the patriarchal acount of Biblical history from the 1606 *Convocation Book,* which he claimed to have seen in manuscript before it was published by Archbishop Sancroft. Seller acknowledged his debt to Filmer but did not quote from him, 'the Enemies of the unaccountableness of Kings, having branded him with the mark of a State Heretick for his Orthodox Opinions, which among all good Men made his Memory reverend, and his works Eminent . . .'.[59]

More interesting perhaps to an analysis of Stuart patriarchalism is the theory's place in the pamphlets supporting the Revolution. The three-volume collection of Revolutionary pamphlets published in 1705–7 and titled *A Collection of State Tracts* abundantly demonstrates that arguments from first principles regularly examined the claims of patriarchalism, either to refute them or to distinguish them from the doctrines that justified the Revolution. Attempts were made to discredit patriarchalism in any way possible. One author said that preachers of this doctrine 'have so few Followers, and the Hypothesis itself is so new, and built upon such uncertain Conjectures, and so contrary to plain Matter of Fact, and the universal Practice of all Nations, that it is not worth any man's contending about'. He advised any reader with 'a mind to know the Mystery' of patriarchalism to consult the second part of Tyrrell's *Bibliotheca Politica* 'and try if he can make anything of it'.[60] Another writer believed that 'the highest Monarchical-Men that ever were of our Church have founded *the right of Kings over their Subjects, upon the Right of Parents over their Children'.*[61] Several tractarians accepted the historical tracing of government to familial beginnings but held that patriarchalism was irrelevent to the present disputes because

---

in 1710 as *A Defence of Dr. Sacheverall; or, Passive Obedience Prov'd to Be the Doctrine of the Church of England, from the Reformation to these Times.*

[59] [Abednigo Seller], *A Continuation of the History of Passive Obedience* (Amsterdam, 1690), pp. 76–82 and 146.

[60] *An Inquiry into the Nature and Obligation of Legal Rights* (London, 1693), reprinted in *A Collection of State Tracts, Publish'd on the Occasion of the Late Revolution in 1688,* 3 vols. (London, 1705–7), II, 393. Cited as *State Tracts.*

[61] *A Friendly Conference concerning the New Oath of Allegiance to K. William and Q. Mary* (London, 1689), p. 20.

no man could legitimately claim lineal descent from a literal father of his country.[62]

The presumed difference between political and paternal authority was one of the most important notions used to attack the moral patriarchal theory. Very few writers actually *demonstrated* that there were distinctions between ruling a family and governing a state; generally, they merely *asserted* that the powers were distinguishable. As Samuel Masters wrote, 'If some plead a Likeness or Analogy between them [fatherhood and kingship] it can serve only a rhetorical Illustration, but not for any logical Proof, such as the present Case requires.' Therefore, it was possible to assert against the Filmerian position that even though man's natural and original condition subjected him to his father's authority, he was still free enough to choose his government for himself.[63]

One very careless tract, supposedly written by a member of the Convention Parliament, alleged that patriarchal authority had been political only so long as the prime fathers were able to govern and defend their subjects. But when the power of the subjects exceeded that of the 'Patriarch or Father of the Family', this form of government might be dissolved. If they wished, the people could 'resume their natural Freedom, or again engage in the Family by Pact or Promise, or else leave it, and by Compact with others submit to what Laws or Measure of living together in a Community they think fit'. The process that followed this breakdown of fatherly rule combined the doctrines of Hobbes and Locke, for the post-patriarchal world was curiously described as a 'Tyranical Government, or State of War' that was 'more intolerable than the Patriarchal Government' and could be escaped only by means of a compact that placed specific

---

[62] [Thomas Long], *A Resolution of Certain Queries concerning Submission to the Present Government* (London. 1689), reprinted in *State Tracts*, I, 442–3; *The Proceedings of the Present Parliament Justified by the Opinions of . . . Hugo Grotius* (London, 1689), reprinted in *State Tracts*, I, 179; and *Inquiry into the Nature, State Tracts*, II, 393.

[63] [Samuel Masters], *The Case of Allegiance in Our Present Circumstances Consider'd* (London, 1690), reprinted in *State Tracts*, I, 319–18. See also N. N., *The Letter Which Was Sent to the Author of the Doctrine of Passive Obedience and Jure Divino Disprov'd &c. Answered* (London, 1689), reprinted in *State Tracts*, I, 383; and [Gilbert Burnet], *An Enquiry into the Measures of Submission* (London, 1687), p. 1.

limitations upon the governors. 'Thus all Governments in the same degree that they differ from Patriarchal and Tyrannical must derive their Originals from Compact, and the Governour must necessarily derive his Power from and by the mutual Consent of the People he governs. . . .' James II, it was concluded, had failed to abide by the contract establishing his authority and was therefore lawfully deposed.[64]

A number of authors identified this era of pre-governmental familial rule with the Biblical period up to the Flood. As Peter Allix said:

It seem'd indeed that the Authority of *Adam*, their common Father, together with that of the Patriarchs, might have been sufficient to contain Men within the Bounds of their Duty, as well as the near Relation and Alliance that was between them. But their Paternal Authority having by the space of fifteen Ages been found incapable to restrain the licentiousness of Men, and too weak to put a stop to their Debaucheries and Murders, which at last drew down the Deluge upon them; we find that God afterwards instituted Magistracy as a stronger Curb, to stop the impetuosity of Mens exorbitant Passions. . . .

. . . Moreover, Men being oblig'd to separate themselves from one another, in order to their peopling of the whole Earth, consequently could not observe the same Principles of Communion which link'd them together under the Patriarchs; wherefore it was natural to substitute to the Patriarchal Authority, a Government more accommodated to the state of Men in their different and dispers'd Habitations.[65]

Another variation of this attitude was the claim that 'Government grew by degrees into Kingdoms, and began in Families,

[64] A. B., *Some Remarks upon Government . . . in Two Letters* (London, 1689), reprinted in *State Tracts*, I, 151–2.

[65] [Peter Allix], *Reflections upon Opinons of Some Modern Divines Concerning the Nature of Government* (London, 1689), reprinted in *State Tracts*, I, 468 and 469.
A Scottish pamphleteer who made the same basic point justified giving only slight attention to the claims of patriarchalism because of the brevity of his tract: 'I intend no tedious Discourse on this Subject, and therefore I pass by the Patriarchal Government of the Fathers of Families, which for a short Season after the Creation and Flood, might have kept some Order and Peace amongst Men.' (*A Vindication of the Proceedings of the Convention of the Estates in Scotland* [London, 1689], reprinted in *State Tracts*, III, 468.)

encreased into Vacinities, Towns, Cities, Common-Wealths and Kingdoms. And that Form of Government was best, which best agreed with the People, and was most conducive to the Publick Benefit.'[66] This interpretation of governmental origins had been employed by Sir Thomas Smith in the previous century and by George Lawson during the Interregnum; the terminology used here is strikingly similar to Lawson's. In what is probably the most representative way in which Stuart political writers fused patriarchalism and consent in an anthropological theory of origins, an unnamed friend of the Revolution wrote that common-wealths emerged from voluntary associations of familial groups. These unions were the results of compacts 'entered [into] by the Fathers of the Families incorporated: for before the Errection of Commonwealths, there was no other Government amongst Man, but the Patriarchal Government of the Fathers of Families'.[67]

The patriarchalism of Sir Robert Filmer was specifically and dramatically made a part of the Revolution controversy by the publication of Locke's *Two Treatises* in late 1689; for some writers—as indeed for their Whig successors in the nineteenth and twentieth centuries—the issue was forever buried. As William Atwood wrote in 1690 in what appears to have been the earliest published reference to the *Two Treatises*, 'The difference between a *Patriarchal* and a *Monarchical* Authority is so well stated and prov'd by my Learned Friend, *Mr. Tyrril*, that few besides the unknown Author of the two late *Treatises of Government* could have gained reputation after him, in exposing the false *Principles* and Foundations of Sir *Robert Filmer* and his admirers.'[68] Atwood, among the least able of the Whig pamphleteers, devoted a nineteen-page appendix of his tract to a pointless criticism of Filmer. Tyrrell apparently still felt Sir Robert was sufficiently important to renew his attack in 1691 in his long-winded *Bibliotheca Politica,* published over the next three years in thirteen dialogues.

[66] *A Friendly Debate between Dr. Kingsman, a Dissatisfied Clergy-man, and Gratian Trimmer, a Neighbour Minister* (London, 1689), p. 29.
[67] *A Discourse Concerning the Nature, Power, and Proper Effects of the Present Conventions in Both Kingdoms* (London, 1689), reprinted in *State Tracts*, I, 218–19.
[68] W[illiam] A[twood], *The Fundamental Constitution of the English Government* (London, 1690), p. 4.

H

Filmer's name was correctly associated with the views of the non-jurors immediately after the Revolution. In June 1689, Locke heard from Benjamin Furley, with whom he had lived in Holland, 'I met with a scrupulous Cambridge Scholar, that thought no thing, could discharge him of the oath of Allegiance that he had take[n] to Ja: 2 & his successors. I had a pleasant sport with him upon Sr. R: Filmers maggot, w$^{ch}$ he soon quitted, because he saw he could not make it lean to his purpose.'[69]

When William Sherlock, the Dean of St. Paul's, finally took the new oath in 1691, he wrote a treatise defending his action. Sherlock examined the nature and origins of governmental authority and observed that patriarchal power

> was the first Government in the World, and is the only Natural Authority; for in propriety of speaking, there is no Natural Prince but a Father. But by what bounds this paternal and Patriarchal authority was limited, we cannot tell; how the extent of this power was stinted, and where new Families, and new Governments began; and it is in vain for us to inquire after it now.[70]

This disclaimer of the relevance of patriarchalism prompted James Parkinson, the Oxford don who had been expelled for teaching anti-Filmerian, Whig principles, to remark of Sherlock, 'And so he has taken leave of Sir Robert Filmer's *Patriarcha*.'[71] Sherlock had denied the right of political patriarchs to give away any of their authority,[72] and Jeremy Collier responded, almost as if Filmer were an author whose views were universally known:

> But suppose a Father can't give away his Authority; I hope the Doctor will permit him to leave it behind him when he dyes. Now this is sufficient for the Patriarchal Scheme: For by this Hypothesis,

[69] Furley to Locke, 6 June 1689, Bodleian Library, MS. Locke c. 9, fol. 39.
[70] William Sherlock, *The Case of Allegiance Due to Sovereign Powers, Stated and Resolved, According to Scripture and Reason* (London, 1691), p. 11. For the theoretical context of Sherlock's abandonment of the non-jurors, see Gerald Straka, 'The Final Phase of Divine Right Theory in England, 1688–1702', *English Historical Review*, LXXVII (1962), 638–58, and *Anglican Reaction to the Revolution of 1688* (Madison, Wisconsin, 1962).
[71] James Parkinson, *An Examination of Dr. Sherlock's Book, Entituled, The Case of Allegiance Due to Sovereign Powers* (London, 1691), p. 11.
[72] Sherlock, *Case of Allegiance*, pp. 23–4.

*Adam* and all the other Patriarchs, who had Sovereign Dominion from God left their Jurisdiction to go by descent to their Heirs; who were Lords, not only of their immediate Brethren, but of all the remoter Branches of the younger Families. So that there is no need of the Resignation of Paternal Power: For the Successive Conveyance of Original Authority, to the Heirs, or reputed Heirs, of the first Head, is as much as the Hypothesis requires. This is the Substance of Sir Robert Filmer's Opinion; and because the Doctor has said nothing to confute it, I shall vindicate it no further.[73]

The patriarchal origins of political authority were an integral part of Sir Isaac Newton's historical theories. In a short manuscript entitled 'The Original of Monarchies' probably composed about 1694, he wrote:

So then upon the first plantation of the earth [after the Flood] there were no standing kingdoms. Every father was a sovereign Lord of his own inheritance during his life & then his sons became sovereign Lords of their several shares & so on till the earth was planted with innumerable scattered families not subject to any other Lords than their own common fathers. For I here reccon every father with all his posterity to be one family & upon the fathers death to break into so many families as he left sons surviving him.

Newton said nothing about the exercise of government over widows and unmarried daughters, an omission that might indicate that the theory had only an anthropological importance for him. Nonetheless, he attributed to every father a 'legislative & judicial power' which was transferred to a council of elders when several independent families united to create a larger and non-familial political unit. Newton believed that his account was a true picture of Biblical history as well as of the settlement of Greece: 'upon the first peopling of Peloponnesus every father shared his territories amongst all his sons (as Moses described) untill there was no more room for division.'[74]

[73] [Jeremy Collier], *Dr. Sherlock's Case of Allegiance Considered, with some Remarks upon His Vindication* (London, 1691), p. 91.
[74] Isaac Newton, 'The Original of Monarchies', King's College, Cambridge, MS. Newton 146, printed in Frank E. Manuel, *Isaac Newton, Historian* (Cambridge, 1963), pp. 199 and 207. The dating of the MS. is from Manuel (p. 198), who analyzes the document and related fragments at pp. 122–38, *et passim*.

The list of writers who either employed or argued against patriarchal political ideas could be greatly extended. George Dawson, for example, wrote a crudely scientific treatise in which he used the patriarchally ruled aboriginal society to demonstrate the historical and anthropological truth of the Old Testament.[75] Daniel Defoe devoted parts of his tedious and long *Jure Divino* (1706) to a criticism of the patriarchal basis of government. Like so many of his contemporaries, Defoe acknowledged that all authority was originally paternal and felt that the familial system eventually became inadequate and was supplanted by a more voluntarily derived political rule. While Defoe added nothing of theoretical worth to anti-patriarchal thought, some of his novel couplets merit quoting. There was a Lockean quality to his insistence that whatever authority had previously existed, 'government', *per se*, was not instituted until the owners of property consented to it.

> Wise Providence, that all Events fore knew,
> Directs the World their Safety to persue:
> *While* in the infant-Ages of the King,
> Nature to *first Paternal Rule* confirm'd;
> The Men untainted, and their Number few,
> The Patriarchal Government *might do.*
> ...............................................
>    First Government was Natural and Free,
> And fixt in Patriarchal Majesty,
> From thence convey'd Right t. *Property*,
> Where he bestows the Soil, and gives the Land,
> The Right of that's the Right of Command.
> There can be no pretense of Government,
> Till they that have the Property consent.[76]

Of the patriarchal monarchy of Adam and its extinction in a later age Defoe wrote:

> Look back to the old Originals of Power,
> Long before Men knew each other how to devour;
> Bring out the Mortal from his Master's Hand,

[75] George Dawson, *Origo Legum: or A Treatise of the Origin of Laws, and Their Obliging Power* (London, 1694), pp. 33–45, 52–3, and 58.
[76] [Daniel Defoe], *Jure Divino: A Satyr*, folio ed. (London, 1706), Bk. II, pp. 4 and 16–17.

Lord of the World and fitted for Command;
Not yet debauched with Tyranny or Pride,
But with his pregnant Reason fortify'd;
Vested with Judgment to direct his Way,
And chuse how he should rule, or who obey:
While his succeeding Sons were just and few,
Paternal modes of Govenment they knew;
But as the king increas'd, they soon found Cause,
To limit Forms of Government by Laws:
Degenerate Nature soon seduc'd by Crime,
Quickly incroached upon the Power sublime;
And Reason found it needful to explain,
Laws to prescribe, and Limits to restrain.[77]

## 5

On the other side, many Tories, Jacobites, and opponents of 1688 continued to rely upon patriarchal arguments to support their pleas of passive obedience and non-resistance. Henry Gandy, who became one of the non-juring bishops, opened his anonymous and confused *Jure Divino* (1707) by declaring that 'GOD made Paternal Power the foundation of all Civil Government— And more reasoning Men agree, that Monarchical Government is best suiting with *God's Ordinance*, and the benefit of Society.'[78] He further argued that the patriarchal kingship of Adam was a manifestation of God's preferance for monarchy. When Providence transformed natural, paternal government into civil authority, 'the whole diffusive body of the Governed were to be (in this respect of change of their Forms of Government) reputed in the state of *Wives*, or of *Children*, or *Minors*'.[79]

---

[77] Ibid., V, p. 1. For patriarchal references in some of Defoe's other political writings see the dedication to his *The Original Power of the Collective Body of the People of England, Examined and Asserted* (1701), 3rd ed. (London, n.d.), p. v.; and his anonymous *Reflections upon the Late Great Revolution* (London, 1689), reprinted in *State Tracts*, I, 246 and 247.

[78] [Henry Gandy], *Jure Divino: or, An Answer to All that Hath or Shall Be Written by Republicans against the Old English* (London, 1707), p. 5. The same argument was made in [Henry Gandy], *Old England: or, The Government of England Prov'd to Be Monarchical and Hereditary* (London, 1705), p. 34.

[79] [Gandy], *Jure Divino*, pp. 7 and 14.

The standard patriarchal arguments were employed by an early eighteenth-century critic of Locke's against the state of nature, natural rights, and consent theories of the *Two Treatises*. This unnamed pamphleteer insisted upon the patriarchal sovereignty of Adam and Noah, the division of the world along familial lines at Babel, the applicability of the Fifth Commandment to civil obedience and the incompatibility of original freedom with the natural authority of fathers over their children.[80] In general, the attacks on Locke followed this same pattern; they were not so much criticisms as they were bland and unsupported assertions that the positions rejected in the *Two Treatises* were correct.

Patriarchal and familial explanations of monarchy are found in the sermon literature of the reign of Queen Anne. Especially noteworthy is the use of the 'nursing mothers' passage from Isaiah[81] as the text for several major sermons. In one respect, use of this passage was a new departure in patriarchal reasoning, for it represents an attempt to reconcile the sovereignty of a woman with the traditional patriarchal doctrine of female inferiority. These ministers, however, did not recognize that Queen Anne's occupancy of the throne conflicted with Eve's subordination to Adam; patriarchal theorists, of course, generally considered this subordination as the establishment of civil authority. (It should be remembered that no attempt was made to reconcile the reign of Queen Elizabeth I with the claims and presumptions of patriarchalism.) John Sharp, Archbishop of York, stressed the gentleness of parents in his Coronation Sermon on the Isaiah text, saying that he envied the people whose rulers thought of themselves as nursing fathers and mothers. Such people 'are out of all fears of *Despotick* or *Arbitrary* proceedings'. However, Sharp did not fail to remind his listeners that their 'nursing mother' was entitled to the filial obedience of her subjects:

But always bear in Mind what returns of *Duty*, and *Gratitude*, and *Filial Obedience*, this Consideration of a Queen's being a *Nursing-*

---

[80] *An Essay upon Government, Wherein the Republican Schemes Reviv'd by Mr. Locke, Dr. Blackal, &c. Are Fairly Consider'd and Refuted* (London, 1705), pp. 7–10, 14, 15, 37, and 40.

[81] Isa. 49: 23: 'And kings shall be thy nursing fathers and their queens thy nursing mothers.'

*Mother to her People* doth call for from us, and all her other Subjects. . . .

If all Subjects did seriously consider this Relation between their *Princes* and *them*, they would think themselves obliged to bear the same *Love* and *Affection*, to pay the same *Honour* and *Reverence* and *Obedience* to their *Nursing-Fathers* and *Nursing-Mothers* as they do their *Natural Parents*.[82]

Nathaniel Hough, Lecturer at Kensington Church, in a sermon of 1713, noted the distinction between Isaiah's 'nursing fathers' and 'nursing mothers' but considered them inseparable. He commented, 'Therefore I could not do justice to the Text, if I should part one Branch of it from the other, and not just mention a King who died this very day, as the *Guardian-Father* of the Church in its Adversity, in my way to a QUEEN, who happily succeeded, now in its Prosperity, a *Nursing-Mother*.'[83] But it remained for Benjamin Hoadly, afterwards known as the controversial Bishop of Bangor and then of Winchester, to raise the issue in a succinct form:

If *Paternal Right* were by *God's* appointment, the foundation of *Civil* Authority; then, either *God's* appointment is of little obligation, or it is impossible that any *Prescription*, or any *Humane Constitution*, can give to a *Woman* a *Right* to *Civil Government*. For tho' *after the innumerable changes that have been made in the Government of all Nations*, it cannot appear which Man hath the ancient *Natural Right* to the *Civil Government* of a *Nation;* yet this must appear that it is impossible a *Woman* should have it. . . . I fear this will reduce the *Title* of any *Queen* to nothing better than *Usurpation*.[84]

Hoadly's comment came at the end of a controversy between himself and Offspring Blackall, one of Queen Anne's favorite preachers, who had been rewarded with the bishopric of Exeter. The thrust of Hoadly's criticism was altogether ignored by the Bishop. One of the chief points dividing Hoadly and Blackall was

[82] John Sharp, *A Sermon Preach'd at the Coronation of Queen Anne* (London, 1702), pp. 11 and 22–3.
[83] Nathaniel Hough, *A Sermon on the Anniversary Day of Her Majesty's Happy Accession to the Throne* (London, 1713), p. 4.
[84] Benjamin Hoadly, *An Humble Reply to the Right Reverend the Lord Bishop of Exeter's Answer*, 2nd ed. (London, 1709), p. 50.

the relationship of patriarchal to political power. In a sermon commemorating the third anniversary of the accession of Queen Anne, Blackall had admitted that the two were at least historically distinct authorities, for civil government had succeeded the patriarchal rule originally established by God.[85] On the same date, three years later, Blackall repeated this point but went on to assert, in familiar fashion, that there had never been a state of nature because all men since Adam were born subjects to their fathers.[86] Hoadly saw the fallacy in this position and claimed that Blackall's distinction between paternal and political power was actually an argument in behalf of the state of nature, for if civil authority *succeeded* patriarchal rule, there must have been a time when there was no civil government. Then, Hoadly said, men lived in 'the *State* of *Nature*, [which] with respect to *civil Government*, is a *State* of *Equality*'.[87] Blackall replied that the distinction he had in mind exists in 'the World, as it is now . . . yet *from the Beginning it was not so*'. For civil authority was originally a part of the paternal title of Adam who had 'as much [of] the Power of a Civil Governour, as any King has now'. Not until after the time of Noah, when colonies were scattered throughout the world, were these authorities separated, as the civil power was 'delegated to (or perhaps Usurp'd by) the Heads of such Colonies'.[88]

This was Blackall's parting shot at Hoadly, but the controversy was far from over. Charles Leslie and a great many other writers had already joined the fray,[89] and what began as a political dispute between a Tory Bishop and deistic clergyman became a

[85] Offspring Blackall, *The Subjects Duty: A Sermon Preach'd at the Parish-Church of St. Dunstan in the West* (1704), 3rd ed. (London, 1709), pp. 7–8.

[86] Offspring Blackall, *The Divine Institution of Magistracy and the Gracious Design of Its Institution* (London, n.d. [1708]), p. 6.

[87] Benjamin Hoadly, *Some Consideration Humbly Offered to the Bishop of Exeter*, 3rd ed. (London, 1709), pp. 15–17, quotation from p. 17.

[88] Offspring Blackall, *The Lord Bishop of Exeter's Answer to Mr. Hoadly's Letter* (London, 1709), p. 17.

[89] The catalogues of the British Museum and Cambridge University Library list at least sixteen tracts written in 1709 on one side or the other of the controversy. It did not end there, but continued for another two or three years. This entire dispute has never been studied in detail.

re-enactment of the Jacobite-Whig battles of the 1688 Revolution.[90]

Leslie, a non-juring clergyman who is remembered for his theological writings, was an unabashed Filmerian. Even though he rarely mentioned Sir Robert, Leslie's primary contentions, references, and methods of argument all suggest that *Patriarcha* was the chief source of his political doctrines. Hoadly, on the other hand, is almost universally regarded as a disciple of Locke's who lacked his master's intellectual acumen.[91]

The root issue between Leslie and Hoadly was still the relevance of patriarchal authority to political power, with Leslie, of course, insisting that they were identical. In three anti-Hoadly tracts and the four volumes of *The Rehearsal*, the penny-paper he published from 1704 to 1709, Leslie did not advance significantly beyond his initial argument or beyond the arguments of Filmer himself, for that matter. 'You spend many Words upon the Differences betwixt *Paternal* and *Civil* Government:' he said to Hoadly, 'Whereas there is none. For the *Paternal* is *Civil* Authority. And it is *Supreme* and *Absolute* (where there is no Superior *Civil* Authority to Controul it) as to *Life* and *Death*, *Liberty* and *Property*, and everything else.' Supporting his position with Abraham's abortive sacrifice of Isaac, Judah's condemnation of Tamar, and Reuben's 'pawning the *Lives* of his *Sons*', Leslie triumphantly concluded, 'Thus *Adam* was both *Father* and *King* of all the World. And therefore *Civil* Government was from the very Beginning.'[92] In the main, Leslie merely recited the standard patriarchal arguments. His final and most lucid contribution, *The Finishing Stroke* (1711), is at least notable

---

[90] Among the pamphlets was a reprinting of the *Judgment and Decree*, which concluded with a special advertisement to Hoadly: 'This is to give Notice, That if Mr. *Hoadly* will not Recant his Rebellious and Seditious Principles which he has Borrow'd from the vile Authors here Condemn'd, he may speedily expect the same Censure from both Universities which they underwent.' (*The Oxford Decree: Being an Entire Confutation of Mr. Hoadly's Book of the Original of Government* [London, 1710], p. 8.)

[91] See Edwin R. Bingham, 'The Political Apprenticeship of Benjamin Hoadly', *Church History*, XVI (1947), 154–65; Stephen, *English Thought in the Eighteenth Century*, paperbound, II, 130; Laski, *Locke to Bentham*, p. 73; and Robbins, *Commonwealthman*, p. 84.

[92] [Charles Leslie], *The Best Answer Ever Was Made and to Which No Answer Will be Made* (London, 1709), p. 42.

for its wit. For example, after discussing Isaac's having acquiesced in his father's preparations to sacrifice him, Leslie remarked, 'But the Authority of a *Father* and *King* is somewhat Abated since those Days! Had *Isaac* been a *Whigg*, he had never Inherited the *Blessing*, he would have held up *Magna Charta* against the *Old Man*, and *Pleaded Original Contract*, and the *Independent State of Nature*!'[93]

Leslie denied the existence of the state of nature,[94] attacked Locke for extracting equality of mothers and fathers from the Fifth Commandment,[95] and generally followed Filmer's interpretation of Biblical history with one important exception. Examining the relationship of inferior fathers to thier common superiors, Leslie eliminated the muddle Bohun had left. 'There are Tributary *Kings* who have *Absolute* Power in their own Dominions,' he wrote, 'and yet are Subject to an Higher King or *Emperor*, who had *Absolute* Authority over them'. The same principle was applicable to the relative authorities of fathers, grandfathers, and great-grandfathers.[96] Therefore, the building of the Tower of Babel had not destroyed Noah's universal monarchy as Hoadly had complained.[97] Noah was king of the entire world 'as long as he Lived'; his sons exercised authority under him and their sons under each of them. 'And thus the World might have been, and thus the World was *Divided* into several Nations.'[98] Eventually this universal monarchy died out (Leslie did not say that it lasted beyond the life of Noah), and the identities of the rightful patriarchal rulers of the world's nations were lost. There was no competition about the rights to crowns, for it has been the '*Rule* in all *Ages* and *Nations*' that the '*Possessor* had the *Right*'.[99] Thus, just as Filmer had done, Leslie made usurpation a valid basis for monarchy and treated prescription as the test of legitimacy.

[93] [Charles Leslie], *The Finishing Stroke: Being a Vindication of the Patriarchal Scheme of Government* (London, 1711), pp. 61–2.
[94] Ibid., p. 21. See also [Charles Leslie], *The Rehearsal (A View of the Times, Their Principles and Practices)*, I, no. 55 (11 August 1705), p. 1.
[95] [Leslie] *Rehearsal*, I, no. 55 (11 August 1705), p. 2. See Locke, *Two Treatises*, I, 61, and II, 53.
[96] [Leslie], *Finishing Stroke*, p. 13.
[97] Benjamin Hoadly, *The Original and Institution of Civil Government, Discuss'd*, 2nd ed. (London, 1710), p. 50.
[98] [Leslie], *Finishing Stroke*, p. 43.
[99] [Leslie], *Rehearsal*, I, no. 144 (2 October 1706), p. 2.

Hoadly's attacks on patriarchalism were no more original than Leslie's defenses. He continued to distinguish between patriarchal and political rights and asserted that the doctrines of usurpation and prescriptive rights of sovereignty unsettled all present titles and invited insurrection.[100] Hoadly also rejected Leslie's derivation of political authority from Adam's patriarchal powers over Eve and their offspring. Making Adam into an absolute monarch, Hoadly claimed, is too subtle an interpretation of the Old Testament. Besides, if God had intended to establish 'an *Universal Monarchy* in *Adam,* Who can think that he would have not done it plainly and effectually?' Why would God 'have obliged *Cain* to have begun the Foundation of a distinct Family and distinct *Nations,* in a part of the World removed from *Adam's* Habitation?'[101] But perhaps the most significant element of Hoadly's criticism was his rejection of the Fifth Commandment as the basis for political obligation. This equation of the duty to obey political superiors with filial piety, he contended, 'is only by way of Common-place; and often for the sake of Brevity'. The doctrine of the catechism 'no more proves that the *Fifth Commandment* founds *Civil Government* upon *Paternal Authority'* than using the Fourth Commandment to justify holidays established long after the time of Moses 'will prove that it was the Design of the *Fourth Commandment* to enjoyn the Observation of Christmas-Day'.[102]

What is important about this argument is that it was written by a man soon to become an Anglican Bishop. On its face, Hoadly's position appears to have been a denial of one of the tenets of his Church, for the strict derivation of political duty from the Fifth Commandment had been taught by Anglicanism at least since the Reformation. Hoadly was not *challenging* this doctrine but was attempting to explain it in rational terms. His views here were at one with the deism of his theological writings, and in that respect Hoadly had nothing to say to his patriarchalist adversary. Hoadly's rationalism—however crude and unintelligent it may have been—was the harbinger of the next step in the development of political discourse, but Leslie and divine right patriarchalism belonged to an earlier age. To be sure, there were exponents of the

---

[100] Hoadly, *Original*, pp. 7–8, 96, and 112.
[101] Ibid., p. 14.
[102] Ibid., pp. 8–9.

# XII

## Thomas Hobbes on the Family and the State of Nature

### I

Among the most celebrated passages in the literature of political philosophy is Thomas Hobbes's classic description of the incommodious, barren, and uncertain life in the state of nature: 'no Arts; no Letters; no Society; and which is worst of all, continuall feare, and danger of violent death; And the life of man, solitary, poore, nasty, brutish, and short'.[1] Seventeenth-century critics assumed that even the most rudimentary social unit, the family, was excluded from the Hobbesian state of nature and often opposed this view of '*the* NATURALL CONDITION *of Mankind*' with the patriarchally governed household. They held that the natural 'warre of every man against every man'[2] never existed. The reaction of Bishop John Bramhall was typical:

there never was any such time when mankind was without Governors and Lawes, and Societies. Paternall Government was in the world from the beginning, and [by] the Law of Nature. There might be sometimes a root of such Barbarous Theevish Brigants, in the same rocks, or desarts, or odd corners of the world, but it was an abuse and a degeneration from the nature of man, who is a politicall creature.[3]

Repeating the same criticism, Sir Henry Sumner Maine wrote in the last century, 'It is some shifting sandbank in which the

[1] Hobbes, *Leviathan*, ch. xiii, ed. Pogson Smith, p. 97.
[2] Ibid., pp. 94 (chapter title) and 98.
[3] John Bramhall, *A Defence of True Liberty from Antecedent and Extrincicall Necessity* (London, 1655), p. 107.

grains are Individual men, that according to the theory of Hobbes is hardened into the social rock by the wholesome discipline of force.' But ancient law, Maine continued, 'knows next to nothing of Individuals. It is concerned not with Individuals, but with Families, not with single human beings, but groups'.[4] And G. P. Gooch has said against Hobbes's conception, 'The unit of primitive society was not, as he imagined, the individual, but the family or some other group. . . .'[5]

All three of these statements echoed the complaints of Sir Robert Filmer. These anti-individualist interpretations rely, in large measure, upon the presumption that the Hobbesian state of nature was intended as an actual historical account of man's pre-political condition, a notion that is generally discredited in the twentieth century. Even more damaging to this whole body of assumptions, however, is Hobbes's own assertion, in the seventeenth chapter of the *Leviathan*, that familial authority existed in the pre-political condition. Thomas Tenison replied to this, 'You rather overthrow than prove your supposed state of Nature.'[6] But Hobbes had gone even further and had identified familial and political authority: 'Cities and Kingdoms . . . are but greater Families'.[7] In his own English translation of *De Cive*, he stated that 'a family is a little city',[8] later writing, 'a great family is a kingdom, a little kingdom a family'.[9] Numerous similar and related comments are scattered throughout Hobbes's writings. Together they comprise a patriarchal element in his political philosophy that has only rarely been recognized.[10] This chapter is an

---

[4] Henry Sumner Maine, *Ancient Law: Its Connection with the Early History of Society and Its Relation to Modern Ideas*, ed. Frederick Pollock, 4th American ed. (New York, 1906), p. 250.

[5] G. P. Gooch, *Political Thought in England: Bacon to Halifax*, Home University Library, reprinted (London, 1946), p. 34.

[6] [Tenison], *The Creed of Mr. Hobbes Examined*, p. 134. Cf. Filmer, *Originall*, pp. 239 and 241.

[7] Hobbes, *Leviathan*, ch. xvii, p. 129.

[8] Thomas Hobbes, *De Cive* (1642), translated by Hobbes as *Philosophical Rudiments Concerning Government and Society* (1651), reprinted as volume II of Hobbes, *The English Works*, ed. William Molesworth, 11 vols. (London, 1839–41), ch. vi, sect. 15, note, p. 84. This work will be cited throughout in accord with the established usage by the Latin title, *De Cive*, and the *English Works* will be cited as *E.W.*, which also corresponds to the standard practice.

[9] *Ibid.*, viii, 1 (*E.W.*, II, 108).

examination of the familial aspects of the *Leviathan, De Cive,* and other works by Hobbes. While I have not attempted to reassess the whole of his political thought, I have, in several places, called attention to some of the problems that this patriarchalism raises for interpretations of other aspects of Hobbes's theory.

2

Political power, Hobbes said, arose either from acquisition or institution; the power of fatherhood was derived from acquisition:

The attaining to this Soveraigne Power, is by two wayes. One, by Naturall force; as when a man maketh his children, to submit themselves, and their children to his government, as being able to destroy them if they refuse; or by Warre subdoeth his enemies to his will, giving them their lives on that condition. The other, is when men agree amongst themselves, to submit to some Man, or Assembly of men, voluntarily, on confidence to be protected by him against all others. This latter, may be called a Politicall Common-wealth, or Common-wealth by *Institution*; and the former, a Common-wealth by *Acquisition*.[11]

So far as Hobbes was concerned, there were no differences between instituted and acquired commonwealths once they were established, for 'The Rights, and Consequences of Sovereignty, are the same in both.'[12] In *De Corpore Politico* he wrote, in a 'monarchy by acquisition . . . the sovereignty is in one man, as it is in a monarch made by *political institution*. So that whatsoever

[10] For previous discussions of Hobbes's patriarchalism see R. W. K. Hinton, 'Husbands, Fathers and Conquerors', *Political Studies*, XVI (1968), 55–8, and a most illuminating essay by Keith Thomas, 'The Social Origins of Hobbes's Political Thought', *Hobbes Studies*, ed. Keith C. Brown (Oxford, 1965), pp. 185–236.

[11] Hobbes, *Leviathan*, ch. xvii, p. 132. The same point was made in *De Cive*, v, 12, viii, 1, and ix, 10 (*E.W.*, II, 70–1, 108, and 121–2). In an earlier work Hobbes made parenthood a distinct and therefore a third source of dominion in the state of nature. (Hobbes, *De Corpore Politico; or The Elements of Law* [1640], II, iii, 2 [*E.W.*, IV, 149].)

[12] Hobbes, *Leviathan*, ch. xx, p. 153. See also p. 154 and *De Cive*, ix, 10 (*E.W.*, II, 121–2).

rights be in the one, the same also be in the other. And therefore I shall no more speak of them as distinct, but of monarchy in general.'[13] It therefore follows that acquisition provided as valid a title as institution,[14] and it appears that Hobbes accepted patriarchal power and consent as equivalent though distinguishable sources of governance.

In fact, in his little-known *Dialogue between a Philosopher and a Student* published in 1666 Hobbes implicitly adopted much of the traditional patriarchal argument and attributed to primitive fathers many of the characteristics of sovereignty:

And first, it is evident that dominion, government, and laws, are far more ancient than history or any writing, and that the beginning of all dominion amongst men was in families. In which, first, the father of the family by the law of nature was absolute lord of his wife and children: secondly, made what laws amongst them he pleased: thirdly, was judge of all their controversies: fourthly, was not obliged by any law of man to follow any counsel but his own: fifthly, what land soever the lord sat down upon and made use of for his own and his family's benefit, was his propriety by the law of first possession, in case it was void of inhabitants before, or by the law of war, in case they conquered it. In this conquest what enemies they took and saved, were their servants. Also such men as wanting possession's of lands, but furnished with arts necessary for man's life, came to dwell in the family for protection, became their subjects, and submitted themselves to the laws of the family.[15]

In his debate with Bishop Bramhall Hobbes admitted, '*It is very likely to be true, that since the Creation there very likely never was a time when Mankind was totally without Society.*' Bramhall, Hobbes continued, '*saw there was Paternal Government in*

---

[13] Hobbes, *De Corpore Politico*, II, iv, 10 (*E.W.*, IV, 159).

[14] Ibid., II, iii, 1 (*E.W.*, IV, 148–9). See also E. F. Carritt, *Morals and Politics: Theories of Their Relation from Hobbes and Spinoza to Marx and Bosanquet* (Oxford, 1935), pp. 31–2.

[15] Thomas Hobbes, *A Dialogue Between a Philosopher and a Student of the Common Laws of England* (1666), *E.W.*, VI, 147. Cf. Hobbes, *Leviathan*, ch. xviii, pp. 133ff., for a discussion of the nature of sovereign power. Hobbes's derivation of a father's authority over his family from the law of nature in the above-quoted passage may perhaps be explained by reference to the fourth law of nature as set forth in the *Leviathan*. See below, pp. 230–1 and 235.

Adam, *which he might do easily, as being no deep considera-tion'*.[16] But in *De Cive* he dismissed as a justification for kingship the argument 'that paternal government, instituted by God him-self at the Creation, was monarchical'. The difficulty, according to Hobbes, was that this claim along with other similar notions made its case 'by examples and testimonies, and not by solid reason'.[17] In the *Leviathan* he asserted that an independent family was a small kingdom:

> . . . a great Family if it be not part of some Common-wealth, is of it self, as to the Rights of Soveraignty, a little Monarchy; whether that Family consists of a man and his children; or of a man and his servants; or of a man, and his children, and servants together: where-in the Father or Master is the Soveraign. But yet a Family is not properly a Common-wealth; unlesse it be of that power by its own number, or by other opportunities, as not to be subdued without the hazard of war.[18]

Breaking sharply with the patriarchalism of the mid-seven-teenth century, Hobbes insisted that paternal power in the state of nature was not derived from fatherhood as such. If patriarchal sovereignty was a product of procreation, he reasoned, then the mother, who is a full partner in the act of generation, should have an equal claim to dominion over the child. However, a sharing of authority was impossible, for it would have violated two axioma-tic principles, that no man can serve two masters and that supreme power is indivisible.[19] Presumably, this judgment was applicable to the power of Adam too, which, as has just been shown, might well have been patriarchal for all Hobbes cared. Hobbes's denial of the generative origins of the governmental authority of fathers allowed him to rest his political doctrine on the proposition that no status among men was natural. Subordination among men was due to convention and human consent, not to nature.[20] The

---

[16] Thomas Hobbes, *The Questions Concerning Liberty, Necessity, and Chance Clearly Stated and Debated* (London, 1656), p. 139.

[17] Hobbes, *De Cive*, x, 3 (*E.W.*, II, 129).

[18] Hobbes, *Leviathan*, ch. xx, p. 157.

[19] Ibid., ch. xx. p. 154, and *De Cive*, ix, 2 (*E.W.*, II, 115).

[20] Cf. the statement quoted above (p. 228) from the later and less philo-sophic *Dialogue*: 'the father of the family *by the law of nature* was absolute lord of his wife and children' (Emphasis added).

power of parents was a virtual reward for preserving the lives of their children when they had the ability and right to destroy them. Since all equals were potential dangers to one another in their natural state, men, as a means of insuring their personal safety, were entitled to keep a subdued individual in a permanently weakened condition. But a man who preserved someone whom he might have destroyed was entitled to obedience from the person he saved. Thus, in the state of nature, 'if the mother shall think fit to abandon, or expose her child to death, whatsoever man or woman shall find the child so exposed, shall have the same right which the mother had before; and for this same reason, namely, for the power not of generating, but preserving'.[21]

Power over a child initially belongs to the mother, according to Hobbes, 'insomuch as she may rightly, and at her own will, either breed him up or adventure him to fortune'. The obligation of the child to obey a mother who does not destroy him results from his tacit or projected consent to her power over him. As Hobbes said in *De Cive*:

If . . . she [the mother] breed him, because the state of nature is the state of war, she is supposed to bring him up on this condition; that being grown to full age he become not her enemy; which is that he obey her. For since by natural necessity we all desire that which appears good unto us, it cannot be understood that any man hath on such terms afforded life to another, that he might both get strength by years, and at once become an enemy. But each man is an enemy to that other, whom he neither obeys nor commands.[22]

The point was expressed more succinctly in the *Leviathan* where Hobbes said that paternal authority 'is not derived from the Generation, as if therefore the Parent had Dominion over his Child because he begat him; but from the Childs Consent, either expresse, or by other sufficient arguments declared'.[23] The future consent of the child was probably based on Hobbes's fourth law of nature, the law of gratitude, which required '*That a man which*

21 Hobbes, *De Corpore Politico*, I, i, 13, and II, iv, 3 (*E.W.*, IV, 85 and 155). See also, *Leviathan*, ch. xvii, p. 132.
22 Hobbes, *De Cive*, ix, 2 and 3 (*E.W.*, II, 116).
23 Hobbes, *Leviathan*, ch. xx, p. 153. See also *De Corpore Politico*, II, iv, 3 (*E.W.*, IV, 156).

*receiveth Benefit from another of meer Grace, Endeavour that he*
*which giveth it, have no reasonable cause to repent him of his*
*good will.*' For if men fail to be grateful for such beneficence,
'there will be no beginning of benevolence, or trust; nor consequently of mutuall help; nor of reconciliation of one man to
another; and therefore they are to remain still in the condition
of *War*'.[24]

Applied specifically to the relationships of fathers and children
in the state of nature, this aspect of Hobbes's theory of consent
provided the means of legitimately transforming what was earlier
termed 'Naturall force' into sovereignty. The key to the process
was the fact that the child did not resist his father's will. It will
be seen that Hobbes apparently included this acquiescence within
the category of consent 'by other sufficient arguments declared'
and could thus assert that paternal domination was derived from
the consent of the child. What was central to Hobbes's political
thesis was, once again, a demonstration that men and not nature
were the authors of their own subjection.[25]

### 3

Howard Warrender concludes that the 'propriety on Hobbes's
part of applying the notion of tacit covenant to the child–parent
relationship is very doubtful'.[26] This observation is based on
Hobbes's having denied the ability of children to make covenants
because they 'have no use of Reason' and the statement later
in *Leviathan* that 'Over naturall fooles, children, or mad-men
there is no Law, no more than over brute breasts; nor are they
capable of the title of just, or unjust; because they had never power
to make any covenant, or to understand the consequences thereof;
and consequently never took upon them to authorize the actions of

---

[24] Hobbes, *Leviathan*, ch. xv, p. 116.
[25] In *De Cive* Hobbes said that in their natural condition men are 'without all kind of engagement to each other'. He specifically limited to
'three ways only' the procuring of 'a dominion over the person of another'. These ways were contract, conquest, and generation. (*De Cive*, viii,
1 [*E.W.*, II, 109].) In *Leviathan* it was asserted that there is 'no Obligation
on any man, which ariseth not from some Act of his own'. (*Leviathan*, ch.
xxi, p. 166.)
[26] Warrender, *Political Philosophy of Hobbes*, p. 124.

any Soveraign, as they must do that make themselves a Common-wealth.'[27] These notions, Warrender suggests, 'would seem to be more consistent with Hobbes's doctrine in general' than the 'tacit covenant children are supposed to make with their parent(s) by whom they are preserved'. He attributes Hobbes's derivation of parental authority from the consent of the child 'perhaps, to an anxiety to forestall at their inception, contemporary paternalistic theories of sovereignty'.[28]

However, Warrender seems to have missed the full meaning of Hobbes's identification of political and familial authority in the state of nature; he therefore fails to appreciate the importance of Hobbes's notion that *all* sovereign power springs from (voluntary) human actions rather than from natural causes. The discrepancy would be removed if the tacit compacts of children were equivalent to the consent given by each child as he came of age and became master of his own reason. This is approximately the conclusion that Hobbes reached in his debate with Bishop Bramhall when he attempted to explain how children could be bound by the laws of their ancestors:

The Conquerour makes no Law over the Conquered by vertue of his power; but by vertue of their assent that promised obedience for the saving of their lives. But when then is the assent of Children obtained to the Laws of their Ancestors? This also is from their desire of preserving their lives, which first the Parents might take away, where the Parents be free from all subjection; and where they are not, there the Civil power might do the same, if they doubted of their obedience. The Children therefore when they be grown up to strength enough to do mischief, and to judgment to know that other men are kept from doing mischief to them, by fear of the Sword that protecteth them, in that very act of receiving that protection, and not renouncing it openly, do oblige themselves to obey the Lawes of their Protectors; to which, in receiving such protection they have assented.[29]

[27] Hobbes, *Leviathan*, ch. xvi, p. 125, and ch. xxvi, p. 208.
[28] Warrender, *Political Philosophy of Hobbes*, pp. 256 n.1, and 124. Cf. Thomas in *Hobbes Studies*, ed. Brown, pp. 189 and 193.
[29] Hobbes, *Liberty and Necessity*, pp. 136–7. The absence of genuine social continuity had been pointed out by Filmer as one of the chief drawbacks of the contract theory. (See *Patriarcha*, p. 65, and *Anarchy*, p. 287.) Hobbes escaped this dilemma on the operational level in two further ways, but neither of them met the logical objections that could have been raised. He

Authority over the child in the state of nature belonged to any-one who had the power to kill it. In the first instance this person was always the mother, and the patriarchal title originated in power over her, not in the inherent rights or superiority of either males or fathers. Fathers have this authority in society, Hobbes reasoned, 'because for the most part Common-wealths have been erected by the Fathers, not by the Mothers of families'. In nature where there are no matrimonial regulations, without individual and specific contracts to the contrary, children are under the dominion of and subject to their mothers. Without laws govern-ing marriage, 'it cannot be known who is the Father, unlesse it be declared by the Mother: and therefore the right of Dominion over the Child dependeth on her will, and is consequently hers'. On the other hand, when the mother is subject to her husband, 'the Child, is in the Fathers power',[30] just as the child in society is the subject of his father's sovereign.[31]

4

It has been customary for modern commentators to draw sharp distinctions between two kinds of sovereignty in Hobbes's writings, that is, between the government that arises 'when a man maketh his children, to submit themselves, and their chil-dren to his government', and that which springs from the 'Covenant of every man with every man'.[32] The former is said

---

said, 'He that hath the Dominion over the Child, hath Dominion also over the Children of the Child; and over their Childrens Children.' (*Leviathan*, ch. xx, p. 155.) Thus, in political society every child was from birth a subject of his father's ruler. The second solution to the problem invoked the Covenant that God had made with Abraham in Gen. 17: 10: '*Abrahams* Seed had not this revelation, nor were yet in being; yet they are a party to the Covenant, and bound to obey what *Abraham* should declare to them for Gods Law; which they could not be, but in vertue of the obedience they owed to their Parents; who (if they be Subject to no other earthly power, as here in the case of *Abraham*) have Soveraign power over their children, and servants.' (*Leviathan*, ch. xxvi, p. 221.)

[30] Hobbes, *Leviathan*, ch. xx, pp. 154–5. See also *De Cive*, ix, 6 and 7 (*E.W.*, II, 118–19).

[31] Hobbes, *Leviathan*, ch. xx, p. 155, as quoted above in n. 29, and *De Cive.*, ix, 6 (*E.W.*, II, 118).

[32] Hobbes, *Leviathan*, ch. xvii, pp. 132 and 131.

to have been the true *historical* beginnings[33] of society recognized by Hobbes whereas the latter is supposed to represent the *logical* basis. An essential corollary to this view stresses the logical existence of the state of nature, falling back upon Hobbes's own words: 'It may peradventure be thought, there was never such a time, nor condition or warre as this; and I believe it was never generally so, over all the world.'[34]

G. C. Robertson was the first commentator to express this view. Despite the great attention devoted to the contract in the *Leviathan*, Robertson said, 'That states had their natural beginning in families when not in conquest, . . . is evidently the real opinion of Hobbes.'[35] The analysis of Leslie Stephen is similar; he also sees an opposition between the two positions and goes even further than Robertson, claiming that the contract thesis is not only 'absurd historically, but is also irrelevant to Hobbes'.[36] Richard Peters too treats familial government as a form of rule apart from that instituted by men and calls attention to Hobbes's 'lack of interest' in patriarchal authority, holding that 'it was *institution* that appealed to his way of thinking'.[37]

The most extreme member of this school is Leo Strauss, who says, Hobbes 'maintained up to the end that paternal authority and consequently patrimonial monarchy is, if not the legal, nevertheless the historical, origin of all or the majority of States'. Strauss further asserts that Hobbes always acknowledged 'the precedence of the natural over the artificial State'. According to Strauss, Hobbes insisted upon 'going beyond the findings of history' that society was originally patriarchal. Instead, he constructed 'a completely defective state of mankind', from which even the most simple human associations had been eliminated. This condition was 'the war of every one against every one'. Hobbes 'derives this war from its origin in human nature', Strauss continues, implying that even human nature and history are in opposition in the Hobbesian scheme. Finally, Strauss says, 'Hobbes

---

[33] Perhaps it should be indicated that by 'history' I do not mean the recapturable pasts of specific states or peoples but the anthropologically real antecedents of human social and political organization in general.

[34] Hobbes, *Leviathan*, ch. xiii, p. 97.

[35] Robertson, *Hobbes*, p. 146.

[36] Leslie Stephen, *Hobbes* (London, 1904), pp. 209–10, quotation from p. 210.

[37] Richard Peters, *Hobbes* (Baltimore, 1956), p. 211.

considered the philosophic grounding of the principles of all judgment on political subjects more fundamental, incomparably more important than the most thoroughly founded historical knowledge.' Therefore, the state of nature is 'not an historical fact, but a necessary condition'.[38]

This interpretation is not altogether satisfactory primarily because it omits two very important statements made by Hobbes: first, that there are no meaningful differences after inception between sovereignty by acquisition (which includes patriarchal power) and institution,[39] and second, that patriarchal power is derived not from the right of the father but from the tacit or projected consent of the child to be bound by the governance of his parent(s) and from the fourth law of nature, the law of gratitude. Further texual evidence—to say nothing of Warrender's persuasive reinterpretation of the status of obligation in the prepolitical situation—suggests that Hobbes conceived of the state of nature as something less than the 'completely defective state of mankind' envisaged by Strauss and not quite the total anarchy seen by his Stuart critics. Warrender is aware of the lack of significant differences between instituted and acquired sovereignty, but he too says, 'In any event, when Hobbes turns to consider the general problem of men in the State of Nature and the erection of a sovereign authority, he is clearly interested in logical and not historical analysis.' He does concede, however, that Hobbes 'bases no important point' upon the distinctions between logic and history and argues that 'it is more likely that he regarded the two types of sovereignty simply as different patterns determined by circumstances, without prejudice to where or how often each of them had been instanced historically'.[40] Even this reading is incomplete, for there is yet a further interpretation possible, one that attempts to assert the similarities between the notions that political societies grew out of the family and, alternatively, that they sprang from the state of nature.

The difficulties of interpretation arise from Hobbes's imprecise use of the state-of-nature concept and his failure to distinguish

[38] Leo Strauss, *The Political Philosophy of Hobbes; Its Basis and Genesis*, trans. Elsa M. Sinclair (Chicago, 1952), pp. 60, 66, and 104.
[39] Hobbes, *Leviathan*, ch. xx, p. 152; and *De Corpore Politico*, II, iii, 1, and II, iv, 10 (*E.W.*, IV, 148–9 and 159).
[40] Warrender, *Political Philosophy of Hobbes*, pp. 238–40.

at all times between two apparently different things he was doing
in his political writings. Hobbes was justifying a particular kind
of political authority and discussing the historico–anthropological
evolution of the state. To be sure, these are analytically separable
operations that are carried out on different levels, and it is to
the credit of previous commentators that they have drawn attention to these distinctions as they may be extracted from the political philosophy of Hobbes. In the seventeenth century, however,
these activities were not always separate. For many political
writers, as I have already pointed out, historical origins provided
a valid justification for authority, and it is not at all apparent that
Hobbes should be *totally* excluded from the authors who accepted this kind of reasoning. In fact, much of what Hobbes wrote
might become more intelligible if we keep in mind the moral significance his age attached to origins. This is especially true of his
theory of the state of nature, for the construct is appropriate to
political and logical justification as well as to historical reconstruction. Hobbes clearly used the state of nature to serve both
ends—and sometimes simultaneously. Seen in this light, Hobbes's
two tasks are revealed as having been very much alike, and the
differences between the historical and logical analyses in his
writings need not be as great as Robertson, Stephen, Peters,
Strauss, and Warrender suggest. If attention is directed primarily
to the place of the family in the state-of-nature theory, it is
possible to argue that there is no difference at all!

## 5

'A son', Hobbes declared in *De Cive*, 'cannot be understood
to be at any time in the state of nature, as being under the power
and command of them to whom he owes his protection as soon as
ever he is born, namely, either his father's or his mother's or him
that nourished him. . . .'[41] This statement was validly inferred
from the conception of the state of nature as the condition in
which 'there were no common Power to feare'.[42] Removal of a

---

[41] Hobbes, *De Cive*, i, 10n. (*E.W.*, II, 10).
[42] Hobbes, *Leviathan*, ch. xiii, p. 97. In *De Corpore* Hobbes wrote, 'The
appetites of men, and the passions of their minds, are such, that unless they

son from the state of nature is doubly significant because, as the context reveals, it was part of an answer to a critic (whom Hobbes failed to identify) and not a possible confusion that had passed unnoticed. Moreover, this position had already been incorporated into the original text of *De Cive* when Hobbes declared that the equality of nature applied only to 'all men of riper years'.[43] It was as if the state of nature extended only to the door of the household but did not pass over the threshold, for Hobbes claimed that there was private property in the family but not in the state of nature. There can only be private ownership where there is sufficient security, a qualification that precluded the state of nature.[44] But a family, Hobbes wrote, 'is a little city. For the sons of a family have a propriety of their goods granted them by their father, distinguished indeed from the rest of the sons of the same family, but not from the propriety of the father himself.'[45] In the *Leviathan*, Hobbes said that the American Indians lived in a virtual state of nature and except for the internal organization of their families were without the benefits of order: 'For the savage people in many places of *America*, except the government of small Families, the concord whereof dependeth on naturall lust, have no government at all; and live at this day in that brutish manner, as I said before.'[46]

As has already been observed, Hobbes regarded a 'great Family if it be not part of some Common-wealth,' as itself a commonwealth so long as 'it be of that power by its own number, or by other opportunities, as not to be subdued without the hazard of war'. A closer examination reveals that these family-common-wealths existed in a state of nature *vis-à-vis* other units, for they would have faced each other with 'no common Power to feare'.[47]

---

be restrained by some power, they will always be making war upon one another.' (*De Corpore* [1655], I, vi, 7 [*E.W.*, I, 74].) These unbridled appetites and passions became the state of nature of the *Leviathan* and *De Cive*.

[43] Hobbes, *De Cive*, ix, 2 (*E.W.*, II, 115). See also the discussion in the *Leviathan*, ch. xxvi, p. 208, of the inability of children to enter into covenants.

[44] Hobbes, *De Cive*, vi, 1 (*E.W.*, II, 72).

[45] Ibid., vi, 15n. (*E.W.*, II, 84). See also *De Corpore Politico*, II, iii, 4 (*E.W.*, IV, 151).

[46] Hobbes, *Leviathan*, ch. xiii, p. 97.

[47] Ibid., ch. xxx, p. 157 (see also ch. xvii, p. 129), and ch. xiii, p. 97.

In the state of nature, independent fathers were 'absolute Sovereigns in their own Families'[48] and were civil rulers because they had authority over their children and servants, which 'has no place but in a State Civill, because before such estate, there is no Dominion of Persons'.[49] It is these fathers who were in the state of nature and engaged in the 'warre of every man against every man'. Thus, 'every man' can certainly be understood as 'every father' without changing Hobbes's basic argument. The members of families were the subjects of their father-sovereigns who secured private belongings for them. 'But fathers of divers families, *who are not subject to any common father nor lord*, have a common right in all things,' Hobbes asserted in *De Cive*.[50]

A small problem arises in attempting to classify the relationships among members of different families, none of whom were patriarchs or independent fathers. They too would undoubtedly have faced one another in a state of nature, for there would have been no authority above them. In these cases, however, the state-of-nature relationships would have been due to the individuals' having figuratively stepped out of their respective families. Patriarchs, on the other hand, were in the state of nature because of their very status and inherent condition. In arguing that independent nations faced each other in a state of nature, Hobbes clearly stated that the rights and liberties of that condition accrued to the commonwealths and their representatives and not to the individual residents of each polity.[51]

All that was missing was a formal statement that the agreement of fathers rather than the consent of all persons established commonwealths by institution. Hobbes said precisely this in two passages that have been overlooked by all his commentators, both seventeenth-century and modern, who have perceived a fundamental conflict between the family and the state of nature. In justifying the authority that fathers have over their offspring in society, Hobbes said:

[It must be remembered] that originally the Father of every man was also his Soveraign Lord, with power over him of Life and

48 Ibid., ch. xxii, p. 180.
49 Ibid., ch. xvi, p. 125.
50 Hobbes, *De Cive*, vi, 15n. (*E.W.*, II, 84). Emphasis added.
51 See *Leviathan*, ch. xxi, pp. 164–5 (quoted below, p. 240).

Death; and that *the Fathers of families, when by instituting a Common-wealth,* they resigned that absolute Power, yet it was never intended, they should lose the honour due unto them [from their children] for their education. For to relinquish such right, was not necessary to the Institution of Soveraign Power.[52]

Similarly, Hobbes write that 'the Parent ought to have the honour of a Soveraign, (*though he have surrendered his Power to the Civill Law,*) because he had it originally by Nature'.[53]

The importance of these statements can be appreciated by contrasting them with Bishop Bramhall's insistence that Hobbes had erred in attributing the institution of civil society to the actions of naturally free men. He 'builds upon a wrong foundation, that all Magistrates at first, were elective', the Bishop charged. 'The first Governours were Fathers of Families; And when those petty Princes could not afford competent protection and security to their subjects, many of them did resign their severall and respective interests into the hands of one joint Father of the Country.'[54] In light of Hobbes's statements, there now appears to have been no disagreement between him and Bramhall on this matter. Filmer's criticism of Hobbes—that the subordination of children to their Fathers left 'little liberty in the subjects of the family to consent to [the] institution of government'[55]—may also be qualified to the extent that dependants were not parties to the contract. On this reading, the Hobbesian doctrine is not far removed from Sir Robert's own statement in *Patriarcha* that 'By the uniting of great families or petty Princedoms, we find the greater monarchies were at first erected. . . .'[56] Thus, both men had far more in common with their contemporaries than is generally acknowledged.

## 6

This interpretation of Hobbes invites a reassessment of certain aspects of his doctrine. In the first place, his state of nature no

---

[52] Hobbes, *Leviathan*, ch. xx, p. 263. Emphasis added.
[53] Ibid., ch. xxvii, p. 237. Emphasis added.
[54] Bramhall, *Defence*, p. 100.
[55] Filmer, *Original*, p. 239.     [56] Filmer, *Patriarcha*, pp. 61-2.

longer appears to have been altogether individualistic; rather it
was composed of familial social units that faced each other as
autonomous entities. As Thomas Tenison observed in his criticism
of the *Leviathan:*

> It is further to be marked, that one Family, as it stands separated
> from another, is as one Kingdom divided from the Territories of a
> Neighbouring Monarch. If therefore the state of Nature remaineth
> in a Family not depending upon another Family, in places where
> there is no common Government; then all Kingdoms which have not
> made Leagues with one another, are, at this day, in the same state.
> . . . I know you esteem all distinct Kingdoms in a state of War in
> relation to each other, and therefore they have a right; if they have
> a Power, of invading: but he that consults *Grotius*, in his Book
> *de jure belli & pacis* (designed chiefly to set forth the Rights,
> not of Domestick, but Forinsick War) will not be much of your
> opinion.[57]

Independent nations, according to Hobbes, *did* face one
another as in the state of nature. He said:

> For as among masterless men, there is perpetuall war, of every man
> against his neighbour; . . . So in States, and Common-wealths, not
> dependent on one another, every Common-wealth (not every man)
> has an absolute Libertie, to doe what it shall judge (that is to say,
> what that Man, or Assemblie that representeth it, shall judge) most
> conducing to their benefit. But withall, they live in the condition
> of a perpetuall war, and upon the confines of battel, with their
> frontiers armed, and canons planted against their neighbours round
> about.[58]

This description is no less applicable to families in the state of
nature than to the relations of sovereign nations. Hobbes in fact
did compare the activities of small, primitive families to cities
and kingdoms of his own day.[59] Operationally, then, the elemental
social unit for Hobbes was not the individual but the family, and
a characterization such as Bertrand de Jouvenel's that 'Hobbes

---

[57] [Tenison], *The Creed of Hobbes*, p. 135.
[58] Hobbes, *Leviathan*, ch. xxi, pp. 164–5.
[59] Ibid., ch. xvii, pp. 128–9.

gives a picture of individuals living each man for himself',[60] cannot be accepted without qualification.

Another consequence of this rereading is the possible revision of the modern estimates of Hobbes's relationship both to his contemporaries and to traditional modes of thought. That Hobbes was an innovator is not open to serious question. Leo Strauss at one time regarded him as the 'originator of modern political philosophy',[61] and George Sabine has remarked that Hobbes's system was 'the first wholehearted attempt to treat political philosophy as part of a mechanistic body of scientific knowledge'.[62] The justification of absolute, undivided sovereignty with arguments 'taken from general principles of psychology and ethics rather than from assertions about Divine Right' was also a new departure,[63] as was the use of consent along with natural freedom and equality as the source of an unlimited rather than a constitutional government. All these Hobbesian innovations have long been known and are frequently commented upon. What has gone largely unnoticed, however, is the relationship of Hobbes's observations on the nature of familial power to the traditional patriarchal political theory. In this instance, too, important new ground was broken.

Although his identification of primitive paternal authority with political power was in keeping with the writings of many of his contemporaries, Hobbes was unique in attempting to derive the father's power over his children from their consents. Buttressing the arguments for original freedom and equality in his manner, he added greater consistency to his doctrine and was not required to explain how men who were subjected to their fathers by nature could ever be sufficiently free to agree to a compact of government. And if it is remembered that the child's consent was projected into the future through the fourth law of nature, the

[60] Bertrand de Jouvenel, *Sovereignty: An Inquiry into the Political Good*, trans. J. F. Huntington (Chicago, 1957), p. 232. It need hardly be added that Hobbes was certainly an 'individualist' in the sense that his doctrine predicted a utilitaritian harmony of separate interests realized in a community rather than a more 'collectivist' notion of the social good.

[61] Strauss, *Political Philosophy of Hobbes*, p. xv. Strauss later attributed the decisive break with the past to Machiavelli (p. xvi).

[62] George H. Sabine, *A History of Political Theory*, 3rd ed. (New York, 1961), p. 460.

[63] Peters, *Hobbes*, p. 27.

law of gratitude, this thesis is no less plausible than anything else about the state of nature.

A more conventional way out of this dilemma was to adopt the anthropological thesis and to insist that while the family was the historical precursor of the state, patriarchal subjugation was distinct from and in no way prejudiced man's natural political right. This argument had been used many times in the past and would be employed again with variations by some of Hobbes's critics, by Temple, as well as by Locke in his answer to Filmer. Another solution was to attempt to extract a normative conclusion from the identity of familial and governmental power and the fact that political society traced its origins to the primitive family. Ultimately, of course, Hobbes did conform to this second pattern and sought to validate the proposition that all status is conventional. To this extent, the alleged natural freedom of mankind was at least *theoretically* preserved. Since this freedom gave way to parental control as soon as the child was born—if only because a child's physical weakness made it dependent upon others at once[64]—my claim that the family rather than the individual was the basic social unit for Hobbes is in no way qualified.

The historical reality of the state of nature is yet another question that might be re-examined in light of Hobbes's use of patriarchal political theories. It need not be argued that the condition of 'meer Nature' *necessarily* corresponded to a genuine historical situation, but the entire matter is placed in a new perspective when it is shown that what recent commentators have regarded as Hobbes's history is potentially compatible with his state of nature. If the thesis of Leo Strauss and others is correct— that is, if Hobbes believed that actual states grew out of expanding families—and if independent, sovereign, familial commonwealths existed in the Hobbesian state of nature, it should follow that the state of nature was a representation of true history. Hobbes himself provided further evidence for this view in his very admission that the state of nature was a logical fiction. What is often overlooked about this admission, however—or allowed to stand without comment—is that Hobbes did not say that there

---

[64] '... to man by nature, or as man, that is, as soon as he is born, solitude is an enemy; for infants have need of others to help them to live, and those of riper years to help them to live well.' (*De Cive*, i, 2n. [*E.W.*, II, 2].)

had never been a state of nature. He wrote, 'I believe it was never *generally so, over all the world*: but there are many places, where they live so now', and he immediately referred to the American Indians, who 'except [for] the government of small Families, . . . have no government at all'.[65] What seems unmistakable clear is the complexity of the problem. *Prima facie* dismissal of the issue is undoubtedly out of place, and it ought not be flatly asserted, to quote Professor Jouvenel again, that Hobbes 'was concerned to build not a historical reconstruction but a social mechanics'.[66]

---

[65] Hobbes, *Leviathan*, ch. xiii, p. 97. Emphasis added. On this interpretation cf. Macpherson, *Possessive Individualism*, p. 20, and F. C. Hood, *The Divine Politics of Thomas Hobbes* (Oxford, 1964), pp. 81–2, both of whom are aware of the partial reality of the state of nature yet still assume that Hobbes regarded the concept as historically irrelevant to his political theories.

[66] Jouvenel, *Sovereignty*, p. 232.

# XIII

## The Family and the Origins of the State in Locke's Political Philosophy

### I

It has been the genius of recent scholarship to question seriously —if not to dispel altogether—one of the standard myths associated with the political philosophy of John Locke—that the target of Locke's *Two Treatises* was the contractual absolutism of Thomas Hobbes. Peter Laslett has presented compelling reasons for believing, on the contrary, that Locke was criticizing the divine-right patriarchalism of Sir Robert Filmer.[1] There has never been any question that Locke's 'First Treatise' was a direct and often belabored criticism of Filmer's political writings. Locke himself described the 'First Treatise' as an essay in which *'The False Principles and Foundation* of Sir *Robert Filmer*, and His Followers, Are Detected and Overthrown'.[2] However, it is no longer sufficient to say that Locke's critique of patriarchalism consisted of a detailed exegesis of Biblical passages, a refutation of Sir Robert's view that Adam had been an absolute patriarchal sovereign, and a demonstration that paternal political power (even if it had once existed) had not descended through Adam's heirs to the English House of Stuart. What must be equally understood is that the very logic and structure of the whole of the *Two Treatises* were responses to Filmer. Only through such a realization is it possible both to appreciate Locke's interest in certain problems and to grasp the implications of some of the very fine distinctions that he drew. By looking at his analysis of the relationship between political and paternal authority in these terms, we are

[1] See Laslett, Introduction to Locke, *Two Treatises*, esp. pp. 45–78.
[2] Title page of the 1698 printing of the *Two Treatises* as reproduced in Laslett's edition, p. 153.

able to see how much of Locke's argument was shaped by the need to answer Filmer and to understand the kind of political theory that could serve as an adequate alternative to moral patriarchalism. For Locke, more fully than anyone else, analyzed the patriarchal political theory and tried to put something in its place.[3]

Locke specifically and emphatically distinguished between the powers of political superiors and fathers throughout his *Two Treatises*, attributing 'the great mistakes of late about Government' and to the 'confounding [of] these distinct Powers one with another'.[4] This difference lay at the heart of his political philosophy, and as early as section two of the 'Second Treatise' he wrote:

> ... I think it may not be amiss, to set down what I take to be Political Power. That the Power of a *Magistrate* over a Subject, may be distinguished from that of a *Father* over his Children, a *Master* over his Servant, a *Husband* over his Wife, and a *Lord* over his Slave. All which distinct Powers happening sometimes together in the same Man, if he be considered under these different Relations, it may help us to distinguish these Powers one from another, and shew the difference betwixt a Ruler of a Common-wealth, a Father of a Family, and a Captain of a Galley.[5]

The distinctions between patriarchal and political authority were evident from their varying origins and ends, Locke contended. *'Nature gives* the first of these, *viz. Paternal Power to Parents* for the Benefit of their Children. ... *Voluntary Agreement* gives the second, *viz. Political Power to Governours* for the Benefit of their Subjects. ...'[6] In the 'First Treatise' Locke denied the political significance of the Fifth Commandment, which, as Laslett comments, was a repudiation of 'far more than the principles of Filmer'. It was an attack on an important doctrine of

---

[3] The only detailed study of Locke's political thought that fully appreciates the importance of the Locke-Filmer relationship is John Dunn's excellent *The Political Thought of John Locke: An Historical Account of the Argument of the Two Treatises of Government* (Cambridge, 1969), which complements and extends the argument of this chapter in many important respects.

[4] Locke, *Two Treatises*, II, 169.

[5] Ibid., II, 2. See also II, 71.     [6] Ibid., II, 173.

I

Protestant Christianity. The Fifth Commandment, Locke wrote, is 'an Eternal Law annex'd purely to the relations of Parents and Children, and so contains nothing of the Magistrates Power in it, nor is subjected to it'.[7]

Locke had not been eager to separate paternal from political authority throughout his life. In 1672, in a topical sketch of knowledge under the general heading 'Sapientia,' he accepted 'Jus Paternum' along with 'Consensus populi' as the 'Fundamentia' of politics.[8] He added 'Arma' in his own hand to a later version of this outline prepared by his copyist, Sylvester Brownover.[9] Similarly, in his early essays on things indifferent—recently published as *Two Tracts on Government*—Locke observed:

> Now I find that there are, among the authors who discuss this question [the sources of civil authority], commonly two such foundations. . . . [S]ome suppose men to be born in servitude, others, to liberty. The latter assert an equality between men founded on the law of nature, while the former maintain a paternal right over children and claim that government originates thence. . . .
>
> To these a third way of constituting civil power may perhaps be added: One in which all authority is held to come from God but the nomination and appointment of the person bearing that power is thought to be made by the people. Otherwise a right to govern will not easily be derived from the paternal right nor a right of life and death from the popular.
>
> However, I offer no conclusion about these theories, nor do I consider it of any relevance to our present controversy whether one or other of them be true.[10]

The young Locke does not appear to have been nearly so interested in the origin of political organization as he was to become by the time he wrote the *Two Treatises*.[11] Then, of course, 'Jus Paternum' and 'Consensus populi' were no longer regarded as equally valid bases for the state.

[7] Ibid., I, 64. Laslett's remarks are in the note to lines 11–14.
[8] Bodleian Library, MS. Locke c. 28, fol. 41. An earlier version of this same division—taken from a 1661 manuscript—has been published as an appendix to Locke, *Two Tracts on Government*, ed. Philip Abrams (Cambridge, 1967), p. 245.
[9] Bodleian Library, MS. Locke c. 28, fol. 157ᵛ.
[10] Locke, *Two Tracts*, pp. 230 and 231.
[11] See Laslett, Introduction to Locke, *Two Treatises*, pp. 19–21 and nn.

**2**

Locke's description of familial power—its origin, nature, and extent—is fundamental to his analysis of the relation between patriarchalism and politics. He held that procreation alone is not the source of paternal authority. God, not man, is the maker of children; the rights of fathers cannot spring from generation when the parents are merely God's unwitting agents. 'They who say the *Father* gives life to his Children, are so dazled with the thoughts of Monarchy, that they do not, as they ought, remember God, who is *the Author and Giver of Life: 'Tis in him alone we live, move, and have our Being,*' Locke wrote. God 'is *King* because he is indeed Maker of us all, which no Parents can pretend to be of their Children'.[12] The parents' role in procreation was succinctly described:

What Father of a Thousand, when he begets a Child, thinks farther than the satisfying his present Appetite? God in his infinite Wisdom has put strong desires of Copulation into the Constitution of Men, thereby to continue the race of Mankind, which he doth most commonly without the intention, and often against the Consent and Will of the Begetter. And indeed those who desire and design Children, are but the occasions of their being, and when they design and wish to beget them, do little more towards their making, than *Ducalion* and his Wife in the Fable did towards the making of Mankind, by throwing Pebbles over their Heads.[13]

Thus, men are 'all the Workmanship of one Omnipotent, and infinitely wise Maker; . . . [and] they are his Property, whose Workmanship they are'.[14] Similarly, Locke wrote in his *Journal* for 1678 that if a man 'comprehends the relation between father and son and finds it reasonable that his son whom he hath begot (only in pursuance of his pleasure without thinking of his son) and nourished should obey, love and reverence him and be grateful to him, he can not but find it much more reasonable that he

---

[12] Locke, *Two Treatises*, I, 52 and 53. See also II, 65 (especially lines 7–9).
[13] Ibid., I, 54.
[14] Ibid., II, 6. Both notions—that men are the workmanship and property of God—are repeated throughout the *Two Treatises*. For references, see Laslett's note to lines 10–14 of this section.

and every other man should obey and revere, love and thank the author of their being to whom they owe all that they are'.[15]

The authority to discipline children was not, according to Locke, a necessary attribute of fatherhood, and since it was exercised over God's creatures, it could be held and executed only through some degree of divine dispensation. Beginning with Adam and Eve, all parents were placed 'by the Law of Nature, *under an obligation to preserve, nourish, and educate the Children*, they had begotten, not as their own Workmanship, but the Workmanship of their own Maker, the Almighty, to whom they were to be accountable for them'.[16] On this ground, Locke said, 'The *Power*, then, *that Parents have* over their Children, arises from that Duty which is incumbent on them, to take care of their Off-spring, during the imperfect state of Childhood.'[17] Thus, in the 'First Treatise', Locke implied that the child was bound to obey whoever nourished and cared for him, whether that person was his natural father or not;[18] and in the 'Second Treatise' he specifically said:

Nay, this *power* so little belongs to the *Father* by any peculiar right of Nature, but only as he is Guardian of his Children, that when he quits his Care of them, he loses his Power over them, which goes along with their Nourishment and Education, to which it is inseparably annexed, and it belongs as much to the *Foster-Father* of an exposed Child, as to the Natural Father of another.... It is but a help to the weakness and imperfection of their Nonage, a Discipline necessary to their education.[19]

Locke assumed that familial authority belonged to the mother as much as to the father, and he never seemed to tire of pointing

---

[15] Locke, *Journal*, 1678, Bodleian Library, MS. Locke f. 3, p. 202 (entry dated 15 July and titled 'lex Na[tur]ae'). The full text is conveniently available as the conclusion to W. von Leyden, 'John Locke and the Law of Nature', *Philosophy*, XXI (1956), 35.

[16] Locke, *Two Treatises*, II, 56. See also II, 60 (lines 17–20).

[17] Ibid., II, 58.

[18] Ibid., I, 100.

[19] Ibid., II, 65. See also II, 69 (lines 4–8). In March, 1679, Locke made the following entry concerning the children of the Canadian Indians in his reading notes: 'Education not generation gives the obligation & affection, for the children taken prisoners when men made wars against their parents & country [lived] as heartily as any....' Bodleian Library, MS. Locke c. 33, fol. 10.

out to Filmer's apologists that the Fifth Commandment ordered children to obey both parents, not just the father as Sir Robert implied.[20] Even if the power to control children came from generation, Locke asserted, 'This would give the *Father* but a joynt Dominion with the Mother over them. For no body can deny but that the Woman hath an equal share, if not the greater, as nourishing the Child a long time in her own Body out of her own Substance.'[21] Thus, Locke contended that paternal power might 'more properly [be] called *Parental Power*. For whatever obligation Nature and the right of Generation lays on Children, it must certainly bind them equal to both concurrent Causes of it.'[22] However, Locke soon forgot his own injunction and reverted to the phrase '*Paternal Power*',[23] subsequently suggesting that the terms were interchangeable.[24]

In most matters Locke treated the husband as the superior mate, since 'the Rule, should be placed somewhere [when there are differences between husband and wife], it naturally falls to the Man's share, as the abler and stronger'. Marriage, according to Locke, is a contractual relationship that 'leaves the Wife in the full and free possession of what . . . is her peculiar Right, and gives the Husband no more power over her Life, than she has over his'. Man's superiority extends only 'to the things of their common Interest and Property,'[25] and the conjugal power does not provide the basis of government. If the subjugation of Eve by divine *fiat* gave Adam a monarchical power over her as Filmer had claimed, 'there will be as many Monarchs as there are Husbands', for what was bestowed upon Adam was 'the Power that every Husband hath to order the things of private Concernment in his Family'.[26] It can certainly be inferred from these remarks, however, that final authority over children, which would

---

[20] Locke, *Two Treatises*, I, 6, 11, and 60–6. Cf. II, 52–3.

[21] Ibid., I, 55.

[22] Ibid., II, 52.

[23] Ibid, II, 69. See Laslett's note to line 1.

[24] '. . . *Paternal* or *Parental Power* is nothing but that, which Parents have over their Children. . . .' (Ibid., II, 170.) At one point, he said, '*Nature gives . . . Paternal Power to Parents. . . .*' (II, 173.)

[25] Ibid., II, 82. See also II, 78. '*Conjugal Society* is made by a voluntary Compact between Man and Woman.'

[26] Ibid., I, 48. The Biblical allusion is to Gen. 3: 16. For Filmer's statement see *Anarchy*, p. 283.

undoubtedly be among 'the things of their common Interest and Property,' belonged to the husband, for Locke does not seem to have questioned this aspect of the traditional patriarchal family.

Parental power is needed, Locke reasoned, because of the inability of infants to take their places in the world of men, a justification that Sir Leslie Stephen described as 'simple utilitarianism'.[27] Discipline exists 'for the Benefit of Children during their Minority, to supply their want of Ability, and understanding how to manage their Property'.[28] The parent–child relationship is, therefore, more properly regarded as 'the Priviledge of Children, and Duty of Parents, than any Prerogative of Paternal Power'.[29] Children are born 'ignorant and without the use of *Reason*'[30] and therefore do not enjoy 'that *equal Right* that every Man hath, *to his Natural Freedom*, without being subjected to the Will or Authority of any other Man'.[31] Thus, Locke escaped the conflict between familial authority and the principle of natural equality, which Filmer had insisted plagued the anti-patriarchalists of his own day.

In addition, subjection to parents—however legitimate—is only temporary, Locke said, for its bonds 'are like the Swadling Cloths they [infants] are wrapt up in, and supported by, in the weakness of their Infancy. Age and Reason as they grow up, loosen them till at length they drop quite off, and leave a Man at his own free Disposal.'[32] Parental control educates and prepares the child for the time when he will be the master of his own actions while simultaneously directing his life by taking the place of the private will and understanding that have not yet developed. But once the child reaches the age of discretion and reason, according to Locke, he achieves the equality of which his infancy had deprived him. The father's 'power of Commanding ends with Nonage',[33] for 'when he comes to that Estate that made his *Father a Freeman, the Son is a Freeman* too'.[34]

The most significant limit on patriarchal authority was presented in Locke's argument that because '*every Man's Children*

[27] Sir Leslie Stephen, *History of English Thought in the Eighteenth Century*, 3rd ed. 1902), paperbound reprint, 2 vols. (New York, 1962), II, 116.     [28] Locke, *Two Treatises*, II, 173.

[29] Ibid., II, 67.     [30] Ibid., II, 57.

[31] Ibid., II, 54.     [32] Ibid., II, 55.

[33] Ibid., II, 69.     [34] Ibid., II, 58.

... [are] by Nature as *free* as himself, or any of his Ancestors ever were, [they] may, whilst they are in that Freedom, choose what Society they will join themselves to, what Common-wealth they will put themselves under'.[35] That is, as Locke expressed it in another context, a man '*cannot* by any *Compact* whatsoever, bind *his Children* or Posterity. For this Son, when a Man, being altogether as free as the Father, any *act of the Father can no more give away the liberty of the Son*, than it can of any body else.'[36] Filmer had insisted that allowing children to be bound by the acts of their ancestors was a denial of the principles of natural equality and original freedom.[37] Locke met this challenge head on and carried these principles and the consent basis of government to their necessary conclusions by acknowledging the right of each man to be the author of his own political obligation. Subjugation to parents did not encroach upon political freedom, and Locke properly asserted in one of his most important and effective statements against Filmerian thesis:

> Thus we are *born Free*, as we are born Rational; not that we have actually the Exercise of either: Age that brings one, brings with it the other too. And thus we see how *natural Freedom and Subjection to Parents* may consist together, and are both founded on the same Principle. . . . The *Freedom of a Man at years of discretion*, and the *Subjection* of a Child *to* his *Parents*, whilst yet short of that Age, are so consistent, and so distinguishable, that the most blinded Contenders for Monarchy, *by Right of Fatherhood*, cannot miss this *difference*, the most obstinate cannot but allow their consistency.[38]

Nonetheless, Locke recognized that parents—and fathers in particular—effectively had great control over their children and could use this control to induce their offspring to become members of their own civil societies. This aspect of familial authority is most clearly seen in Locke's discussion of inheritance and of the rights of fathers and governments to impose conditions on the acceptances of bequests. Even though children expect to inherit the possessions of their parents and ordinarily do so, Locke said, 'it is commonly in the Father's Power to bestow it with a more

---

[35] Ibid., II, 73.
[36] Ibid., II, 116.
[37] See Filmer, *Patriarcha*, p. 65, and *Anarchy*, p. 287.
[38] Locke, *Two Treatises*, II, 61.

sparing or liberal hand, according as the Behaviour of this or that Child hath comported with his Will and Humour'.[39] This power was justified by Locke as a consequence of the property right and not as an inherent right of fatherhood: 'That Estate being .... [the] Fathers Property, he may dispose or settle it as he pleases.'[40]

Locke realized that this power 'is no small Tye on the Obedience of Children' and that it led to very significant social and political consequences.[41] As we have seen, Locke had previously declared that there were two major restrictions on patriarchal authority: a father was not entitled to give his child's consent to be bound by a government; nor could he exercise his parental power beyond the nonage of the child. Inheritance provided a *practical* means of overcoming these limitations without disturbing their *moral* validity. Locke knew that sons were usually members of their fathers' states and that they often continued to obey their fathers after coming of age. The cause in both cases was the continued paternal power that resulted from inheritance. But this 'is no natural Tye or Engagement', Locke asserted; rather, it is 'a voluntary Submission', for children are free to reject inheritances. However,

if they will enjoy the *Inheritance* of their Ancestors, they must take it on the same terms their Ancestors had it, and submit to all the Conditions annex'd to such a Possession. By this Power indeed Fathers oblige their Children to Obedience to themselves, even when they are past Minority, and most commonly too subject them to this or that Political Power. But neither of these by any peculiar right of *Fatherhood*, but by the Reward they have in their hands to inforce and recompense such a Compliance.[42]

More pertinent here than the continuing obedience to fathers beyond the years of nonage is the allegiance to government that follows from the inheritance of property. It was Locke's firm conviction that a son could not own his father's possessions 'but under the same terms his Father did; by becoming a Member of the Society: whereby he puts himself presently under the Government, he finds there established, as much as any other Subject of

[39] Ibid., II, 72.     [40] Ibid., II, 116.
[41] Ibid., II, 73.     [42] Ibid.

that Commonwealth'.⁴³ Acceptance of a bequest obligated one to a government because it was an act that Locke termed 'tacit consent':

every Man, that hath any Possession, or Enjoyment, of any part of the Dominions of any Government, doth thereby give his *tacit Consent*, and is as far forth obliged to Obedience to the Laws of that Government, during such Enjoyment, as any one under it.⁴⁴

The power of a civil society to attach conditions—including political obligation—to the ownership of property had already been claimed by Locke in a statement in the 'Second Treatise' that seems to have escaped the attention of most commentators on his theory of property: 'For in Governments the Laws regulate the right of property, and the possession of land is determined by positive constitutions.'⁴⁵ It is difficult to reconcile this doctrine with the pre-political natural right to property. However, the tacit consent and obligation that were consequences of heirship demonstrate Locke's acceptance of institutional pressures as a major reason for men's moral and social compatibility. Thus, Locke incorporated genuine social continuity into an essentially individualist political theory by joining tacit consent to inheritance.

Locke was able to provide this continuity without accepting the metaphysical complexities and societal organicism of Rousseau and Hooker. Locke combined social and political continuity (as well as the *prima facie* restraints implied by historical conditioning) with moral freedom by distinguishing between natural and habitual obedience.⁴⁶ What is equally important is the fact

---

⁴³ Ibid., II, 117. Locke was not consistent about his intentions. As the next passage quoted in the text shows, heirs presumably satisfied this requirement by tacitly consenting to the government. But in II, 122 Locke said that tacit consent would not make a man a 'member' of a civil society: 'Nothing can make any Man so, but his actually entering into it by positive Engagement, and express Promise and Compact.'

⁴⁴ Locke, *Two Treatises*, II, 119.

⁴⁵ Ibid., II, 50. See also II, 120 (esp. lines 1–11).

⁴⁶ This distinction is implicit in the assertion that obedience elicited by an anticipated inheritance 'is no natural Tye or Engagement, but a voluntary Submission' (Ibid., II, 73) and will be seen again in Locke's explanation of the ease with which a family could become transformed into a civil society.

that this separation was a part of Locke's answer to Filmer. Sir Robert had complained that the theories of natural equality, individual freedom, and political voluntarism, consistently maintained, were destructive of political stability. These doctrines 'well practised,' he said, 'layeth all open to constant anarchy'.[47] Locke's response, in effect, was that men generally do join the commonwealths of which their fathers were members even though they always have the *right* to refuse to do so by withdrawing. If this doctrine is *philosophically* anarchic, that is an unavoidable result of political voluntarism, for the only way to demonstrate that men do not have the right of choice is to place political obligation on a naturalistic and involuntary basis. In fact, the *practical* result is not anarchy, for men are generally inclined to accept the governments of their fathers. This acceptance, however, is a contingent factor and not a natural result or necessary consequence of being born under a particular political authority.

3

Despite the importance to Locke of the differences between the subordination of children to their parents—and especially to their fathers—during their nonage and man's subjugation to political authority, the familial association played a major role in the *Two Treatises* in the explanations of the origins of the state and man's emergence from the state of nature. Next to self-preservation, Locke felt, the strongest drive 'God Planted in Men' was that of 'propagating their Kind, and continuing themselves in their Posterity'.[48] This urge to procreate was presumably one of the 'strong Obligations of Necessity, Convenience, and Inclination' that man had been placed under by God 'to drive him into *Society*', for man had been so created that 'in his own Judgment, it was not good for him to be alone'. Locke accordingly observed, 'The *first Society* was between Man and Wife, which gave begin-

---

[47] Filmer, *Originall*, p. 260.
[48] Locke, *Two Treatises*, I, 88. Locke did not attempt to reconcile this conscious drive to propagate with the argument based on involuntary parenthood that he had previously used against the derivation of paternal power from generation. Note also that Locke has shifted his grounds somewhat, for in I, 54 (above, p. 247) this drive was reduced to a desire to copulate, but here procreation has become a conscious act.

ning to that between Parents and Children; to which, in time, that between Master and Servant came to be added.' Nonetheless, Locke contended that even the complex household 'came short of *Political Society*'.[49] But he went on to say that the familial society could be *transformed* into a state. What must be determined, then, are the reasons why the household was not political and how civil society was established on the foundation of this non-political association. Only then can the relationship between state and family in the *Two Treatises* be properly ascertained.

It should be clear that this familial group existed in the state of nature and was therefore a pre-political society; the state of nature emerges at least from *this* context as an historically real condition.[50] It is equally apparent that Locke distinguished between society and political society, a differentiation that has the very important consequence of making social (albeit non-political) institutions perfectly compatible with the historical state of nature.[51] Admittedly, this distinction was not uniformly maintained throughout the *Two Treatises*, but any attempt to extract a rigorous consistency from Locke on this matter would obscure an important feature of his political philosophy. By not always making clear the apparent differences between political and non-political societies while simultaneously contending that non-civil societies existed in the state of nature, Locke developed a conception of politics in which the transition from the state of nature to government was almost effortless; it was, in addition, barely perceptible.

A non-political condition does not appear to have lasted very

[49] Ibid., II, 77. In II, 79, Locke said that the purpose of the '*conjunction between Male and Female*' is 'not barely Procreation, but the continuation of the Species'. Therefore conjugal society ought to endure 'so long as is necessary to the nourishment and support of the young Ones, who are to be sustained by those that got them, till they are able to shift and provide for themselves'.

[50] The question of whether Locke's state of nature was a logical construct or an historical reality has been much debated. It is my feeling that Locke accepted both an historical and a logical conception, his use varying with his context. See Richard Ashcraft, 'Locke's State of Nature: Historical Fact or Moral Fiction?' *American Political Science Review*, LXII (1968), 898–915.

[51] See Locke, *Two Treatises*, II, 28 and 211, and J. W. Gough, *John Locke's Political Philosophy: Eight Studies*, corrected ed. (Oxford, 1956), p. 92 (Additional Note).

long after people began to live in societies and to recognize their mutual social relations, for Locke said, 'Government is hardly to be avoided amongst Men that live together.'[52] There was also an element of necessity behind the transformation of pre-political society into government; in explaining why '*History* gives us but a very little account of Men, *that lived together in the State of Nature*', Locke wrote, 'The inconveniences of that condition, and the love, and want of Society no sooner brought any number of them together, but they presently united and incorporated, if they designed to continue together.'[53] In other words, the provision by government of 'an *establish'd*, settled, known *Law*', '*a known and indifferent Judge*', and '*Power* to back and support the sentence [of the judge] when right, and to *give* it due *Execution*'[54]—the three things that were so conspicuously absent from the state of nature—were essential to preserve not only the society into which men were driven by their natures but the resultant advantages and values of social life as well.

Thus, an important and persistent acceptance of what is at base Aristotelianism can be extracted from Locke's conceptions of society and government, and the moral aspects of his notion of political origins can be seen to have had much in common with the later theory of Rousseau's *Social Contract*. For it was only by uniting into societies and then setting up governments that the men of the *Two Treatises* were able to develop their personalities and to enjoy fully and permanently the benefits that were potentially theirs by the gift of God and nature.[55] This is true whether the state emerged from the family or from some other pre-political association, but our interest here is in the transformation of paternal power.

'In the first Ages of the World,' Locke wrote, 'and in places

---

[52] Locke, *Two Treatises*, II, 105. See also II, 127: 'we seldom find any number of Men live any time together in this State [of nature]'.

[53] Ibid., II, 101.

[54] Ibid., II, 124, 125, 126.

[55] Geraint Parry ingeniously argues that according to Locke each person has an obligation as a human being to cultivate his rationality and that this cultivation will lead him to the realization that the state is necessary. However, Parry does not carry his analysis to a teleological conclusion. See his 'Individuality, Politics and the Critique of Paternalism in John Locke', *Political Studies*, XII (1964), 165–6.

still, where the thinness of People gives Families leave to separate into unpossessed Quarters', it was very easy 'for the *Father of the Family to* become the Prince of it'. Since men living together will always need a formal government and because the children had grown accustomed to patriarchal authority, it was most likely that political power should, 'by the express or tacit Consent of the Children, when they were grown up, be in the Father, where it seemed without any change barely to continue'. In this manner a father might be endowed with a monarchical power, and Locke hastily added that 'this was not by an *Paternal Right,* but only by the Consent of his Children'.[56] However, this 'express or tacit Consent' successively deteriorated. 'Thus 'twas easie, and almost natural for Children by a tacit, and scarce avoidable consent to make way for the *Father's Authority and Government,'* Locke wrote[57] and then asserted that 'the natural *Fathers of Families,* by an insensible change, became the *politick Monarchs* of them too'.[58]

The meaning of 'insensible change' is not apparent, but the words seem to qualify Locke's political history *vis-à-vis* his state-of-nature assumptions. In the first place, it is now clear that the presumed gulf between patriarchal and political authority that is so important to the argument of the *Two Treatises* could in practice be bridged—and with very little difficulty—by the transformation of the father into a political ruler. Moreover, government need not have been established in the first instance by the agreement of men who consciously recognized the inconveniences of the state of nature. Instead, mankind may well have casually drifted into political society with the help of acquired social habits. Locke described and justified the process:

the Father having, by the Law of Nature, the same Power with every Man else to punish, as he thought fit, any Offences against that

[56] Locke, *Two Treatises,* II, 74. On the need for government, see in addition, II, 105 (lines 19–21).

[57] Ibid., II, 75. In the first three printings of the *Two Treatises* the key phrase was 'tacit, and almost natural consent'. (See Laslett's Collation of the Second Treatise, ibid., p. 480.)

[58] Locke, *Two Treatises,* II, 76. In II, 99, Locke similarly wrote that governance was begun 'by barely agreeing to *unite into one Political Society* . . .'. These passages should all be read in conjunction with Locke's insistence that consent is the only means by which one could become subject to authority, discussed below, pp. 261ff.

Law, might thereby punish his transgressing Children even when they were Men, and out of their Pupilage; and they were very likely to submit to his punishment, and all joyn with him against the Offender, in their turns, giving him thereby power to Execute his Sentence against any transgression, and so in effect make him the Law-maker, and Governour over all, that remained in Conjunction with his Family. He was fittest to be trusted; Paternal affection secured their Property, and Interest under his Care, and *the Custom of obeying him, in their Childhood, made it easier to submit to him, rather than to any other.*[59]

Locke admitted that monarchy was probably the first form of government in the world because of its compatibility with the unitary rule of the family by the father. He was almost apologetic as he defended the claim of monarchy to historical priority:

First then, in the beginning of things, the Father's Government of the Childhood of those sprung from him, having accustomed them to the *Rule of one Man*, and taught them that where it was exercised with Care and Skill, with Affection and Love to those under it, it was sufficient to procure and preserve to Men all the Political Happiness they sought for, in Society. It was no wonder, that they should pitch upon, and naturally run into that Form of Government, which from their Infancy they had been all accustomed to; and which, by experience they had found both easie and safe. To which, if we add, that *Monarchy* being simple, and most obvious to Men, whom neither experience had instructed in Forms of Government, nor the Ambition or Insolence of Empire had taught to beware of the Encroachments of Prerogative, or the Inconveniences of Absolute Power, which Monarchy, in Succession, was apt to lay claim to, and bring upon them, it was not at all strange, that they should not much trouble themselves to think of Methods of restraining any Exorbitances of those, to whom they had given the Authority over them, and of ballancing the Power of Government, by placing several parts of it in different hands. . . . 'tis no wonder they put themselves into such a *Frame of Government*, as was not only as I said, most obvious and simple, but also best suited to their

[59] Ibid., II, 105. Emphasis added. See also II, 75 (lines 5–10), where Locke emphasized the gentleness of the father. Again, note the contrast between the earlier insistence upon apparently overt consent and the assertion here that sons *'in effect* make him [their father] the Law-maker' (emphasis added).

present State and Condition; which stood more in need of defence against foreign Invasions and Injuries, than of multiplicity of Laws.[60]

Locke's reconstruction of the historical origins of the state was not vastly different from the position of Sir Robert Filmer, for Locke acknowledged that government had, in all probability, begun in the family and that the first ruler was a patriarchal monarch. But the similarity stopped at these points of superficial agreement. Sir Robert rested his patriarchalism upon a genetic method of political justification; he believed that it was only necessary to determine the origins of political authority to understand what the nature and essence of government ought to be. Filmer saw no logical gap between the presumed beginnings of the state and his own ethico-political doctrine, and he treated the latter as a valid inference from the historical fact. Locke, on the other hand, held that origins have almost nothing to do with subsequent duty. 'An Argument from what has been, to what should of right be, has no great force', he wrote. Therefore, if the patriarchalists 'can give so many instances out of History, of *Governments begun* upon Paternal Right', Locke was quite willing, 'without any danger, [to] yield them the cause'.[61] Similarly, he said, 'if Princes have their Titles in the Fathers Right, and it be a sufficient proof of the natural *Right of Fathers* to Political Authority, . . . [this argument] will as strongly prove that all Princes, nay Princes only, ought to be Priests, since 'tis as certain, that in the Beginning, *The Father of the Family was Priest, as that he was Ruler in his own Household*'.[62]

In other words, Locke separated the two components of Sir Robert's argument; he made the history into a descriptive and politically neutral anthropology and then inserted his own theory of consent and a doctrine of governmental trust in place of the moral patriarchalism Filmer had improperly derived from history. Yet, Locke was obviously not willing to explain the nature of politics without looking into the past. In fact, he recognized that history was a valuable source of *information*. By themselves,

[60] Ibid., II, 107. (In the early part of this passage Locke does not seem to have maintained the distinction between society and government.)
[61] Locke, *Two Treatises*, II, 103.
[62] Ibid., II, 76. See also Sanford A. Lakoff, *Equality in Political Philosophy* (Cambridge, Mass., 1964), p. 69.

however, historical examples could not produce values, but they could be used in support of normative claims founded upon reason.[63] Had Locke ignored the problem of origins, his accounts of the state of nature and the natural right to property, for instance, would have been superfluous. But the framework within which he wrote forced Locke to examine these and other questions in order to compose a full answer to Filmer's patriarchalism.[64]

The analysis of origins in the *Two Treatises* was due as much to the very nature of the philosophic task Locke set for himself, a task that was similar to Rousseau's proclaimed goal of reconciling man's free birth with the chains of society. 'To understand Political Power right, and derive it from its Original,' Locke said, 'we must consider what State all Men are naturally in, and that is, a *State of Perfect Freedom* to order their Actions, and dispose of their Possessions, and Persons as they think fit, within the bounds of the Law of Nature, without asking leave, or depending upon the Will of any other Man.'[65] Further analysis revealed, as has already been seen, that man was naturally somewhat sociable and needed the help of others to enjoy and retain the benefits of nature. By looking at man in his original, prepolitical condition, Locke was able to determine what kind of government would be most consistent with human nature.

In Locke's writings origins thus led to government in a prudential rather than necessary sense. The existence of political authority was justified by an appeal to something more functional and tangible than divine mystery or the nature of things. It was the purpose of government, in general, to protect the life, liberty, and property of the citizens. So long as these protections were offered by an agency that drew its authority from the consent of the people and did not degenerate into absolutism, political obligation appears to have been complete. However, when the natural rights of the citizens were flouted or when a government became absolutist, the duty to obey the state ceased to be binding.

[63] See, e.g., Locke, *Two Treatises*, II, 105 (lines 1–3), and Ashcraft, 'Locke's State of Nature', pp. 898–900 and 912–13.
[64] See Thomas I. Cook, Introduction to his edition of Locke, *Two Treatises of Government*, Hafner Library of Classics (New York, 1947), pp. xii and xv.
[65] Locke, *Two Treatises*, II, 4.

The insistence upon consent provided a further basis for Locke's claim that the patriarchal and kingly origins of government were irrelevant to contemporary obligation. He asserted that it is '*the Consent of Free-men, born under Government*, which only *makes them Members of it.* . . .'.[66] Even the transformation of a family into a state could only be accomplished through the consent of the children. To Locke there was no question 'That the *beginning of Politick Society* depends upon the consent of the Individuals, to joyn into and make one Society', and he believed that reason and history clearly showed that 'the *Governments* of the World, that were begun in Peace, . . . were *made by the Consent of the People*'.[67] Locke's doctrine of consent is excessively vague and of limited use as an explanation of political obligation in the *Two Treatises*.[68] Still, his commitment to what he called 'consent' is unassailable. What Locke presumably sought was a means of basing political authority on the voluntary actions of free individuals;[69] that he might not have succeeded in no way detracts from his intentions. What is singularly important about the consent thesis in relation to the patriarchal origins of government is that Locke used it to show that however unnoticed the transformation might have been, the state and the family rested on altogether different moral bases.

It is now possible to appreciate the full significance for Locke of Filmer's remarks about the inconsistency of allowing children to be bound by the acts of their ancestors while simultaneously proclaiming a doctrine of natural freedom and equality. Filmer's argument is worth re-examining in detail, for it throws important light on Locke's answer. After asserting that there never would have been any time when all people might have assembled and agreed to a contract of government and further complaining that

[66] Ibid., II, 117. See also, II, 95, 112, 119–21, 192, 197, and 198.
[67] Ibid., II, 106 and 104.
[68] See the penetrating analysis by John Dunn, 'Consent in the Political Theory of John Locke', *Historical Journal*, X (1967), 153–82. Dunn cites and ably analyzes almost every modern commentary on Locke's theory of consent.
[69] See Joseph Tussman, *Obligation and the Body Politic* (New York, 1961), pp. 32–9; S. I. Benn and R. S. Peters, *The Principles of Political Thought: Social Foundations of the Democratic State*, paperbound (New York, 1965), pp. 376–82; and Hanna Pitkin, 'Obligation and Consent—I', *American Political Science Review*, LIX (1965), 994–7.

K

those who did not participate—especially children—'ought not to lose their liberty without their own consent', Sir Robert said:

> But in part to salve this, it will be said that infants and children may be concluded by the votes of their parents. This remedy may cure some part of the mischief, but it destroys the whole cause, and at last stumbles upon the true original of government. For if it be allowed, that the acts of parents bind the children, then farewell the doctrine of the natural freedom of mankind; where subjection of children to parents is natural, there can be no natural freedom. If any reply, that not all children shall be bound by their parents' consent, but only those that are under age: it must be considered, that in nature there is no *nonage*; if a man be not born free, she doth not assign him any other time when he shall attain his freedom: or if she did, then children attaining that age, should be discharged of their parents' contract. So that in conclusion, if it be imagined that the people were ever but once free from subjection by nature, it will prove a mere impossibility ever lawfully to introduce any kind of government whatsoever, without apparent wrong to a multitude of people.[70]

The context clearly indicates that Filmer was attacking the historical inadequacies of the *original contract* of government. But his arguments were valid on logical grounds as well, for he was ultimately claiming that no one could *legitimately* give away or limit what belonged to someone else by nature. Locke accepted this principle and incorporated it into his own position, essentially, by placing very little reliance upon the contract and its inevitable dependence upon the acts of ancestors; he emphasized instead individual *consent*. This distinction between contract and consent is not often drawn. Consequently, the dependence of the contract theory upon genetic justification—and its closeness to the patriarchal theory in this respect—has seldom been appreciated. Locke did recognize this aspect of the contract doctrine and was driven by this awareness to formulate his theory of consent as a direct response to Filmer's argument. Consent represented the personal and contemporary manner in which individuals could claim the same freedom that had belonged to their fathers before them.

---

[70] Filmer, *Anarchy*, p. 287. Locke did not refer to this passage in the *Two Treatises*; he introduced the concept of nonage as if Filmer had never criticized it. Still, his treatment of the problem was clearly an answer to Filmer.

From this perspective, it is misleading to regard Locke as a 'social contract' theorist and to ask such questions as whether there are one or two contracts in his doctrine.[71] Locke used to contract to explain how *some* political societies *may* have *first* been established. But this appeal to the contract was equivalent to the anthropological tracing of the state to patriarchal authority; it was a descriptive, historical statement about the genesis of commonwealths. Like fatherly power, the compact was not used by Locke to justify the duty of later citizens to obey civil authority. Men were not obligated because they lived under a government that had begun in voluntary association but because some, by acts of their own, had personally consented (however tacitly and unnoticed!) to be bound by a just authority that did not violate its trust.[72] However, governments that originated contractually were initially just, and Locke presumed that they would tend to remain so. If they did not, they had no more *moral* claim to the allegiance of their members than did absolute monarchs, tyrants, unjustified conquerors, or others whose positions were based upon force rather than trust.

A further escape from genetic reasoning was provided for Locke by his belief that governmental power—despite its patriarchal origins—exists only for the benefit of the governed. Political authority could therefore be regarded as part of an on-going process; it is held as a sacred trust for the 'publick Good and Safety'.

Thus, whether *a Family* by degrees *grew up into a Commonwealth*, and the Fatherly Authority being continued on to the elder Son, every one in his turn growing up under it, tacitly submitted to it, and the easiness and equality of it not offending any one, every one acquiesced, till time seemed to have confirmed it, and settled a right of Succession by Prescription: or whether several Families, or the Descendants of several Families, whom Chance, Neighbourhood, or Business brought together, uniting into Society, the need of a

[71] See, for instance, Sir Ernest Barker, 'The Theory of the Social Contract in Locke, Rousseau, and Hume', reprinted in his *Essays on Government*, 2nd ed. (Oxford, 1951), p. 98. In this very influential essay, Sir Ernest continually incorporated Locke's language of consent into a theory of the contract. The same is true of Gough, *Social Contract*, 2nd ed., pp. 127–46, esp. p. 145.

[72] See Dunn, 'Consent in the Political Theory of John Locke', Pitkin, 'Obligation and Consent', and the discussion following this note.

General, whose Conduct might defend them against their Enemies in War, and the great confidence the Innocence and Sincerity of that poor but vertuous Age (such as are almost all those which begin Governments, that ever come to last in the World) gave Men one of another, made the first Beginners of Common-wealths generally put the Rule into one Man's hand, without any other express Limitation or Restraint, but what the Nature of the thing, and the End of Government required: which ever of these it was, that at first put the rule into the hands of a single person, certain it is that no body was ever intrusted with it but for the publick Good and Safety, and to those Ends in the Infancies of Commonwealths those who had it, commonly used it: And unless they had done so, young Societies could not have subsisted: without such nursing Fathers tender and carefull of the publick weale, all Governments would have sunk under the Weakness and Infirmities of their Infancy; and the Prince and the People had soon perished together.[73]

4

Basic to this important doctrine of trust are the moral and psychological assumptions that Locke made about human nature. The men of the *Two Treatises* were potentially good—that is, they were capable of recognizing their obligations and, in general, could be counted on to act upon them[74]—and were other-regarding rather than hedonistic.[75] Such men would have little reluctance about placing great powers in the hands of others, for they would not feel the need to guard continually against potential abuses of authority. Therefore, Locke said, men 'chuse to be under the Conduct of a *single Person*, without so much as by express Conditions limiting or regulating his Power, which they

[73] Locke, *Two Treatises*, II, 110 (quoted *in toto*). Locke's reference to 'nursing Fathers' suggests Isaiah 49: 23, *q.v.* Also noteworthy is the use of 'young *Societies*' (emphasis added) where the context clearly called for a more specifically political concept. This, of course, is another instance in which the society–government distinction of the *Two Treatises* was not consistently maintained.

On Locke's doctrine of trust, which is central to my argument at this point, see Gough, *Locke's Political Philosophy*, ch. vii, and Laslett, Introduction to Locke, *Two Treatises*, pp. 112–15.

[74] See Locke, *Two Treatises*, e.g., II, 11 (line 31); 14 (lines 17–19); 124 (lines 8–9); and 136 (lines 5–6).

[75] See ibid., e.g., II, 6 (lines 19–25), and 33 lines 1–3).

thought safe enough in his Honesty and Prudence'. And when this '*single Person*' was a father whose authority had been allowed to become political, the people did not subsequently believe that 'Paternal Power [ought] to have a right to Dominion, or to be the Foundation of all Government'.[76] Beyond this, it cannot be emphasized too strongly that it was the gentleness of the father that made him a suitable political ruler. Because of 'Paternal affection',[77] the 'tenderness' a father had for his offspring,[78] and his consequently 'easie and safe' rule of his family,[79] children were content to pass out of nonage into maturity without changing the external ordering of their lives. In short, they believed that their fathers would not become tyrants.

Therefore, in the early days, when fathers were governors and watched over the people 'for their good, the Government was almost all *Prerogative*. A few establish'd Laws served the turn, and the discretion and care of the Ruler supply'd the rest.' This was as it should be, 'For *prerogative is nothing but the Power of doing publick good without a Rule*'.[80] Locke had said the same thing of political authority in general in section three of the 'Second Treatise':

*Political Power* then I take to be *a Right* of making Laws with Penalties of Death, and consequently all less Penalties, for the Regulating and Preserving of Property, and of employing the force of the Community, in the execution of such Laws, and in the defence of the Common-wealth from Foreign Injury, and all this only for the Publick Good.[81]

When rulers failed to act 'for the Publick Good', the bonds of political obligation were dissolved, and power potentially reverted to the people.[82] Historically, it was abuse of the prerogative and violation of the trust of government by rulers that led to the establishment of specific laws. 'And thus declared *limitations of*

---

[76] Locke, *Two Treatises*, II, 112.
[77] Ibid., II, 105.
[78] Ibid., II, 75. On both affection and tenderness, see II, 170, lines 8–12).
[79] Ibid., II, 107.
[80] Ibid., II, 162 and 166.
[81] Ibid., II, 3 (*in toto*).
[82] See Ibid., II, 221, 222, and 240, and Laslett's Introduction, p. 113 and n.

*Prerogative* were by the People found necessary in Cases, which they and their Ancestors had left, in the utmost latitude, to the Wisdom of those Princes, who made no other but a right use of it, that is, for the good of their People.'[83]

Another of Locke's important departures from the patriarchal tradition was his denial of the natural origins of hereditary succession. Even in the early days of paternal rule, the succession of the son to his father's title was generally dependent upon his merit. But when 'the Father died, and left his next Heir for want of Age, Wisdom, Courage, or any other Qualities, less fit for Rule: ... There, 'tis not to be doubted, but they [the people] used their natural freedom, to set him up, whom they judged the ablest, and most likely, to Rule well over them.' 'Almost all *Monarchies*,' Locke wrote, 'near their Original, have been commonly, at least upon occasion, *Elective*.'[84] As these patriarchal kings 'chanced to live long, and leave able, and worthy Heirs, for several Successions, or otherwise; So they laid the Foundations of Hereditary, or Elective Kingdoms ...'.[85] This description was not merely an account of life in the hypothesized state of nature; it seems to have been based upon the actual government of the Canadian Indians. As Locke wrote in his *Common-Place Book,* presumably in March, 1679:

The Kings of Canada are elective but the sons never faile to succeed their fathers when they are equal to their virtues, otherwise not; & their Kings are rather obeyed by consent & persuasion, then by force and compulsion, the publique good being the measure of their authority. Sagard, p. 418. And this seems to have been the state of regall authority in its Original at least in all this part of the world. JL[86]

[83] Ibid., II, 162.
[84] Ibid., II, 105 and 106.
[85] Ibid., II, 76.
[86] Locke, *Common-Place Book*, Bodleian Library, MS. Locke c. 42, pt. B, fol. 6. Passage slightly modernized. The probable dating is derived from Locke's having made a similar entry in his reading notes on 25 March, 1679. (Bodleian Library, MS. Locke c. 33, fol. 10.) This entry was lightly crossed out by Locke, indicating that it was recopied somewhere else, presumably in the *Common-Place Book*. The reference is to Gabriel Sagard's *Canada*, published in 1636, and used extensively by Locke in 1679. (See Laslett, Introduction to Locke, *Two Treatises*, Appendix B, no. 72, p. 143, and his notes to II, 58 and 106 lines 16–18.

Thus, the state of nature, the probable beginnings of political commonwealths, and the primitive structure of American society and government were assimilated and used to reinforce the proposition that the end of governance could be nothing but the public good. As understood by Locke, civil authority was always held in trust and never by right.[87]

In terms of the patriarchal explanation of political obligation, the doctrine of trust was one of the most important components of the theory of the *Two Treatises*. It enabled Locke to say that the familial origins of government were of no value in understanding the nature of man's political commitments. It was precisely Locke's polemic purpose to show how irrelevant the Filmerian analysis of politics was! Locke believed that allegiance was due to the state because of the trust that it held and only so long as that trust was not violated. Thus, each generation and, in fact, each individual person theoretically retained the right to determine whether or not a government was properly performing its functions. If the answer was no, the base of political authority was liable to be withdrawn. On this reading, the state was conventional, a contrivance that was the creature of those whom it was to serve. At the same time, Locke certainly believed that the state was essential to human existence, but its necessity was functional rather than moral. The political order as he described it did not endow men with additional rights or more personality and individuality, but by providing positive and sure protections, the state did make it possible for them to enjoy what was already naturally theirs.

[87] See Locke, *Two Treatises*, I, 93.

# XIV

## Conclusion

### I

For almost 1,500 years prior to Locke, the family had been seen as the organizational precursor of the political order. Political writers from Plato and Aristotle to Bodin and Hooker regularly traced governmental authority to its beginnings in the household. And in seventeenth century England, this almost universally accepted historical doctrine was the basis of an absolutist theory of political obligation. The family was regarded by many Stuart thinkers as a proper symbolic representation of the state; for these men, the natural and purportedly unlimited authority of the father revealed the nature of political power. There were, of course, criticisms of this view, but it remained for John Locke to complete the destruction of this symbol—by asking all the right questions, by rejecting the presumptions on which patriarchalism rested, and—most importantly—by supplying new presumptions and a new symbol. In short, Locke's dissection of Filmer convincingly fortified what many other writers had said with less force and grace: moral patriarchalism would no longer suffice as a theory of political obligation because it did not conform to the way of viewing the world that Locke himself did so much to establish. If men had once thought the doctrine valid, it was because they had accepted untenable premises and had failed to understand the nature of both politics and freedom.

Locke, of course, rejected far more than patriarchalism; the premises he replaced were parts of a world view or belief system that was being undermined by the growth of historical consciousness, by the rise of empirical science and philosophy, by the growth of deism, and by social and political events themselves. But changes in intellectual modes are not cataclysmic and abrupt; Locke did not suddenly speak a new 'truth' for his contemporaries to recognize. The patriarchal symbol and its supporting assumptions were overthrown by a rival body of attitudes that had been present for some time. The consent theory was not truly a 'new view'. Its triumph had been preceded by a persistent and growing contractual criticism of the old style. As the implications of the contract thesis became more fully understood, the doctrine itself was transformed from an historical to a rational political theory. Eventually, Locke combined the chief criticisms of patriarchalism more clearly than his predecessors had done, adding something of his own in the process. He then became the spokesman of the critics and has been looked upon ever since as their leading representative. How little Locke actually added to the substantive arguments against patriarchalism is appreciated when it is remembered how much of his position had been stated by Edward Gee some thirty years prior to the publication of the *Two Treatises*. The essential difference was that Locke saw far more clearly than Gee—or any other anti-patriarchalist, except perhaps Tyrrell—the dimensions of the problem and had the subtlety and ability to appreciate the implications of his own positions. It is also very important that Locke wrote better and more tersely than Gee and published at a more propitious time. And so it is Locke's *Two Treatises* and not Gee's weighty *Divine Right and Original of the Civil Magistrate* or even Tyrrell's *Patriarcha non Monarcha* to which we turn for the most cogent and useful statement of the anti-patriarchal case.

2

The patriarchal defense of absolutism can be reduced to two propositions and a conclusion that allegedly followed from them:

(1) Familial authority is natural, divinely sanctioned, and—in its pristine form—absolute and unlimited.
(2) Political power is identical to the power of fathers

Therefore, political power is natural, divinely sanctioned, and—because it still enjoys the ancient and original rights of fatherhood—absolute and unlimited.

The doctrine was attacked on all fronts. As we have seen, neither of the propositions was universally accepted or regarded as self-evident. Moreover, because political argument is not just a matter of logical validity but includes rhetoric and persuasion as well, the conclusion could be rejected without reference to the supporting propositions.

The first proposition, the description of the familial symbol itself, was criticized in several ways. Most writers denied that fathers possessed unlimited powers; the Biblical examples of paternal absolutism were given different interpretations and were opposed by instances in which fathers apparently lacked the authority to act as rulers. It was possible to go even further—as Hobbes did—and deny that paternal power was natural. It could have been argued on this basis—although no one seems to have done so—that any conventional limits placed upon fathers were legitimate since their superiority was a human contrivance in the first place.

Also, as was shown at the end of chapter four, perceptions of the family were changing by the latter part of the Stuart period. Locke and Bishop Fleetwood had emphasized the reciprocity and contractual nature of family life rather than its status relationships. Once the notion of paternal absolutism had been destroyed, it was possible to accept the patriarchal derivation of politics from the household. It could have been pointed out to a patriarchalist that since fatherhood was characterized by gentleness and affection as well as by limits imposed by God, any government established upon this model would also have to be limited and responsible rather than absolute and arbitrary. This argument would have been difficult to sustain, however. As the examination of family structure showed, it was generally agreed that fathers had important duties and obligations to their dependants and that they were entitled to exercise a great deal of authority over inferiors within their legitimate spheres. Nonetheless, Locke came very close to suggesting an analogy between the tenderness a father was to show for the children who had been entrusted to his care by God and the trust and concern for the public good that would be found in a properly designated political society. Hobbes also argued from the conventional origins of fatherly right and familial status to an artificial polity.

The attack on the political relevance of the family was the

most interesting and important aspect of the anti-patriarchal doctrine. To claim that a particular symbol is inappropriate to political discourse is necessarily to assert the superiority of an alternative image. For what was being said, in effect, was, 'The patriarchalists are totally incorrect. Politics is not natural and patriarchal as they maintain. Rather, it is conventional and contractual.' It is most important that the presence of a different symbolic account be recognized. In order to assert that a proffered concept or image is not appropriate, one must at least implicitly have a different understanding of politics in mind; otherwise, he would be incapable of even knowing whether or not something else was suitable. Undoubtedly, the process of examining and criticizing a political symbol itself often brings to the surface a vaguely held and imperfectly grasped conception of one's own.

As I have frequently suggested, the articulation of the distinction between the state and society arose from the need to defend the state-of-nature and social contract theories against the patriarchal claim that men born subject to their fathers were never free. The same need produced in Locke, Tyrrell, and Sidney overt movements away from genetic justification; in addition, Locke replaced the contractual theory of how men became subject to political authority with a doctrine based on consent. The state/society distinction and the rejection of genetic theories provided the most damaging attacks on patriarchalism. Now it could be said, with Sidney for instance, that it did not matter what kinds of power God had bestowed on Adam or how extensive they were, for what applied in one age was not necessarily the rule for all time.

The rejection of absolutism was a less direct and much more subtle attack on patriarchalism than was the denial that paternal authority was unlimited or refusing to accept the implicit identification of state and family. What is involved here is the notion that no matter what arguments are advanced in its behalf, political absolutism is untenable. The experiences of the English government in 1649 and 1688 certainly stood as evidence against the *factual* appeal of absolutism. Like the distinction between political and familial authority, the theoretical attack on unlimited kingship necessarily embodied its own conception of the nature of the political order. It was claimed that any arguments that led to unlimited sovereign power must be incorrect, for *politics* properly so-called was not free of human control. Therefore, acceptance of a symbol such as patriarchalism that supported absolutism would have had drastic and unfortunate consequences: it would have brought about an undesirable reorganization of society and redistribution of power. This was not so much a reasoned argument against the patriarchal theory of obligation as it was an *ad hominem* attack on its implications; it was a plea to the faint-hearted and uncommitted not to be persuaded by apparent logical consistency or clever reasoning alone.

Locke resorted to precisely this kind of appeal when he said that absolute monarchy is '*inconsistent with Civil Society*, and so can be no Form of Civil Government at all'.[1] The point was, simply, that even if Filmer's patriarchal defense of divine right absolutism turned out to be logically and historically irrefutable, Englishmen were not thereby required to have an absolute sovereign to whom they owed obedience. Politics was not what Filmer thought it was. The source and present stability of the political order were not derived from God's ancient grant of patriarchal power to Adam; they depended upon the government's performing its duties without violating its trust.

The subtlety in this argument lies in its implicit statement to the reader not to *adopt* a particular political symbol. He was not told that the arguments advanced in behalf of the symbol were faulty or inadequate but that the symbol itself did not merit his consideration. An author who advocated such a position came very close to recognizing the nature and importance of symbolic political discourse, for he acknowledged that the way in which civil authority was perceived would have a major bearing on the actual shape it took. Usually, of course, writers attack one conception of politics while simultaneously arguing for their own without understanding the process of symbolization itself. They see the dispute as their own 'correct' or 'truthful' formulation versus one that is 'wrong'; it is not a matter of 'better' or 'more suitable'. In a polemical situation, the strength of a normative thesis comes from its relationship to presumed 'reality'; it would not be convincing to very many people to tell them that the 'reality' behind a particular symbol is plastic. Moreover, few

[1] Locke, *Two Treatises*, II, 90. See also, II, 13 (lines 14–29), 137 (lines 1–5), 174 (lines 4–6).

political writers are sufficiently aware of their own limitations and of the nature of debate to realize that they are arguing for a symbol. Nevertheless, when their doctrines are carefully analyzed —as in the case of Locke's assault on the patriarchal theory— the various strands of their positions can be separated and dealt with in these terms. One purpose of the present analysis is to illustrate how large a portion of political philosophy is actually the result of rationalization rather than of honest and careful reasoning.

Locke began with his conclusions, that is, with a presumption in favor of limited political authority and with a bias against absolutism. He *then* worked out arguments in support of these related positions. He was certainly mindful of the need to refute Filmer, and his defense of political voluntarism is a suitable corollary to his critique of patriarchal naturalism. There is no point in asking where Locke 'got' his political 'preconceptions', for that would ultimately be a matter of his intellectual biography. The doctrine was 'there'; it has already been seen that the basic position set forth by Locke was at least as old as moral patriarchalism. And by the time of the Exclusion Controversy, the 'keepers' of the emerging liberal doctrine—the early Whigs, whose most prominent leaders included Locke's patron, the Earl of Shaftesbury—were in need of theoretical support. Filmer had to be answered. And it is not surprising to discover that while the Exclusion Parliaments were meeting, Locke was writing what was to become one of the classic justifications of 'liberalism'. What must be remembered, however, is that Locke consciously *created* an answer to Filmer; he did not invent a political doctrine by arguing from first principles to irresistible and inescapable conclusions. The conclusions were the givens—the starting point —that Locke defended as best he could and *in terms that were appropriate to the occasion.*

3

The rapid decline after 1690 of patriarchalism as a viable political ideology cannot be attributed solely or even largely to Locke's *Two Treatises*. Not only had Locke's main arguments against patriarchalism been articulated earlier without discrediting the doctrine, but confirmed patriarchalists such as Leslie and Jonathan Boucher, the American Tory minister who will be discussed later in this chapter, showed no reluctance to reject Locke and his premises. It is certainly true that Locke's criticisms could not be ignored, but they were not unanswerable. Leslie had counter-arguments, and Bohun had dealt with some of Tyrrell's versions of those same criticisms. What destroyed moral patriarchalism was its own irrelevance as a political symbol. The collapse of two attitudes in the larger belief system of seventeenth century England made it impossible to argue from familial status to political obligation. These attitudes were, first, the appeal to origins to discover the nature of political authority and thus to justify (or condemn) specific institutions or policies and, second, the identifications of all status relationships with one another and specifically the social and familial with the political. They were replaced by a rational outlook and a distinction between state and society. Locke did not invent either of these new modes of viewing the world, but he used them most effectively. Thus, his *Two Treatises* was not the immediate cause of the downfall of patriarchalism so much as it was symptomatic of the changes that were taking place in English social and political philosophy.

The movement away from genetic justification can be accounted for in part by calling attention to the deepening of historical awareness and acceptance of historical change that were becoming apparent by the end of the century. With increasing regularity history was viewed as neutral chronology—or at least as prudential rather than morally determinative. David Hume's famous declaration of the logical gap between 'is' and 'ought'— which itself raised questions about the validity of inferring values from past events—had been anticipated by Locke's claim that 'An Argument from what has been, to what should of right be, has no great force'.[2] Not far removed was Hobbes's rejection of the use of Biblical history to prove that patriarchal monarchy enjoyed God's sanction because this notion was supported 'by examples and testimonies, and not solid reason'.[3] In both cases what was demanded was a shift from historical to rational argumentation. Supporting this new attitude were the belief in the malleability of man and his institutions as well as the doctrine of

[2] Locke, *Two Treatises*, II, 103.
[3] Hobbes, *De Cive*, x, 3 (*E.W.*, II, 129).

'progress', both of which were characteristic notions of the eighteenth century. Malleability meant that the future was indeterminate, that it could be shaped by men to conform to their needs. Progress dictated that the future would be better than the present which itself was superior to the past. The similarity between these two conceptions and their mutual relationship to the repudiation of genetic justification is that both implied that the standards by which the future was to be judged would be generated by the future itself and not derived from some historically remote beginning.

We can sense in Locke's use of consent an attempt to free man from tradition and to establish an immediacy for his activities and life. One was not required to become a member of the commonwealth of his father but had the right to seek a civil society more to his liking. An implication of this doctrine is that the ends served by a government might become outmoded with the passage of time; what answered the father's needs might be inadequate for the son's. Behind this type of reasoning was the 'individualism' born of the Protestant Reformation. The discriminate, self-contained, and personally responsible being that Protestant man was becoming was surely entitled to affect if not control his own life. Man is real, and his institutions—to the extent that they are not held to be established by God—are artificial; they are contrivances designed to serve man's needs. And if a man's needs differ from those of his ancestors, it would follow that he is not bound to maintain the institutions of an earlier age.

This same individualism and the view of political institutions as artifacts also underlay the theoretical separation of social and political relationships. If, as Locke maintained, man in his natural condition was sociable and the establishment of politics removed him from the state of nature, the conventional political order had to be distinguished from the natural social order, and the latter included the family. Thus, it was inappropriate to draw political inferences from familial life. The political naturalism of the patriarchal theory was plainly incompatible with the voluntarism of the individualist thesis. Again, however, Locke was not being original when he called for a distinction between fatherly and magisterial right. Not only was this position implicit in the anthropological patriarchal assertion that familial rule eventually became outmoded and was replaced by political authority, but Aristotle had explicitly criticized Plato for identifying the household and the polity. There was no way of settling this issue between the moral patriarchalists and their critics, for the conflicting views about the relationship of the family and the state rested upon mutually exclusive premises. All that can be said is that if an individual held one set of views about man, political life, and the proper way of justifying normative propositions, he would be inclined to hold the position *vis-à-vis* the patriarchal theory of obligation that was more compatible with them.

Individualism, political conventionalism, and rational justification were the counterpart to the family/state distinction. A more communitarian view, naturalism, and the use of genetic-historical arguments supported the union of all forms of authority under the patriarchal rubric. By the end of the Stuart period, for both historical and philosophic reasons, the former of these two sets of ideas was the more compelling and widespread. Thus, while Locke was not the cause, we can conclude that his *Two Treatises* marked the beginning of a different direction in English political thought. After 1690, genetic justification and the identification of familial and political power were becoming dead issues.

4

Patriarchal theories of obligation did not simply disappear after the Stuart period, but they are to be found with considerably less frequency in eighteenth-century political literature. Matthias Earberry, in 1716, argued in what he described as a 'Mathematical Method' from a set of definitions and axioms to a number of propositions that supported patriarchalism. Among Earberry's propositions were the following: 'If there ever was Naturally a Right of Fathers over Children, Men were not born at that time in a state of Equality'; 'All men have a Natural Right over their Children'; and 'If the Paternal Power extends to the same Actions that pertains also to the Civil, they must be Mutual.' Thus, since

every Father has still a Right over his Children: ... the King, who is the Supreme Parent, has by vertue thereof a Superiour Power over all other Parents or Heads of Families, which aggregately constitute a Commonwealth. So that Kings are included in the Command, *Honour thy father and thy Mother*.[4]

Another author, Andrew Ramsay, used the patriarchal origins of government to demonstrate that:

Monarchy moderated by *Aristocracy*, is the most antient, and most natural of all Governments. It hath its Foundation and Model from the paternal Empire, that is to say, from Nature itself, for the very Origine of Civil Societies proceeds from paternal Power: In a family well-governed, the common Father doth not determine Matters after a Despotical manner, according to his own Fancy; in publick Deliberations he consults the most aged and wise of his Children; young Persons and Domesticks have not an equal Authority with the Father of the common Family.[5]

Viscount Bolingbroke criticized the notion that society and government arose from contractual agreements. He suggested instead that men were naturally sociable and had always lived in families.[6] But Bollingbroke disowned Filmer, whose arguments he did not regard as worth serious consideration. Locke had 'condescended' to refute Filmer, he said, 'more out of regard to the prejudice of the time, than to the importance of the work'.[7] On the Continent, in his 1755 *Encyclopaedia* article on 'Political

---

[4] M[atthias] E[arberry], *Elements of Policy, Civil and Ecclesiastical in a Mathematical Model* (London, 1716), pp. 10–16; and see pp. 1–23 generally. The next year, Earberry repeated these arguments in a tract directed against Bishop Hoadly. He concluded, 'That as the Civil Government is a Branch of the Paternal, it ought to be rever'd as such a King is our common Parent, and we cannot strike him and be guiltless.' M[atthias] E[arberry], *The Old English Constitution Vindicated, and Set in a True Light* (London, 1717), p. 23.

[5] [Andrew Ramsay], *An Essay upon Civil Government* (London, 1722), p. 187. See also pp. 27–37 and 49–53 for Ramsay's discussions of the family as an indication of natural human sociability, the nature of familial relationships, and the patriarchal origins of government.

[6] [Henry St. John, Viscount Bolingbroke], *A Dissertation upon Parties*, 3rd ed. (London, 1735), p. 155; and Kramnick, *Bolingbroke and His Circle*, pp. 92–3.

[7] Henry St. John, Viscount Bolingbroke, *The Idea of a Patriot King* (1749), ed. Sidney W. Jackman, Library of Liberal Arts, paperbound (Indianapolis, Indiana, 1965), p. 30.

Economy', Jean-Jacques Rousseau expressed a similar contempt. '*Public* economy' must be distinguished from '*private* economy', he wrote. Therefore

> the State having nothing in common with the family except the obligation which their heads lie under of making both of them happy, the same rules of conduct cannot apply to both. I have considered these few lines enough to overthrow the detestable system which Sir Robert Filmer has endeavoured to establish in his *Patriarcha*; a work to which two celebrated writers have done too much honour in writing books to refute it.[8]

David Hume found the beginnings of political authority in the primitive kinship group, but his purpose was not to prove that government arose from either a patriarchal right or a primeval contract. Hume intended to demonstrate that neither account was meaningful and that political societies were founded upon natural human sentiment and the need for coercive education that would teach men the social utility of justice and obedience. His patriarchalism was purely anthropological.[9] Hume's undeservedly ob-

---

[8] Jean-Jacques Rousseau, 'A Discourse on Political Economy', in Rousseau, *The Social Contract and the Discourses*, ed. and trans. G. D. H. Cole, Everyman Edition, reset (New York, 1950), p. 288. Cf. *Social Contract*, I, ii (pp. 4–5 of the Cole edition): 'The family then may be called the first model of political societies: the ruler corresponds to the father, and the people to the children; and all, being born free and equal, alienate their liberty only for their advantage. The whole difference is that, in the family, the love of the father for his children repays him for the care he takes of them, while in the State, the pleasure of commanding takes the place of the love which the chief cannot have for the peoples under him.' For Rousseau's comments about the natural status of the family, see his long note to the 'Discourse on the Origin and Foundation of Inequality among Men' (1755), in Rousseau, *The First and Second Discourses*, ed. and trans. Roger D. Masters (New York, 1964), pp. 213–20. Also relevant are Arthur O. Lovejoy, 'The Supposed Primitivism of Rousseau's *Discourse on Inequality*', in his *Essays in the History of Ideas* (Baltimore, 1948), pp. 29–30; and Judith N. Shklar, 'Rousseau's Two Models: Sparta and the Age of Gold', *Political Science Quarterly*, LXXXI (1966), 40–1.

[9] David Hume, 'Of the Origin of Government' and 'Of the Original Contract', in his *Essays Moral, Political and Literary* (1741 and 1742; reprinted: Oxford, 1963), pp. 35–9 and 452–73. A more systematic and philosophic account of the familial origins of the state is contained in Hume's *A Treatise of Human Nature* (1739–1740), III, ii, 2, 7, and 8, ed. L. A. Selby-Bigge (Oxford, 1888), pp. 484–501 and 534–49.

scure contemporary John Millar also derived the state from the family, but he dismissed Filmer's claim, saying, 'The opinion of Sir Robert Filmer, . . . seems, at this day, unworthy of the serious refutation which it has met with, and could only have gained reputation when men were just beginning to reflect upon the first principles of government. To say that a king ought to enjoy absolute power because a father has enjoyed it, is to defend one system of oppression with another.'[10]

Josiah Tucker, Dean of Gloucester, published a lengthy attack on the *Two Treatises* in 1781 and specifically disclaimed the patriarchal thesis. 'There can be no Controversy between Mr. LOCKE's disciplines and me about the patriarchal Scheme in any of its Branches,' Tucker wrote, 'or indeed about any Sort of an indefeasible hereditary Right whatever:—Much less about unlimited passive Obedience, and Non-Resistance'.[11] Nonetheless, Tucker was criticized the next year for his closeness to Filmer. Joseph Towers, who defended Locke, maintained, 'Had Dr. Tucker lived in the days of Filmer, he would probably have been one of his disciples; but the doctrines of that writer are too much exploded, in the present age, for any man to venture to maintain them; and therefore all that the Dean of Gloucester can now do is not formally to vindicate Filmer, but to downgrade Locke as much as possible.'[12]

Perhaps the entire patriarchal case had been most adequately buried as an irrelevant historico–philosophic argument as early as 1727 by the American Cadwallader Colden who commented on the social structure and government of the New York Indians:

As I am fond to think, that the present state of the Indian Nations exactly shows the most Ancient and Original Condition of almost every Nation; so I believe, here we may with more certainty see the Original Forms of all Government, than in the most curious Speculations of the Learned; and that the Patriarchal, and other

[10] John Millar, *The Origins of the Distinctions of Ranks*, 3rd ed. (1779), reprinted in William Lehman, *John Millar of Glasgow, 1735–1801* (Cambridge, 1960), pp. 243, 244, and 246, quotation from p. 243.
[11] Josiah Tucker, *A Treatise Concerning Civil Government, in Three Parts* (London, 1781; fascimile reprint: New York, 1967), pp. 3–4. For Tucker's critical remarks about Filmer, see pp. 81–4.
[12] Joseph Towers, *A Vindication of the Political Principles of Mr. Locke* (London, 1782), p. 31.

Schemes in Politicks are no better than Hypotheses in Philosophy, and as prejudicial to real Knowledge.[13]

There were thinkers who adopted patriarchal principles despite the intellectual climate represented by the attitudes of Rousseau, Hume, Millar, and Colden. Jeremy Bentham in a manuscript fragment entitled 'Locke, Rousseau and Filmer's System' said:

Filmer's origin of government is exemplified everywhere: Locke's scheme of government has not ever, to the knowledge of any body, been exemplified any where. In every family there is government, in every family there is subjection, and subjection of the most absolute kind: the father, sovereign, the mother and the young, subjects. According to Locke's scheme, men knew nothing at all of governments till they met together to make one. Locke had speculated so deeply, and reasoned so ingeniously, as to have forgot that he was not of age when he came into the world.[14]

Jonathan Boucher, the Loyalist Tory minister of colonial Maryland, opposed the American Revolution with arguments that were unabashedly Filmerian. He wrote in defense of his source:

As the idea of a patriarchal government adopted in this Discourse is now very generally rejected, chiefly on the authority of Mr. Locke's answer to a treatise on the subject by Sir Robert Filmer; and as that book is now antiquated, and where known at all, known only through the medium of the answer to it; and also as I have lately perused the book, and did not find it deserving of all that extreme contempt with which it is now the fashion to mention it, I could not easily reconcile myself to the neglect of this opportunity to recommend it to my readers to peruse the book, and to judge for themselves.[15]

[13] Cadwallader Colden, *The History of the Five Indian Nations Depending upon the Province of New-York in America* (1727 and 1747), paperbound (Ithaca, 1958), p. xxi. I owe this reference to John Dunn of King's College, Cambridge.

[14] Jeremy Bentham, 'Locke, Rousseau and Filmer's Scheme', University College, London, MS. Bentham 100, as printed in the Appendix to Elie Halvey, *La Formation du Radicalisme Philosophique*, 3 vols. (Paris, 1901–1903), I, 418. Cf. Bertrand de Jouvenel, *The Pure Theory of Politics* (Cambridge, 1963), p. 45: '"Social Contract" theories are views of childless men.'

[15] Jonathan Boucher, *A View of the Causes and Consequences of the American Revolution* (London, 1797), pp. 528–9n. At the same time,

Another late eighteenth-century work that consciously argued from a set of patriarchal assumptions was John Whitaker's *The Real Origin of Government* (1795). However, while Whitaker acknowledged that his arguments 'were more familiar to the nation eighty or ninety years ago, than they are at present', and *Patriarcha* could well have been his text, he did not mention Filmer or any other patriarchal author.[16] Bentham, Boucher, and Whitaker were the exceptions. The day of the Filmerian was long since over, and the intellectual descendants of Locke and Hume did not even bother to challenge these patriarchalists in their own terms.

---

Boucher agreed that 'There are, no doubt, in several of Sir Robert Filmer's Treatises, many weak things.' He further acknowledged that 'the author of Patriarcha entertained some very extravagant notions on monarchy, and the sacredness of kings: and (what is perhaps still less pardonable) some disparaging and unjust opinions respecting the supremacy of law'. (Ibid., p. 530n.) See also pp. 495–560 *passim* and for further discussions of Boucher and Filmer, William H. Nelson, *The American Tory* (Oxford, 1961), pp. 186–8; Bernard Bailyn, *The Ideological Origins of the American Revolution* (Cambridge, Mass., 1967), pp. 311–19; and Michael D. Clark, 'Jonathan Boucher: The Mirror of Reaction', *Huntington Library Quarterly*, XXXIII (1969–70), 19–32.

[16] John Whitaker, *The Real Origin of Government* (London, 1795), Advertisement, sig. A2. See also pp. 4–25.

# Index

# Biblical Passages Cited